Reasons
For
Faith

Answering Objections
And Obstacles to Belief

Judy Salisbury

Logos Presentations
EQUIPPING - MOTIVATING - LIFE CHANGING

Published by
Logos Presentations
Woodland, WA

Reasons for Faith:
Answering Objections and Obstacles to Belief
by Judy Salisbury

Published by Logos Presentations
Woodland, WA 98674

Originally published as *A Christian Woman's Guide to Reasons for Faith: Understanding Why You Believe.* Copyright © 2003 by Judy Salisbury, Harvest House Publishers Eugene, Oregon 97402. Re-released in 2011 through Wipf & Stock Publishers, Eugene, Oregon as *Reasons for Faith: A Common Sense Guide for Christian Women* by Judy Salisbury. *Reasons For Faith: The First Apologetic Guide For Christian Women On Matters Of The Heart, Soul, And Mind* by Judy Salisbury Updated and Expanded Second Edition Copyright © 2017 by Judy Salisbury, Published by Christian Publishing House, Cambridge, Ohio 43725

ISBN: 9798644502905

ENDORSEMENTS

"Judy Salisbury's book is a powerful tool for the defense of the faith, one that combines fascinating facts with true spiritual understanding and a refreshing sense of humor. Judy encourages, exhorts, and powerfully persuades us to remember how vitally important it is to understand why we believe."

JILL MARTIN RISCHE
Co-founder of Walter Martin's Religious InfoNet and
Coauthor of *Through the Windows of Heaven*

"Judy Salisbury is a gifted writer and teacher whose work and life exhibit the ideal combination of intellectual integrity with an attractive, gracious, and winsome personality. Her latest work is an important contribution to the cause of Christ in our world. I highly recommend it."

FRANCIS J. BECKWITH
Author of *Defending Life* and Associate Professor of
Church-State Studies, Baylor University

What an accomplishment—to make a book on Christian apologetics delightfully entertaining! Judy's common sense language and powerfully memorable examples give life to each topic she tackles so that reading her book is pure joy. Her book and her approach is a rarity."

JUNE HUNT
President/Founder, Hope for the Heart

"Judy Salisbury's unique approach to Christian apologetics gives the reader a firm foundation—and in a society of relativism, it's nice to know there is an Absolute to whom we can cling. Judy not only reminds us to remember our first love, the Lord Jesus Christ but also illustrates that love by way of her often humorous and always thought-provoking examples. A must-read for believers and seekers alike."

JOAN PHILLIPS
Founder and president of G&E Enterprises and G& E Services

"There are many books available that teach mothers how to raise their children in a godly way, but this is the first I've seen that equips them to answer their children's spiritual questions with biblical insight and accuracy. The author's practical, day-to-day illustrations give the reader a deeper understanding of Scripture and a desire to ask the hard questions that will bring God and His Word more into focus. This book will prepare every woman, wife, or mother to answer those one-on-one questions brought to them by their children, friends, family members, or even complete strangers."

SALLY E. STUART
Author of *Christian Writer's Market Guide*

DEDICATION

To my darling daughter,

Nicole:

Retain the standard of sound words which you have heard from me,
in the faith and love which are in Christ Jesus.
Guard, through the Holy Spirit who dwells in us,
the treasure which has been entrusted to you.
—2 Timothy 1:13-14

I could not be prouder of the woman you have become since the
original publication of this work in 2003. You are a wonderful
daughter, wife, and mother. You are an absolute blessing to me.
I am so thankful that we are not only mother and daughter,
but also sisters in Christ and best friends.
You are my sunshine. Never stop shining Christ for all to see!
With immense love and affection,

Mom

TABLE OF CONTENTS

ACKNOWLEDGMENTS

My deepest appreciation and very special thanks to the late Dr. Norman Geisler for encouraging me to write this book and for his gracious words in the foreword. I would also like to express my humble gratitude to the apologists who have dedicated their lives to providing a vast array of resources that help equip the Christian community to offer sound reasons for our faith; you will find their names and resources throughout this book.

Thanks also to Professor Frank Sherwin for his input, suggestions, and review of the 2017 version of chapter 6 and for his patience and timely answers to all my questions or concerns. It was an honor to have had the late Dr. Duane Gish review chapter 6 for the original 2003 manuscript as well. May God continue to bless his memory.

Special thanks to the Hubbell family for sharing their immense love and powerful testimony. To my dear friends Connie and Nan, who ask me the deepest and most challenging questions, thank you for keeping me on my spiritual and intellectual toes! I am truly indebted to many brothers and sisters in Christ at Calvary Chapel Woodland, and Pleasant View Community Church for their prayers, love, and support of my ministry. Thank you so, so much; your humility and service to the Lord are jewels in your ever-growing crowns.

Very special thanks to my understanding and patient children, Nicole and Mikael. They were only 10 and 3 when I wrote the original manuscript. They, along with my awesome son-in-law, Kamden, and my adorable grandson, Caius, remain the best reasons to become equipped with reasons.

To my beloved husband, Jeff, thank you for your unwavering, passionate, and compassionate love for me; I am so thankful that we are, and always will be, each other's best friend.

To my Lord and Savior Jesus Christ—I am so thankful that the foolishness of God is wiser than men, for if it weren't, I'd never stand a chance (Acts 4:13). May You alone be glorified.

FOREWORD

Do you have reasons for your faith? As Christians, it is vitally important that we do. For many years, I have had a growing concern over the lack of available and appropriate resources specifically designed for women, written by women, in the area of Christian apologetics.

Simply put, Christian apologetics is the ministry of offering sound reasons for the Faith to those who have a variety of questions, believer and unbeliever alike. Since women, and especially mothers, seem to have the greatest number of spontaneous opportunities to share and defend their faith, filling this need is crucial.

What a breath of fresh air it was to meet a woman who knows how to do what the Bible commands each of us to do, yet in a way that "puts the cookies on the bottom shelf." Judy Salisbury is a trained professional speaker and a competent defender of the Christian Faith, as well as a dedicated wife and mother. Her message not only transforms the heart, but it satisfies the mind. I know of no book on the market that better meets the spiritual needs and fills the intellectual hunger of women who want to see their friends, family, and children in the kingdom of God than *Reasons for Faith*.

Judy not only writes in an engaging, dynamic, and biblical way, but her common sense answers also will help mothers—and fathers too—prepare their children for the pagan and anti-Christian world in which they find themselves. After all, studies show that children who grow up without good reasons for the faith of the parents tend to discard it in high percentages while in college.

In short, this book is a stimulating, informative, oftentimes witty and encouraging resource for women with a desire to impact their sphere of influence for the Lord Jesus Christ in a manner that indeed reaches the heart, soul, and mind.

DR. NORMAN L. GEISLER
Author or co-author of over one-hundred books
Cofounder Veritas International University

CHAPTER 1 ~ *Making the Case: My Journey*

God has a sense of humor. I never really knew, until the Lord called me to write this book, how careful a woman should be about whining too loudly or too often—because she just might be the one God taps on the shoulder to meet the challenge.

For a long time, I grumbled in front of the apologetics section (or the woman's section) in Christian bookstores, unable to find a resource that would help equip me with reasons for my faith while addressing my spiritual and emotional needs as well. I remember thinking, *Wouldn't it be great to own a resource without sports analogies that I can't understand because I don't play golf or football, but instead includes anecdotes I can relate to—anecdotes that will help me remember a particular answer or spiritual truth?* Well, I guess this book is an example of *she who complains the most will find herself engaged in the task*.

Several events and situations motivated me to become better equipped with reasons for my faith. One of them was that it simply amazed me, shortly after I gave my life to the Lordship of Jesus Christ, how everyone around me appeared to have a sudden interest in spiritual matters. (Perhaps it's like when you purchase a new car—it feels as if just about everyone on the freeway is driving the same model and color.) Because spiritual matters seemed to be the talk of the town, I felt I needed a resource to help me become better equipped.

You might feel the same way. Opportunities abound with friends, family, neighbors, grocery store clerks, co-workers, and the list can go on. For example, I never in my life had a cultist knock on my door until I gave my life to Christ. After that, I thought my doorbell had a magnet on it! (This is not why we later moved to the woods.)

Divine Appointments Abound

Even before committing my life to Christ, I had vast and varied opportunities to discuss spiritual matters with hurting or searching individuals. I wish I could relive those spontaneous divine appointments that just seemed to fall into my lap back then. I would enthusiastically seize them today. Unfortunately, though I considered myself a Christian, my heart was far from Christ. In the yesterdays of my pursuit of self rather than a relationship with God or others, my career in corporate sales took center stage in my life, along with aspirations to become an entertainer. Though many felt convinced I would someday become the next Carol Burnett, I am eternally grateful that God was not so convinced. After all, it is a far more significant achievement to be a servant rather than a celebrity.

My Missed Divine Appointments

My heart breaks with regret over one individual, in particular, a sales assistant, who I will refer to as Lance, whom I worked with at one specific corporation based in San Fransico, California. Lance was as open as anyone could be to discussing spiritual matters. There were about eight of us sales folk whom he would assist with essential secretarial duties. I had a soft spot in my heart for Lance and his usually upbeat and flamboyant personality, yet I was insensitive to his spiritual hunger.

Every Monday morning, for example, for the first three months I worked for that organization, I would blow through the office doors, scuttle past Lance's desk with a hot cup of tea, and go straight to my desk so I could hit the phones to set appointments for the week. Once I left at about noon, my co-workers didn't catch a glimpse of me until Friday. That was when I would yet again blow past everyone with a straight-faced, monotone "morning," and disappear into my cubicle until late in the evening to complete paperwork and follow-up with customers or potential sales prospects.

My whole demeanor was strictly business, and everyone around me knew it. My abrupt personality and *nose to the grindstone* approach to my work were a carryover from being a recent transplant from the Metropolitan Area of New York City where I was raised and where I had also worked in corporate sales.

Within my first year at that San Francisco-based company, I had won two national sales awards and landed their first three international contracts. Because I appeared so focused, to say I was unapproachable would be a gross understatement, and this, along with my now long lost harsh New Jersey/Booklyneeze accent, prompted my co-workers to keep their distance. However, one day, all that changed.

"Good morning, everyone!" I practically sang as I whirled by Lance with a single red rose in my hand. "It's a great day, isn't it?" My assistant's jaw almost hit his desk. No, I hadn't met the Lord Jesus Christ just yet. However, I had just met my husband, Jeff, who left that single red rose on my car's windshield, along with a sweet note, the morning after our first date. I will never forget how people wandered out of their cubicles and offices with the same bewildered look on their faces as Lance while I, without being asked, jubilantly told everyone in earshot about the wonderful time I had had with this *guy* who had taken me to the de Young Museum in San Francisco. Light entered my life, and it brought me to share a tiny bit of myself with others.

Well, it seemed the change had a positive effect on everyone. Soon I was having lunch with the gang at work, and I even elected to change my schedule so I could attend company-paid events. I enjoyed Giant's baseball games at what was then Candlestick Park in San Francisco and a variety of other fun company-paid outings with my co-workers. (I still have several extra innings CROIX DE CANDLESTICK reward buttons and no—they are not for sale.) After a while, the other sales staff didn't mind teasing me about how standoffish I was before I met the man I would marry just seven short months later.

Lance seemed to be the happiest for me when he heard that Jeff and I had impulsively eloped. He said assuredly, "You two must have known each other in a past life—that's why you connected so quickly."

To which I quipped, "Lance, this world could only handle me once. I guarantee you I never had a past life." Oh, how I wish we could have that conversation now.

I also remember hearing one of the other sales representatives repeatedly in tears as she talked over the telephone with her ex-husband, begging him for cooperation and help with their four children. Daily I could see she carried a tremendous burden, yet she turned to the stars for answers. I know now she never got the right ones. Since I was not equipped at the time, she certainly didn't get any helpful counsel or answers from me.

Perhaps you have had the same experience. A friend or co-worker, desperately needing the Savior's touch, tugs at your heart, but you hesitate because you feel ill-equipped to answer her concerns. You may wonder, *Where and how do I even begin the task of becoming equipped to reach the lost or hurting?* My dear sister, our Lord has not only provided you with vast opportunities to share your faith but also a resource that can help you do that confidently and competently.

My 180° Life and Attitude Change

How sad for me that, unlike many Christian women, I did not recognize the need to reach those around me with the truth they needed. Through life's circumstances, while on the road as a salesperson, God brought me to my knees in a little hotel room by way of a Gideon Bible. There I truly gave Him my life. Once again, I was in for a huge life and attitude change. Mine was a dramatic transformation of heart, soul, mind, and then eventually a career, which brought about new opportunities to share my faith.

Three-and-a-half years after Jeff and I eloped, the physical birth of our daughter, Nicole, came on Christmas Eve—almost exactly one year after my spiritual birth. She was huge—ten pounds, three ounces—but to us, she was our tiny, precious baby girl. Once the swelling in her face had subsided, my husband was right—she was exquisite. Since I had never had the opportunity to babysit, I was somewhat embarrassed to ask the nurses—at almost

30 years of age—"Now, just *how* do I change that diaper?" I learned quickly.

I will never forget, as I cuddled her, reflecting on what seemed like a full year that I had carried her. Now, here she was in my arms. After a few days, Jeff felt safe enough to return to work and leave me alone with Nicole, fully confident that I had mastered diaper changing. I had no ambivalence or misgivings for having left the corporate world for the precious little bundle I snuggled close to me. By making me Nicole's Mommy, I recognized that God was entrusting to me my highest and richest calling.

So many thoughts flooded my mind. However, as I looked at Nicole's tiny face and delicate little hands, I must say the most compelling thought was the realization that my daughter was going to ask serious questions about our faith and beliefs. It did not take a pediatrician or a parenting class to tell me that one day Nicole was going to ask, "Why?"

How awful it would be, I thought, *for my little girl to turn to someone else rather than her mommy and daddy for the answers.* At this point in my relationship with the Lord, I was acutely aware there would be those who would just love to give her answers that would sound good on the surface but would lead her to spiritual death. When I thought back on my days in corporate sales, I could not imagine the pain of seeing my daughter swept away, as the daughters of several of my colleagues were. I then realized a profound responsibility to do what I could to try to prevent that from happening.

I was thankful I spent the first year of my Christian infancy reading the Holy Bible cover to cover. What an amazing experience it was! Prophecies regarding the long-awaited Messiah seemed to jump off the pages. I never realized just how many common expressions, such as "the handwriting is on the wall," had come from the Bible. They were certainly fun to discover. More importantly, I learned parenting skills, which I desperately needed, from the perfect heavenly Parent. Soon I began to know, love, and draw closer to the God in whom I finally put my trust.

Now, I know this won't come as a surprise to you, but by age three, Nicole was off and running with, "Why this...?" "Why that...?" "How come...?" As a new believer, I also had questions. Therefore I began the arduous task of becoming equipped. For me, it was arduous because, by the end of the day with a little one, I found that my mind was downright fried. Not only that, but I must also admit I had always had difficulty in the past with reading and studying in an attempt to retain information. Regardless of my challenges, God was faithful to answer my prayers when I got on my knees and cried to Him for help in understanding, retaining, and recalling the material I felt compelled to study.

FINAL THOUGHTS

What you have in your hand is a bit of fruit from my study effort. This book was born out of a desire to understand what I believed and why. It was born out of a desire to help others meet our risen Lord. With the arrival of our son, Mikael, it was born out of a deep desire to offer my children sound reasons for our faith. Finally, *Reasons for Faith* was born out of a desire to ensure that Christian women would have a safe, practical, relatable, and fun place to start their task of becoming better prepared when facing a crisis of belief or when facing challenges to their faith.

I sincerely believe you will find this book an asset when sharing with others your love for our precious Lord Jesus Christ, His Word, His truth, and His offer of eternal life. *Reasons for Faith* is a resource that will help you answer your children's concerns and that of their friends as well. It is a dynamic resource that will help you reach your friends, family, and co-workers who are seeking something—Someone.

Further, my earnest hopes and prayers are that when you fully understand *why* you believe *what* you believe, you will experience strength and will be immovable when you face life's most turbulent storms. So, pop a little popcorn, make a nice hot cup of cocoa, slip a peppermint stick into it, and may the Lord richly bless you as you become better equipped with sound, common sense, memorable reasons for your faith.

QUESTIONS & RESOURCES

1. What is prompting you to read this resource?

2. What do you hope to gain from it?

3. Are there, or have there been, people you desired to reach for Christ, but you hesitated? What happened?

4. The chapter titles give you an idea of what I will address in this resource. At this point, how would you address these issues?

5. Do you feel a sense of responsibility to become better equipped to share your faith? Why, or why not?

At this point, my concern is that you be sure to read your Bible from cover to cover. If you profess Christ and have not done this already, then this should be your priority to becoming equipped. Therefore, my suggested resource for this chapter is a reading of your Bible, Genesis to Revelation.

CHAPTER 2 ~ *Trusting the Word*

"God said it. I believe it. That settles it." That is a rather bold saying, to be sure. However, as a new believer, though I was without a doubt committed to trusting Jesus with my life and eternity in December 1991, I must admit I was also somewhat apprehensive about trusting the Bible as well. Nevertheless, I realized that if I were to grow closer to God and know His will for my life, the Bible was the place to turn. Like many other people, I had questions—and yes, concerns. One of which was whether or not the Bible was indeed God's Word.

Thankfully, our merciful and loving Heavenly Parent did not leave us without answers. He did not give us a burning desire to seek Him and grope for Him, according to Acts 17:27, only to leave us frustrated in our quest to find Him. God, in His immense love for His image-bearers, gave not just what so many refer to as *Life's Little Instruction Book*—no, it is so much more than that. God gave us His Word, a window to His heart, and to His love for fallen humanity, which we call the *Holy Bible*.

Is it okay to question the validity of the Bible? Is it okay to have doubts? Is it okay to wonder if there is any difference between it and other so-called holy books from the vast array of world religions? In a nutshell, is it okay to ask, "Why should we believe that the Holy Bible is the inspired Word of God?" The answer is that it is perfectly fine to have doubts because those doubts prompt us to pursue reliable answers to our questions, and God loves to prove Himself true.

Because the answers are plentiful, I will share just a few points from several areas. First, I will uncover some fundamental misconceptions regarding the Bible. Second, I will turn my focus to the reliability of the Old and New Testament manuscripts. Third, I will review some fascinating biblical prophecies and their fulfillment. Fourth, I'll explain the attitude Jesus had toward the Scriptures and how He used them. Lastly, I'll share just a few thoughts on the importance of the Word of God in our lives.

The Bible: Must Reading

Indeed, one can turn to the Holy Bible for life's little instructions. If we turned to it for that purpose alone, to help us on our day-to-day journey through life, it would undoubtedly be a worthy read. Unfortunately, though it is the most widely purchased book in North America, it is still the least read. Something that amazed me as a new believer—and always does after walking with Him for decades—is the multitude of professing Christians who have never read their Bible cover to cover. However, I am just as amazed at the number of disbelieving individuals who, likewise, have never read it. It is no wonder that so many people have a difficult time defending or refuting it when this is the case.

Therefore, due to the dust buildup on many a Bible, I think there are several misconceptions I should briefly touch upon to help perhaps strengthen our confidence when presenting God's Word to others.

Divine Inspiration

I think it could be possible that those who feel a bit ambivalent about the Bible's trustworthiness just might picture a bunch of guys in tunics sitting around jawing about a great book idea that could change the world. Some folks might believe that a handful of individuals with overactive imaginations concocted the whole thing. Perhaps the ambivalent people might even think that some wise guys offered their interpretation of what God communicated. However, the apostle Peter assures us that this is not the case. In classic passionate Peter fashion, he emphatically wrote:

> But know this first of all, that no prophecy of Scripture is a matter of one's own interpretation, for no prophecy was ever made by an act of human will, but men moved by the Holy Spirit spoke from God.[1]

---

[1] 2 Peter 1:20

A fascinating statement, one that prompts an interesting question. Did those who were "moved by the Holy Spirit" have the sense that they were speaking for God? A turn to the Scriptures provides us our answer.

King David believed the Lord spoke to and through Him as we read 2 Samuel 23:1-2:

> Now these are the last words of David.
> David the son of Jesse declares,
> The man who was raised on high declares,
> The anointed of the God of Jacob,
> And the sweet psalmist of Israel,
> "The Spirit of the LORD spoke by me,
> And His word was on my tongue."

Jeremiah the Prophet knew the words he communicated were not his own:

> The word which came to Jeremiah from the LORD, saying, "Thus says the LORD, the God of Israel, 'Write all the words which I have spoken to you in a book.'"[2]

In the same chapter where we find the Lord re-writing the Decalogue on stone tablets with His finger to replace the ones Moses threw down out of anger at the sin of his people at the foot of Mt. Sinai, we find this statement from God to Moses:

> The LORD said to Moses, "Write down these words, for in accordance with these words I have made a covenant with you and with Israel."[3]

I could cite many more examples. However, I think the apostle Paul explained quite nicely how the Spirit of God communicated to him and the other apostles, and why believers who hear the message can recognize it as being from the Spirit of God.

> We have received, not the spirit of the world, but the Spirit who is from God, so that we may know the things

---

[2] Jeremiah 30:1-2

[3] Exodus 34:27

freely given to us by God, which things we also speak, not in words taught by human wisdom, but in those taught by the Spirit, combining spiritual thoughts with spiritual words [or, "interpreting spiritual things to spiritual men"]. But a natural man [or, "an unspiritual" man] does not accept the things of the Spirit of God, for they are foolishness to him; and he cannot understand them, because they are spiritually appraised.[4]

Second Timothy 3:16 states, "all Scripture is inspired by God." That appears pretty straightforward. But let's take a closer look. The word *inspired* in the Greek literally means *God-breathed*. The word *all* means just that—*all!* Not some, not pick-and-choose, but "*all* Scripture is inspired by God."

To sum up the above passages, the Holy Spirit of God, Who gave all Scripture, inspired individuals of His choosing, at a time of His choosing, to write them down. As believers, we can grasp the Scriptures by the Holy Spirit as well. Therefore, while many individuals can write beautifully inspiring messages or songs, it is quite another matter to claim that their writings are *divinely* inspired.

For example, if you were holding a book in each hand that claimed to be "holy," there are ways of knowing which one of them was genuinely inspired by God, if either. We can apply a simple fact that no two contradictory statements can both be accurate at the same time and in the same sense to test their claim of divine inspiration. Therefore, the first question to ask is, "Do the messages contained in these books contradict each other?" If one states, for example, that you are to worship many gods, yet the Bible states that there is only one true and living God who said, "You shall have no other gods before Me,"[5] that is an apparent contradiction. Both books cannot be true on the subject of God and worship. Hence, it would be time to put these books to the test. That is precisely the purpose of this chapter: to discover if the "Good Book" is actually "God-breathed."

---

[4] 1 Corinthians 2:12-14. Quoted material in brackets is the alternate rendering from the NASB margin.

[5] Exodus 20:3

Touchy Topics

I find that, while we are more than happy to get the Word of God into the hands of eager seekers, some topics in the Bible make us bristle when we read them. Often these are passages that folks feel are obstacles to belief. The following are just a few of the prickly items that often rock the believer and rouse the unbeliever.

Slavery

The subject of slavery is always a sticky one, yet we must consider the topic in light of biblical times. Though it was part of the culture at that time, thankfully, it was far from what we imagine when we think of slavery today. Some individuals became slaves as a means of paying their debts—however, the Bible does not advocate abuse but rather states that slaves were to be treated with dignity and respect.

For example, if a slave ran away from his master, he was able to live where he wished without fear of being returned.[6] Job, for example, recognized that he and his slaves were on equal footing before God, and he understood that if he mistreated them, he would stand accountable before God for that mistreatment. In his words:

> If I have despised the claim of my male or female slaves
> When they filed a complaint against me,
> What then could I do when God arises?
> And when He calls me to account, what will I answer Him?
> Did not He who made me in the womb make him,
> And the same one fashion us in the womb?[7]

---

[6] Deuteronomy 23:15-16
[7] Job 31:13-15

Bigamy

The practice of bigamy, as recorded in the Bible, is another issue that causes concern. We might well ask, "If Solomon's wealth and wisdom were a gift from God, how could he have chosen to have so many wives?" While Solomon was very wise, he did not apply that wisdom to his fleshly, wayward lusts, which led to his despair. The book of Ecclesiastes, which he penned, reveals his view of the self-indulgent life quite appropriately. "Vanity of vanities! All is vanity."[8] Quite literally, "Futility of futilities! All is futile." Sadly, Solomon's lust for multiple wives drew his heart *away* from God, not to Him.

When God spoke on the subject of matrimony, an institution created by Him, He was unambiguous regarding His design and intent, beginning with the fashioning of Eve. In Genesis 2:21-25, we read:

> So the LORD God caused a deep sleep to fall upon the man, and he slept; then He took one of his ribs and closed up the flesh at that place.
> The LORD God fashioned into a woman the rib which He had taken from the man, and brought her to the man.
> The man said, "This is now bone of my bones,
> And flesh of my flesh;
> She shall be called Woman,
> Because she was taken out of Man."
> For this reason a man shall leave his father and his mother, and be joined to his wife; and they shall become one flesh. And the man and his wife were both naked and were not ashamed.

Notice just a few essential aspects of this passage. 1) God did not take more than one rib to fashion several wives for Adam. 2) The passage states that the man will "be joined to his wife," singular not plural and that they "shall become one flesh." 3) By

---

[8] Ecclesiastes 1:2

using the term "wife," we have the definition of marriage and the qualifications for it, according to God, Who alone instituted it.

In Matthew 19:4-6, Jesus was particular when he reiterated the Genesis account as he was questioned on His view of divorce:

> "Have you not read that He who created them from the beginning MADE THEM MALE AND FEMALE, and said, 'FOR THIS REASON A MAN SHALL LEAVE HIS FATHER AND MOTHER AND BE JOINED TO HIS WIFE, AND THE TWO SHALL BECOME ONE FLESH'? So they are no longer two, but one flesh. What therefore God has joined together, let no man separate."

Our Lord's words would also imply, *let no human being re-define*, even for the claim of being *in love*. Marriage has an even higher calling than merely two individuals who feel warm and fuzzy toward each other.

As I look at the lives of individuals throughout the Bible, it is evident that the departure from God's standard for marriage by those who pursued the cultural practice of bigamy brought nothing but trouble upon themselves. Who can ignore the rivalry between Rachel and Leah? Even though they were the mothers of the children of Israel, their antagonism and jealousy toward one another when it came to Jacob, their shared husband, brought about deep resentment and turmoil. It is by God's grace that He redeemed the human circumstance, which resulted from sin, by bringing about a great nation. Though we never read that God condoned the practice, it appears that He simply tolerated bigamy as a part of Israel's culture for only a season.

Other Sordid Events

We would have to agree that, aside from bigamy or slavery, there are several unflattering, and at times ungodly, circumstances recorded by biblical writers. When Abraham embroidered the truth before Pharaoh, and again before King Abimelech, about Sarah being his sister rather than his bride,[9] or Leah purchasing from

---

[9] Genesis 12:13, 20:2

Rachel a night with Jacob for a handful of mandrakes,[10] are just two examples. Of course, we can add to those the David–Bathsheba affair.[11]

When you think about it, the fact that personalities in the Bible are not always pictured in their best light—but in their frailty, during their less than godly decisions—certainly affords more credence to the Scriptures. The events reported and recorded were as they happened. No doubt, if biblical writers contrived the events in the Scriptures, many would portray themselves as super saints of the century.

However, they, like all of us, were far from that. Peter, for example, constantly put his foot in his mouth, and in a very cowardly way, he swore that he did not know Jesus—not once but three times.[12] What a failure on the part of the man who promised our Lord just hours before that if everyone else deserted Him, he alone would die for Him! Yet, we all have our Peter moments, don't we? Praise God for His immediate forgiveness and restoration when we seek it, and, like Peter, we then have the opportunity to lead thousands to Christ as well.

Perceived Inconsistencies

Sometimes, spotting an inconsistency in the Scriptures can sure knock us for a loop. For example, in the Gospel of Mark, we read that the crucifixion took place at the third hour. However, John's account states that at the sixth hour, Jesus was still on trial! Both can't be true—or, can they? Dr. Norman Geisler and Thomas Howe easily explain this little difficulty in their most handy resource *When Critics Ask: A Popular Handbook on Bible Difficulties*:

> Both Gospel writers are correct in their assertions. The difficulty is answered when we realize that each Gospel writer used a different time

---

[10] Genesis 30:14-16
[11] 2 Samuel 11
[12] Matthew 26:73-75

system. John follows the *Roman* time system while Mark follows the *Jewish* time system.

According to Roman time, the day ran from midnight to midnight. The Jewish 24-hour period began in the evening at 6 P.M. and the morning of that day began at 6 A.M. Therefore, when Mark asserts that at the third hour Christ was crucified, this was about 9 A.M. John stated that Christ's trial was about the sixth hour [6 A.M. Roman time]. This would place the trial *before* the crucifixion and this would not negate any testimony of the Gospel writers.[13]

As we ponder this, it makes more sense for John to rely upon Roman time, since he wrote his Gospel to reach the Gentiles. Mark, documenting the words of Peter, penned from a more Jewish perspective (especially when we consider that Mark's Gospel opens with a quotation from Isaiah the Jewish prophet).

In any case, while there are some variations in the records of the same event, the differences are not contradictions. Moreover, there are always variations in eyewitness testimony. The good news is that they do not discredit the validity of the accounts—in actuality, the differences in the biblical accounts *validate* the Scriptures since if all the reports were identically written, we might well suspect the authors of collaboration or collusion.

In sum, any apparent inconsistencies in the Bible are just that—*apparent*. What we might perceive as an inconsistency or contradiction can be understood by taking into account the language, idioms, customs, or culture of that time.

---

[13] Norman Geisler and Thomas Howe, *When Critics Ask: A Popular Handbook on Bible Difficulties* (Wheaton, IL: Victor Books/SP Publications, Inc., 1992), p. 376

Testing the Old Testament

Remember the telephone game? Someone whispers something in your ear, and you whisper it in the next person's ear, and so on until the message travels all around the room. By the time the message reaches the last person, it is dramatically different from the original. When I played the telephone game, I just couldn't resist the temptation to alter the original message to something rather silly and bizarre. Why? Because it's a game—and the more the message changes, the funnier the game becomes.

Unfortunately, some people believe that relying on the Scriptures is equivalent to trusting the message the last person in the telephone game transmits. They think that with each copy of the text, alterations must have occurred from the original message. However, since Old Testament scribes understood their task as copying what *God-breathed*, they viewed it as anything but a *game*, as Dr. Geisler aptly notes:

> With respect to the Jewish Scriptures, however, it was not scribal accuracy alone that guaranteed their product. Rather, it was their almost superstitious reverence for the Bible. According to the *Talmud* there were specifications not only for the kind of skins to be used and the size of the columns, but there was even a religious ritual necessary for the scribe to perform before writing the name of God. Rules governed the kind of ink used, dictated the spacing of words, and prohibited writing anything from memory. The lines, and even the letters, were counted methodically.
>
> If a manuscript was found to contain even one mistake, it was discarded and destroyed. This scribal formalism was responsible, at least in part, for the extreme care exercised in copying the Scriptures. It was also the reason there were only a few manuscripts (as the rules demanded the destruction of defective copies).[14]

---

[14] Norman L. Geisler, *Baker Encyclopedia of Christian Apologetics* (Grand Rapids, MI: Baker Books, 1999), p. 552

Perhaps you have heard of the Dead Sea Scrolls and wondered what was so significant about the find. Well, among the scrolls discovered in 1947 in the caves of Qumran was the entire book of Isaiah. This scroll turned out to be about a thousand years older than the oldest manuscript of Isaiah available at the time. Proving Dr. Geisler's point, it is word-for-word identical to our standard Hebrew text today. Due to the meticulousness of the scribes, overall, our Old Testament Scriptures are 95-percent pure. The 5-percent variation is only in punctuation or spelling, nothing that would affect any significant doctrine.[15]

Testing the New Testament

When we consider the reliability of the New Testament, it is essential to note that it was written entirely during the first century A.D. Why is this important? Since the majority of the New Testament was written between A.D. 47 to 70, those who might be concerned with legends creeping into the text can put their mind at ease. The period between the documentation of the events and the actual events was simply too short for a legend to develop. Since many contemporaries of Jesus were still alive at the time the texts were written, anything false would have been recognized as a legend. Therefore, they would have been immediately refuted by those who were actual eyewitnesses to the events.

Though there are several ways to prove that the New Testament was written between A.D. 47 and 70, I'll share just one way for simplicity's sake. We can know, approximately, when the New Testament Scriptures were written by what is *not* recorded. For example, you would think that the destruction of Jerusalem and the temple and the dispersion of the Jewish people by the Roman general Titus in A.D. 70 might get even a little mention had the events occurred before the writing of the texts. It would be like me writing a book on the recent history of the United States and omitting September 11, 2001. Since the events of that day so dramatically affected our country as a whole, surely you would

---

[15] Norman L. Geisler, *Baker Encyclopedia of Christian Apologetics* (Grand Rapids, MI: Baker Books, 1999), p. 553

have to assume that my omission meant that I wrote my manuscript before the horrific events of that memorable day.

The other exciting bit of information to note is that there is a time-lapse of only 25 years between the original writing of the New Testament and the oldest available copies. In contrast, the period between Plato's original manuscripts and the earliest existing texts is approximately 1,200-years. In the case of Aristotle, there are around 1,400-years between his original writings and the most ancient copies, and for Homer's *Iliad*, we have about a 500-year gap.[16] Therefore, if we can accept the texts of Plato, Aristotle, and Homer as authentic, surely we can trust the New Testament texts as well—especially since the New Testament is 99.5-percent pure in its accuracy to the original.[17] As with the Old Testament, the only variations are in style or spelling, but nothing that would influence any significant doctrine.

Of all the works of antiquity, the New Testament has the most considerable amount of surviving manuscript evidence. With a whopping 24,000 ancient manuscript copies of the New Testament, comparisons bear out the accuracy of the text. No other ancient writing even comes close. For Plato's writings, there are less than ten ancient manuscript copies, for Aristotle, 50, and Homer's *Iliad*, approximately 640 surviving manuscript copies.

Rest assured that the Gospels of Matthew, Mark, and John are documented eyewitness accounts. Though Luke, the author of the Gospel of Luke and the Acts of the Apostles, was not an eyewitness, the good doctor was also a meticulous historian. It is widely acknowledged that Luke's background information is historically, geographically, and archeologically verifiable. According to the late Dr. Norman Geisler, a contemporary and world-renowned apologist:

> Luke has proven himself to be a reliable historian even in the details. William Ramsay spent twenty years of research in the area Luke wrote about. His conclusion

---

[16] Josh McDowell and Bill Wilson, *A Ready Defense* (Nashville, TN: Thomas Nelson, Inc., 1992), p. 45

[17] Norman L. Geisler, *Baker Encyclopedia of Christian Apologetics* (Grand Rapids, MI: Baker Books, 1999), p. 533

was that in reference to thirty-two countries, fifty-four cities, and nine islands Luke made no mistakes! That is a record to be envied by historians of any era.[18]

Testing Biblical Prophecy

Since questions regarding the future occupy the mind of many people, biblical prophecy is by far one of the most exciting proofs for the reliability of the Holy Bible. Prophecy truly sets the Bible apart from any other professed holy book of other world religions—and it sets the Bible's God apart from any other so-called god, as Isaiah 46:9-11 reveals:

> Remember the former things long past,
> For I am God, and there is no other;
> I am God, and there is no one like Me,
> Declaring the end from the beginning,
> And from ancient times things which have not been done,
> Saying, "My purpose will be established,
> And I will accomplish all My good pleasure";
> Calling a bird of prey from the east,
> The man of My purpose from a far country.
> Truly I have spoken; truly I will bring it to pass.
> I have planned it, surely I will do it.

God certainly has declared "the end from the beginning, and from ancient times things which have not been done" because, as Psalm 103:19 proclaims, "The LORD has established His throne in the heavens, And His sovereignty rules over all."

Incredibly detailed biblical prophecies concerning cities like Sidon, Samaria, Gaza, Edom—and the list can go on—were fulfilled in explicit detail. So precise and accurate are the

---

[18] Geisler, N. L. 1999. *Baker encyclopedia of Christian apologetics*. Baker reference library. Baker Books: Grand Rapids, Mich.

prophecies recorded in the book of Daniel—including the succession of the empires of Babylon, Medo–Persia, Greece, and Rome—that some critics have made the unsubstantiated claim that the book was written after the events took place.[19] Unfortunately, for these critics, the dating of the book of Daniel is historically verifiable as Norman Geisler and Thomas Howe explain:

> The Book of Daniel contains supernatural prophecies that, from Daniel's time, extended hundreds of years into the future (Daniel 2:7). Daniel 11 presents a sweeping display of detailed prophecy that stretches from the reign of Cyrus the Great to the reign of antichrist, to the millennial kingdom, to the end of the age and into eternity.
>
> The record of the movement of nations and events is so accurate, it reads as the historical account of an eyewitness. However, conservative scholarship places the date of the Book of Daniel at a time before any of these events took place. The book itself claims to be predictive prophecy (Daniel 9:24ff).
>
> To avoid the conclusion that Daniel's prophecy was a supernatural act of God, modern scholars have proposed a number of explanations including a late date of writing. However, the historical accuracy of Daniel's record confirms a 6th century composition, and the best conclusion is that the Book of Daniel is a revelation from God about historical events that were future to Daniel, many of which are still future to us today.[20]

---

[19] Norman L. Geisler, *Baker Encyclopedia of Christian Apologetics*, **Daniel, Dating of.** (Grand Rapids, MI: Baker Books, 1999), p. 178

[20] *When Critics Ask: A Popular Handbook on Bible Difficulties* by Norman Geisler & Thomas Howe, copyright © 1992, Victor Books: Wheaton, Ill, p. 291

Consider Just One

I think you just might agree that a fascinating prediction concerned the city of Tyre. In Ezekiel 26, God decreed several remarkable prophecies against this city, which included the following:

- King Nebuchadnezzar of Babylon would besiege the mainland city of Tyre.

- The city walls would be destroyed, the towers would be broken down, and Tyre would be scraped down to the bare rock.

- The stones, timber, and debris from the city would be thrown into the water.

- It would become a place for fishermen to spread their nets.

- The city would never again be rebuilt.

In 585 B.C., three years after Ezekiel's dramatic prophecy, King Nebuchadnezzar began a 13-year siege of mainland Tyre. By 573 B.C., mainland Tyre was destroyed. Several hundred years later, the Tyrians who lived in the island city bruised the ego of Alexander the Great by refusing to open their city gates upon his request to do so. Enraged at their refusal, Alex proceeded to besiege the city. Since he did not possess a naval fleet at the time, he had the debris of mainland Tyre scraped into the sea, thus building a causeway to the island city of Tyre and leaving mainland Tyre a bare rock. The mainland city was never rebuilt to its former grandeur, and if you decide to go there for your next vacation, you will find fishermen drying their nets upon the shore.

As I looked into this intriguing prophecy when I first wrote about it in 2002, I became a bit more curious and wanted to investigate today's Tyer. After I had perused the Internet, I came across a site that included information and a visitor's guide. The website mentioned something I found most interesting. "Whether it was the Hellenistic, Roman, or Byzantine conquerors of the ancient world or the Crusaders and Ottomans of the Middle Ages, they all came and went, like the ebb and flow of Tyre's beautiful shoreline." Now, you might be thinking, *What's so interesting about that?* Well, it just happens to be yet another prophecy fulfilled. Ezekiel 26:3 reads, "Thus says the Lord GOD, 'Behold, I am against you, O Tyre, and I will bring up many nations against you, as the sea brings up its waves.'"

Specific Prophecies for Specific People

There are scores of biblical prophecies concerning events, such as the return of the Jewish people to their homeland from around the globe, the deserts of Israel agriculturally flourishing, and the increase of communication, knowledge, and travel in the last days.

There are also a variety of prophecies highlighting individuals—including, of course, the long-awaited Messiah (I will go over some of those in a later chapter). For now, let's take a look at what the Lord declared in Isaiah 44:28 concerning one man, in particular, a man named Cyrus.

> "It is I who says of Cyrus,
> 'He is My shepherd!
> And he will perform all My desire.'
> And he declares of Jerusalem,
> 'She will be built,'
> And of the temple,
> 'Your foundation will be laid.'"

The passage above outlines a specific prophecy that refers to a particular man named Cyrus. Astonishingly, the prophecy was recorded approximately 150 years before Cyrus was even born! Not only that, but the prophecy predicted the rebuilding of Jerusalem and the temple at a time when they were still standing. It would be as if I said on August 11, 2001, "Of the World Trade Center in New York City, it will be rebuilt." You'd think me crazy! It wasn't until one-hundred years after Isaiah's prophecy that Jerusalem and the temple were destroyed. King Nebuchadnezzar took care of that in 586 B.C. However, after the Persians conquered the region in 539 B.C., Cyrus, king of Persia, as recorded in Ezra chapter 1, made his proclamation for the Jewish exiles to return and "rebuild the house of the LORD ... in Jerusalem." Fascinating. Cyrus did just what the Lord said he would do. Again, God foretold Cyrus's actions through the prophet Isaiah 150 years before the man was even born. "The LORD of hosts has sworn, saying, 'Surely, just as I have intended so it has happened, and just as I have planned so it will stand.'"[21] Therefore, "Many plans are in a man's heart, but the counsel of the LORD will stand."[22]

Every prophecy in the Bible regarding the past, right up until today, has come true. "In his comprehensive catalog of prophecies, Encyclopedia of Biblical Prophecies, J. Barton Payne lists 1817 predictions in the Bible, 1239 in the Old Testament and 578 in the New (674–75)."[23] We can also look forward to some exciting fulfillment yet to come.

No human being in history, from before the time of Nostradamus to today's leading psychics, could make predictions with 100-percent accuracy. Also, unlike the Psychic Hot Line, the Bible needs no disclaimers regarding the accuracy of its prophecies. You will never find the small print "for entertainment purposes only" under the biblical prophetic writings.

It is encouraging to know that since every prophetic word was fulfilled in the past, every word God declared concerning this time forward will also take place. I cannot help but recall Jesus' words in Matthew 5:18: "Truly I say to you, until heaven and earth pass away, not the smallest letter or stroke shall pass from the Law until all is accomplished"—which leads us to our next segment.

The Word on the Word

If the Scriptures were a bit suspect, I think you could safely conclude that our Lord Jesus Christ would not quote them but rather would expose them to prevent us from deception. However, it is evident from the New Testament (which we learned is trustworthy and reliable) that Jesus viewed the Scriptures as authoritative. After all, He confirmed

---

[21] Isaiah 14:24

[22] Proverbs 19:21

[23] Geisler, N. L. 1999. *Baker encyclopedia of Christian apologetics*. Baker reference library . Baker Books: Grand Rapids, Mich. P.609

their validity, referred individuals to them, quoted them when facing His greatest enemy, and rebuked the Pharisees for treating their traditions with higher esteem than the Scriptures.[24]

In John 10:35, Jesus said that "the Scripture cannot be broken," and He also claimed to be the fulfillment of them. Now, one would assume that since He believed Himself the fulfillment of them, He would have to regard them as authoritative. Consider the words of Jesus in the following passages:

- *To Satan in Matthew 4:4,7,10:* "It is written, 'MAN SHALL NOT LIVE ON BREAD ALONE, BUT ON EVERY WORD THAT PROCEEDS OUT OF THE MOUTH OF GOD.'"

  "It is written, 'YOU SHALL NOT PUT THE LORD YOUR GOD TO THE TEST.'"

  "Go, Satan! For it is written, 'YOU SHALL WORSHIP THE LORD YOUR GOD, AND SERVE HIM ONLY.'"

- *To the Pharisees in Mark 7:6-8:* "Rightly did Isaiah prophesy of you hypocrites, as it is written: 'This people honors Me with their lips, but their heart is far away from Me. But in vain do they worship Me, teaching as doctrines the precepts of men.' Neglecting the commandment of God, you hold to the tradition of men."

- *To the rich young ruler in Luke 18:20:* "You know the commandments, 'Do not commit adultery, do not murder, do not steal, do not bear false witness, honor your father and mother.'"

---

[24] Mark 7:1-13

• *To the crowds in John 7:38:* "He who believes in Me, as the Scripture said, 'From his innermost being shall flow rivers of living water.'"

It only makes sense that Jesus viewed the Word of God as authoritative—after all, He is the Word made flesh. "In the beginning was the Word, and the Word was with God, and the Word was God."[25] (I'll share a bit more on this in chapter 8.)

Nix the Magic Eight Ball Approach

The manuscript evidence, the internal evidence such as fulfilled prophecies and eyewitness accounts, and external evidence such as history and archeology, all prove the validity of the Scriptures. However, unlike any other writing, ancient or otherwise, it is a living document, and its impact is supernatural. Anyone sincerely desiring a relationship with the living God will find Him by searching the Scriptures. As you know, what I am referring to is not merely a warm, fuzzy feeling that's fleeting, but an abiding relationship with the Word made flesh.

Isn't it a shame that so many people turn to their Bible as they would to a *Magic Eight Ball?* Have you ever seen those silly things? A former co-worker of mine in sales would keep one on her desk. If a deal wasn't working out quite right, she would shake the little ball and flip it over to see her answer float to the top. Most of the time, it read, "Try again later." Just as frivolous is the approach, some professing believers take to the Scriptures. They flip through it with eyes closed, and wherever their finger lands, that must be God's will for the day. God wants His Word to be so much more than that in our lives because it *is* so much more.

The apostle Paul, in his persuasive final letter before his tragic beheading, passionately reminded young Timothy of the vital importance of Scripture in his life. Even though we know these things, like Timothy, we need a reminder.

---

[25] John 1:1

You, however, continue in the things you have learned and become convinced of, knowing from whom you have learned them, and that from childhood you have known the sacred writings which are able to give you the wisdom that leads to salvation through faith which is in Christ Jesus.

All Scripture is inspired by God and profitable for teaching, for reproof, for correction, for training in righteousness; so that the man of God may be adequate, equipped for every good work.[26]

The Bible helps us discover the living God and reveals the path for entering into an abiding relationship with our heavenly Father. The Bible also encourages us in our walk with our Lord and painfully convicts us when we meander off that narrow path. Have you ever noticed that? Isn't it funny how, at those times when we know we are out of His will, specific passages in the Bible are the last thing we want to read? Hebrews 4:12 tells us why:

For the word of God is living and active and sharper than any two-edged sword, and piercing as far as the division of soul and spirit, of both joints and marrow, and able to judge the thoughts and intentions of the heart.

That's deep stuff—no wonder so many people become inflamed when we quote it!

From the Scriptures, we can discern truth from error, like the Bereans, who offered an excellent example of how we are to do just that.

The brethren immediately sent Paul and Silas away by night to Berea, and when they arrived, they went into the synagogue of the Jews. Now these were more noble-minded [intellectually honest I'd say] than those in Thessalonica, for they received the word with great

---

[26] 2 Timothy 3:14-17

eagerness, examining the Scriptures daily to see whether these things were so.[27]

Also along these lines is the exhortation to "Be diligent to present yourself approved to God as a workman who does not need to be ashamed, handling accurately the word of truth."[28] In other words, no *Magic Eight Ball* approach to the Scriptures. Since it is a living document, our attitude should be with prayer and "great eagerness."

In light of what we've learned, who could ignore this life-impacting gift that the God of the universe gave us to know Him more intimately, learn how to live a truly fulfilled life, and understand His clear path which leads to our salvation?

FINAL THOUGHTS

When my children were small, and even now as a grandmother, wouldn't it be foolish to have them memorize verses from a collection of books that are not what they claim to be? Wouldn't it seem like a waste of time to study that collection of books if they were filled with myths and legends? Wouldn't it seem silly to trust that same collection of books as a roadmap for this present life and the next if they simply were not authoritative? The spectacular truth is that the Holy Bible is what it claims to be. It is reliably the inspired Word of God.

What you've read in this chapter regarding the reliability of the Holy Bible is not new information—and there is so much more I wish I could include. However, at the end of this chapter (and of each chapter in this book), you will find a list of suggested resources. My hope is that you will read those helpful volumes because they will serve you well in answering any further questions that might arise regarding the validity of the Holy Bible and many other concerns.

For far too long, the Christian community has been uneasy about defending the Holy Bible against objections. Some of them

---

[27] Acts 17:10-11, bracketed comments mine.
[28] 2 Timothy 2:15

seem rather convincing. Nevertheless, take heart and don't take it personally if someone snickers at your love of the Word. Keep in mind that anyone's quarrel with the reliability of the Holy Bible is not with the one who honors it as such, but with the One who provided it for any person who seeks a love relationship with the Almighty.

Jot down your seeking friend or relative's concern if you are unsure of an answer. If you can't find the answer in this simple guide for addressing popular objections and obstacles to belief, you will most certainly find the answer in my suggested resources. Also, keep in mind that just because you aren't sure of a solution, that does not mean there isn't one available. God has indeed provided answers.

My dear reader, there is no doubt about it—you can trust the Holy Bible because it is divinely inspired, historically reliable, indestructible, infallible, and life-changing. So go right ahead and pick one up at a nightstand near you—and feel confident to encourage someone you know and love to do the same.

QUESTIONS & RESOURCES

1. Is relying on the Bible like relying on the last person in the *telephone game*? Why or why not?

2. Can you name three things that make the Bible unique?

3. What makes the Bible much more than a mere instruction book?

4. Have you ever read your Bible cover to cover? If so, what impact has this had on your life? If not, are you convicted of beginning the task?

5. Why is it vital that we have a large volume of manuscripts for the Old and New Testaments?

6. After reading this chapter, do you have a greater appreciation for God's Word? What points would you share with someone who questions the Bible's reliability?

When Critics Ask: A Popular Handbook on Bible Difficulties by Norman Geisler and Thomas Howe, Baker Books, 1992.

Halley's Bible Handbook, Revised and Expanded Edition by Henry H. Halley, Zondervan, 2014.

The New Inductive Study Bible (NASB), Precept Ministries International, Harvest House Publishers, 2013.

CHAPTER 3 ~ *God's Existence*

The existence of God—quite an overwhelming subject to ponder, isn't it? At one time in my life, even the thought seemed overwhelming. I must admit that from the ages of nineteen to twenty-eight, I was among those who questioned God's existence. My thinking was that even if He did exist, He must have been utterly aloof to my circumstances. God had other things to occupy His time, like keeping the universe running, rather than concerning Himself with what concerned me.

I suppose this is why I have great empathy for those who struggle in this area—because I know that not all individuals who classify themselves as atheists or skeptics are, in fact, hostile to the idea of God's existence. I meet many individuals who are as I once was. I was frustrated that, while intellectually, I could recognize the evidence, yet when it came to trusting and having faith, for me, it was not a leap into the Everlasting Arms. It seemed more like falling headlong into a dark, bottomless chasm. Still, as I think back on those years of doubt, I suspect that the Lord was calling out to me all the while, as in the old Dr. Seuss story *Horton Hears a Who*, "I am here! I am here! I am here!"

God, are You there? It is the human heart's deepest longing. How difficult it is for our mind to grasp that when we make that heartfelt cry toward heaven, He readily replies, "Of course I am." Seeking the answer to the question of God's existence is a worthy pursuit since the Scriptures state that "without faith it is impossible to please Him, for he who comes to God *must believe that He is* and that He is a rewarder of those who seek Him."[29]

It is God's greatest desire that we know, not only that He is, but that He loves us and longs to bring us into the fold for all eternity and to bless us with Himself. After all, He said, "I have loved you with an everlasting love; therefore, I have drawn you

---

[29] Hebrews 11:6 emphasis added

with lovingkindness."[30] He also knows that some of us need a bit more help in the *drawing* process because, more often than not, the reply is, "If God is there and does exist, why doesn't He *show* Himself?" He has certainly done that and in some rather obvious ways.

The psalmist wrote, "The fool has said in his heart, 'There is no God.'"[31] Aside from the fact that there is ample evidence for God's existence, I imagine what is so foolish about the unbeliever's disbelief is that to deny His existence, a person would have to possess the attributes of omniscience and omnipresence. The foolish unbeliever would have to know *every* nook and cranny in the universe and would have to dwell *in* every nook and cranny to make sure God wasn't lurking behind some supernova in an attempt to hide. However, if the unbeliever did possess the attributes of omniscience and omnipresence, he would *be* God. Thus his argument against God's existence would be self-refuting, in that God would be asserting that God does not exist!

Perhaps, since belief in God is intuitive, you also recognize the folly of the atheist. However, when it comes to articulating reasons for belief, you would simply like to share something a bit more concrete than personal intuition. The purpose of this chapter is to guide you in doing just that. Before I present several tests for the existence of God, I will address the popular challenges that we, as believers, face. Once I have addressed these concerns and posed three basic tests, I will then put forth evidence that the God of the tests and the God of the Bible are, without a doubt, the same.

Santa, Dark Chocolate, and Wishful Thinking

I think we have all encountered individuals who attempt to suppress a hearty chuckle at our profound belief in God. For them, the notion of an eternal Being whose power is as unlimited as His presence and knowledge seems too fantastic to be true. Perhaps, they feel we should reserve the idea of such a Being for a child's bedtime story. They seem to discount God's existence and the

---

[30] Jeremiah 31:3

[31] Psalm 14:1

validity of even asking the question because they view belief as mere *wishful thinking*. They feel that believers see God as an imaginary Santa Claus reserved for the gullible to lean upon when the rigors of life seem too much to bear. However, *wishful thinking* does not prove or disprove the existence of God.

Think of it this way. Imagine, for example, that because of your extraordinary gardening abilities, you received an invitation to speak at your local garden party's yearly banquet. It is a spectacular black tie event. Though you are thrilled with the opportunity and are having a lovely time hobnobbing thus far, your nerves are getting the better of you. At the last minute, you decide to dash off to the restroom for a quick visit. Knowing time is short, you leap out of the bathroom stall, turn on the faucet to wash your hands—and lo and behold, the water shoots out with blinding speed, ricochets off the porcelain sink, and soaks the front of your gown. Flustered, you attempt to dry it with a paper towel, only to find that hundreds of teeny-tiny white balls are now plastered across the beautiful sapphire-blue material.

Suddenly, you hear a muffled voice and realize the host is in the process of introducing you. You leave the restroom nearly panic-stricken and move as swiftly as possible down the center aisle of the rather large ballroom, then gracefully ascend the stairs to find your place on the stage behind the podium. You take a deep breath and smile casually at your audience, all the while, hoping no one will notice the huge wet spot and paper towel lint on the front of your gown. Nevertheless, you can hear the muffled snickers and chuckles from every corner of the ballroom.

Still maintaining your composure, you smile graciously and comment lightly, "It's just water—it'll dry soon, I'm sure," while gently brushing off the front of your dress. Just then, Mrs. Snodgrass, the senior executive administrative director of the garden club, steps behind you, cups her hand over the microphone, and whispers in your ear. Horrified by her words—you had no idea that you had inadvertently tucked the back of your dress into your undergarment before your hasty exit from the bathroom stall. Unfortunately, *this* is the best thing that happened to you all day.

Now imagine further that, as soon as you enter the front door of your home, dejected and humiliated, you throw yourself onto your couch and wishfully think about or desire a large box of dark chocolates. You plan to eat the entire box as fast as possible. After all, everyone knows that, next to bacon, dark chocolate is *the* comfort food. Now, the simple fact that you desire dark chocolate, or wishfully think about dark chocolate, does not mean there is no such thing as dark chocolate. Wishing for, or hoping for, or desiring something to exist does not disprove its existence.

When applying this to God, we can take it one step further. The fact that human beings share a deep-seated need for God *confirms* His existence, in that we only desire or need that which exists. When I was pregnant with my son, my deep-seated need wasn't for dark chocolate. What I craved—and will tell you without a moment's hesitation, *needed*—(though much to the chagrin of my poor husband, who tried not to watch me eating them) were anchovies delicately wrapped around little green capers. Good stuff! My craving, my desire, my deep longing was for something that existed—namely, anchovies delicately wrapped around tiny green capers. Such is our need for the existence of God.

Continuing along these lines, we can thank computer scientists Christoph Benzmüller and Bruno Woltzenlogel Paleo for their work on mathematician Kurt Gödel's (1906-1978) calculations to prove God as a necessary being. Their findings show that Gödel's work does indeed add up, though, as computer scientists, proof for the existence of God was not their original intent when working with Gödel's calculations.[32]

Gödel's theorem was to prove that God is the greatest power conceivable, and if believed (desired) as a concept, then God does indeed exist in reality. The following words are of Chris and Bruno from their peer-reviewed paper entitled, *Automating Gödel's Ontological Proof of God's Existence with Higher-order Automated Theorem Provers:*

---

[32] If you like math and would like to read their peer reviewed work see: http://page.mi.fu-berlin.de/cbenzmueller/papers/C55.pdf

"[We] decided to tackle, with automated reasoning techniques, a philosophical problem that is almost 1000 years old: the ontological argument for God's existence, firstly proposed by St. Anselm of Canterbury and greatly improved by Descartes, Leibniz, Gödel and many others throughout the centuries.

"*...we were able to automatically reconstruct and verify Gödel's argument*, as well as discover new facts and confirm controversial claims about it. This is a landmark result, with media repercussion in a global scale, and yet it is only a glimpse of what can be achieved by combining computer science, philosophy and theology."[33]

We hunger for what exists, not what doesn't—otherwise, how would we know to hunger for it? This urgent need for God is an ingrained aspect of the human condition, and on a global scale, no less. Now that's what I call a craving!

You're in Good Company

Similar to the "wishful thinking" camp of individuals would be those who think belief in the existence of God is merely anti-intellectual. I think anti-intellectualism is a rather weak excuse to abandon the topic. Besides, as far as the intelligence test goes, believers are in good company. Perhaps you are familiar with Francis Bacon, Blaise Pascal, and Sir Isaac Newton, the latter considered by many to be the greatest scientist who ever lived. The renowned physicist Michael Faraday, Gregory Mendel, Louis Pasteur, the famous archaeologist William Ramsay—and one of my favorites, who produced hundreds of uses for the peanut, George Washington Carver—all had an abiding faith in and held to a biblical worldview regarding the existence of God.[34]

Now, lest my readers misunderstand me, I do not list these brilliant individuals to show that belief in God is not anti-

---

[33]http://page.mi.fu-berlin.de/cbenzmueller/papers/C40.pdf
emphasis added

[34] Henry M. Morris, *Men of Science—Men of God* (Green Forest, AR: Master Books, 1988)

intellectual and thus prove God's existence. I think that, if what a simpleton believes in is the truth, then no matter what the subject, that is all that should matter to any of us. *Truth* itself is our measuring rod, not the intellectual capacity of those who recognize that truth.

The Universes' Universal Questions

Have you ever been asked the question, "Mom, where did I come from?" For me, when my daughter was tiny, the answer, "California," satisfied her curiosity. However, I knew someday the question would take on an all-new dimension. "Where did I come from?" would turn into "Where did California come from?" then to "Where did this planet come from?" and to—you guessed it— "Where did the universe come from?" That last question, in particular, is a valid one that more individuals seem to ask. After all, if the universe does exist, from where *did* it come? What caused it? Thankfully, there are only a few possible options.

Is it an Illusion?

I wrote, "*if* the universe exists" because perhaps, just perhaps, the universe is merely an illusion—something I created in my mind. However, to have a mind to ponder these heady things, *I* must myself exist—and since I am not floating around in nothingness, the material world around me must exist as well. You are reading my book, correct? At the very least, the two of us exist! I think if we keep going along on this course, it could quite possibly lead to silliness at best, madness at worst. It reminds me of a telephone conversation I once had with a woman who was convinced I did not genuinely exist. When she asked me to prove my existence to her, I simply replied, "You're talking to me." (Actually, I didn't feel too insulted, since she was convinced she didn't exist either!)

We know the universe is not an illusion because certain events are predictable; for example, my desk calendar notes when full moons will occur. From this invaluable information, I can then plan those cozy evening marshmallow roasts in the backyard with the family. Since an illusion exists only in the mind of the one suffering from it, the company that made my calendar would also have to suffer from the same illusion as the astronomers and us, the marshmallow-roasters. Therefore, I think it is safe to conclude that the universe is not an illusion.

Is it Eternal?

Our next option is that the universe is eternal. It merely has always existed. Herein lies what I believe is yet another self-evident concept, one that even small children can recognize. Simply listen to them arguing on a playground: "*You* started it first." "No, *you* started it." Back and forth, it goes. Why? Because everyone knows, everything and everybody had a beginning, from quarrels on a playground to the grandeur of the universe. Aside from the fact that this notion of a beginning point is intuitive, we can see that everything around us is running down and wearing out (Hello, reading glasses!). Therefore, it *must* have had a beginning.

Just to prove wrong, a high-school science teacher who once wrote in a progress report to my parents, "Judy never, NO NEVER, pays attention," I do remember learning about the second law of thermodynamics. This law states that our universe, and everything in it, is running out of energy, is wearing down, and is subject to decay. If the second law of thermodynamics were not a reality, Pluto would not be encased in ice, and cosmetic manufacturers would go broke. Therefore, the universe is not eternal. It had a beginning.

Is it an Effect?

Another option is that the universe suddenly emerged from nothing. However, I also remember—just to greatly encourage that poor science teacher who was so concerned about my limited attention span—that from nothing, nothing comes. Every cause has an effect. Just as one of those children on that playground caused the argument, so also the universe is the effect of a cause.

It Has a Cause

Since the universe is not an illusion, nor is it eternal, nor could it have emerged from nothing, I think our final option is the most reasonable one. Something or Someone independent of the universe had to cause it to come into being. Something or Someone beyond or greater than the universe had to cause its existence. The universe could not have produced itself. It could not have brought itself into being. After all, it was not there to bring about its existence.

The answer lies not in *what* caused the universe, but *Who* caused or created it. What we observe is the effect of an eternal, uncaused First Cause of everything—an omniscient (all-knowing), omnipotent (all-powerful), omnipresent (everywhere present) Being who transcends (is above and independent of) the material universe.

In a nutshell, the universe was brought into existence at a particular moment in time from nothing (no pre-existing material) by the power of an eternal, ultra-dimensional, creative, relational Being, Who brought it about expressly to have a love relationship with those He created in His image. (I will share a bit more on that later.)

Now, though it never occurred to my daughter, when my son, Mikael, was tiny, he did move beyond, "Where did the universe come from?" to, "Where did God come from?" or "Who created God?" Nevertheless, if God were a created being, He would not be God since one of God's greatest attributes is that He is eternal. If another God created Him, He would not be eternal. Instead, He would be immortal, and thus finite, or limited, by the fact that He had a beginning. Nevertheless, as Mikael's mommy, I felt compelled to offer a response to his question. "Mikael, even if His God created God, it really wouldn't make much difference since, as the Creator of us, we all remain accountable and answerable to Him alone."

I guess we can think of it this way. Try as they might, children can appeal to their grandparents for that extra scoop of ice cream, but the decision rests with the parents. Mom and dad are their final authority as their—for lack of a better term—*creators*. Therefore, their appeals for extra ice-cream before dinner are futile since, as their "creators," mom and dad can exercise their authority by answering, "No, the three scoops of chocolate-chip-mint ice cream that you had for lunch should be plenty!" Now that I am a Grammy and remember what it was like when my children were small, I'll do my best to stay in line. Nevertheless, it sure is hard!

The Billboard Test

A couple of very dear friends of mine with whom, for three years, I had vibrant discussions with regarding spiritual matters before leading them to the Lord, told me of an incident that happened as they drove to Washington State from Idaho. In an attempt to test the validity of my claims for God's existence, while traveling along in their car, they began yelling, "God, if You're *really* out there, show us a sign!" Just then, they noticed an enormous billboard reading:

YOU WANTED A SIGN?
HERE IT IS.
GOD.

They were stunned. Now, you might think my friend's experience just a funny coincidence. However, when we discussed the cause of the cosmos by an uncaused First Cause of the universe, I used the words *creative* and *relational* to describe God. I also said He created us for a love relationship—that this vast universe is specifically for those He created in His image. If this is true, two things should follow:

1. The billboard "sign" was not a funny coincidence.

2. Neither is the universe and all it contains.

The Sign

There are certain aspects, aside from the obvious, I think are worthy of considering when contemplating that *God sign*. I believe it just might help us to recognize other "signs" that answer the question of God's existence and confirm His particular interest in human beings. Think, for a moment, about the following aspects of the "God" billboard.

1. The letters were not posted upon the board haphazardly.

2. The letters were centered neatly in three rows.

3. The letters were written with a particular font and style.

4. The letters were written in a particular order, and the order formed words.

5. The punctuation and spelling of those words were correct.

6. The words conveyed a coherent message.

Upon seeing such a sight, the next obvious questions would be, "Who wrote it?" and, "Who put it there for all to see?" The reason why we would wonder *who* and not *what* is that the billboard sign conveyed a message. The message communicated an idea. We say *who* because the sign has a purpose. Its purpose is to send the message that God will respond when asked to do so. The sign speaks of *design*. The sign has purpose and meaning, which means there is a mind behind the design—a rational, intelligent, thinking mind that wishes to communicate a vital message to individuals who can respond. It is the same with God's universe.

The Design: Made for a Reason

When I consider Your heavens,
The work of Your fingers,
The moon and the stars,
Which You have ordained;
What is man that You take thought of him,
And the son of man that You care for him?[35]

---

[35] Psalm 8:3-4

What is so awe-inspiring about the above passage of Scripture is that, immediately after a consideration of the heavenly bodies, the psalmist realized and communicated to us that God made them spectacular for a particular reason. The psalmist believed that God made them with humankind in mind. This passage of Scripture is a beautiful reminder that God made the heavenly bodies exquisite so that human beings could gaze upon them and worship, not the created, but rather the Creator.

"The heavens declare the glory of God; and the firmament showeth His handiwork."[36] "Handiwork" directs us to a *Handiworker*. There is a reason why modern science was born out of a Theistic worldview. Since a rational, intelligent, orderly Being created the universe, scientists recognized that it, and all it contains, can be observed, tested, and verified. Johannes Kepler, considered to be the founder of physical astronomy, summed up the whole matter quite nicely when he stressed that he was simply "thinking God's thoughts after Him."[37]

At this point, let us consider God's creation as a whole, as we look for further *signs* of His existence or His handiwork by way of two key questions that need answering:

1. Does the universe show any signs of design, thus proving the existence of an Intelligent Designer?

2. Is there any evidence that would lead us to conclude that the Mind behind the design "cares" or "takes thought of" human beings in particular, as mentioned by the Psalmist?

The Design: Made Just for Us

I believe we can sufficiently answer the above questions through what is known as *the anthropic principle*. Do not let that term frighten you. Patrick Glynn, in his book *God: The Evidence*, offers an excellent, easy to understand definition:

---

[36] Psalm 19:1 ASV

[37] Henry M. Morris, Men of Science Men of God: Great Scientists Who Believed the Bible (Green Forest, AZ: Master Books, 1988) p.13

The anthropic principle says that all the seemingly arbitrary and unrelated constants in physics have one strange thing in common—these are precisely the values you need if you want to have a universe capable of producing life. In essence, the anthropic principle came down to the observation that all the myriad laws of physics were fine-tuned from the very beginning of the universe for the creation of man—that the universe we inhabit appeared to be expressly designed for the emergence of human beings.[38]

What are some of these constants and values that must be precise for human life, and specifically on Earth? The following barely scratches the surface:

• Oxygen comprises 21 percent of the atmosphere. If it were 25 percent, fires would erupt. If 15 percent, human beings would suffocate.

• A shift in the force of gravity by only 1 part in 100,000,000,000,000,000,000,000,000,000,000,000,000,0 00, (that should be 41 zeroes) would mean our sun would not exist, and our moon would either crash into Earth or sheer off into space.

• Even a slight increase in the force of gravity would result in all the stars being much more massive than our sun, with the effect that the sun would burn too rapidly and erratically to sustain life.

• If the centrifugal force of planetary movements did not precisely balance the gravitational forces, nothing would hold an orbit around the sun.

• If the universe were expanding at a rate one-millionth— think about that—just one-millionth slower than the current rate, the temperature on Earth would be 10,000° Celsius. (Never mind your sunscreen!)

---

[38] Patrick Glynn, *God: The Evidence* (Rocklin, CA: Forum, 1999)

• The smallest variation in the speed of light would alter the other constants of physics, preventing the possibility of life on Earth.

• If Jupiter were not in its current orbit, space material would inundate our humble planet. Jupiter's gravitational field attracts and thus clears away asteroids and comets that would otherwise strike our planet.

• If the thickness of Earth's crust were greater, too much oxygen would be transferred to the crust to support life. If it were thinner, volcanic and tectonic activity would make life untenable.

• If the rotation of Earth took longer than twenty-four hours, temperature differences would be too vast between night and day. If the days were shorter than twenty-four hours, atmospheric wind velocities would be too high.

• If the axial tilt of Earth were slightly altered, surface temperature differences would be too great to sustain life.[39]

So much for *random chance.* (More on that in chapter 6.) This mind-spinning information is not a recent discovery. In 1973, the established astrophysicist and cosmologist Brandon Carter presented a primary thesis before the world's most renowned "scientific minds of our time." Minds reeled over his paper, entitled *Large Number Coincidences and the Anthropic Principle in Cosmology.* Coincidences?

All one has to do is consider the intricacies of the human body, or even a bug, to recognize a Mind behind the design. The anthropic principle, I think, reveals that as far as appropriate accommodations for a specific entity, namely human beings, planet Earth was God's precisely placed, perfectly designed abode. Now, don't you feel special?

---

[39] For more on this see Norman L. Geisler, *The Baker Encyclopedia of Christian Apologetics* (Grand Rapids, MI: Baker Books, 1999), pp. 26-28.

The Fred C. Dobbs Test

Are you like me in that you genuinely enjoy the golden oldie movies? I am not talking about the 1970s. I mean great black and white films from the 1930s, '40s, and '50s. I sincerely appreciate them—and *The Treasure of the Sierra Madre* is one of my favorites. In that dramatic 1948 film, Humphrey Bogart played a hobo, Fred C. Dobbs, who turned to gold prospecting along with a fellow down-and-outer. At the beginning of their adventure, Dobbs is shocked at even the suggestion that greed might get the better of him, but unfortunately, it surely does—along with intense paranoia.

Toward the end of the movie, Dobbs (Bogart's character), assumed the perception that his companion and friend, had suddenly become his rival and enemy. Intense hatred overcame him, as he feared his fellow prospector would murder him for his gold. Finally, after a long, turbulent, sleepless night for both men, Dobbs shot his innocent former friend. Believing he killed the man, prospector Dobbs tossed the gun to his victim's side and then left the scene of the crime.

What happened afterward is fascinating. Dobbs, alone in the middle of the night and wilderness, tried to comfort himself, as he lay beside his campfire. He then muttered nervously:

> "Conscience, what a thing. If you believe you got a conscience, it'll pester you to death. But, if you don't believe you got one, what could it do to you? It makes me sick, all this talk and fussing about nonsense."

Just then, he rested his head on his arm, closed his eyes as if to sleep—and not a moment later, opened them wide as he stared, with a guilt-ridden, horrified expression on his face, into the roaring flames of the campfire before him.

The Treasure of the Sierra Madre brings us to the third test for the existence of God. Bogart's character, Fred C. Dobbs, could not escape the turmoil within his soul no matter how hard he tried to talk himself out of it. Though some individuals vigorously wish to escape any acknowledgment of God, they cannot escape their innate sense of right and wrong, guilt, and impending judgment.

This perception of a moral standard, this thing within us that C.S. Lewis referred to as our *sense of oughtness*,[40] is experienced in all cultures, through all ages, among all human beings.

Nevertheless, from where did it come? From where did this innate *sense*, this self-evident notion of right and wrong, come? Why would you experience a sinking feeling if you slipped into someone's long-awaited parking space during the Christmas rush? It is not illegal—and if might makes right, perhaps the Smart Car driver should freely give the parking space to you since you drive a gas-guzzling, environmentally abusive, nine-person SUV. However, you would experience a bit of inner turmoil and thus would proceed to do one of four things:

1. *Condone it:* "Perhaps I shouldn't have done that, but I just had to, I'm in a terrible hurry!"

2. *Justify it:* "That always happens to me—it's about time I did it to someone else."

3. *Deny it:* "I did *not* take her spot; she was waiting for one further down."

4. *Own it:* "Oh my—I'm sorry. I *know* it was wrong of me to do that. I'll just back out right away. "

Why would we think twice about that situation? Is this *sense* of right and wrong—this feeling of justice or injustice that leads each of us to condone, justify, deny, or confess—only our opinion, or is it just possible that we intuitively appeal to a higher Authority outside or beyond ourselves?

The only answer is that this exclusive thing within human beings, known as the conscience or the *Moral Law*, this universal feeling we experience, is a gift bestowed upon us by our Moral Lawgiver.

Is the Moral Law unique to humans? Yes. Queenie, the family cat, does not feel the burden of guilt because she ate the family's pet hamster. Queenie does not go to the family and say, "I've

---

[40] C.S. Lewis, *Mere Christianity* (New York: Harper Collins, 2001 edition)

sinned. Forgive me, for not only have I eaten the hamster, but I have wrongly accused Fluffy the dog!"

Dolphins, after killing one of their own for sport, do not gather a group of their dolphin peers to conduct a trial. The accused does not bear remorse and seek redemption for its soul or reconciliation with the bereaved dolphin family.

Yes, every human being—and only human beings—recognize the Moral Law. It is evident within, or self-evident, as Romans 2:14-15 clearly states:

> When Gentiles who do not have the Law do instinctively the things of the Law, these, not having the Law, are a law to themselves, in that they show the work of the Law written in their hearts, *their conscience bearing witness, and their thoughts alternately accusing or else defending them.*[41]

Guilt: It's a Good Thing

Now, you might be wondering why I would refer to the conscience as a gift from God. Indeed, the Moral Law, when followed, is a blessing to humanity. At the very heart of the Moral Law is the commandment to love God above all else and to love our neighbor as we do ourselves. When we deny that spiritual check in our conscience, we harm others and ourselves. However, when we respond to that God-given burning in our conscience and obey our internal conviction, the product is an individual with self-restraint, and our society experiences the benefits of following the Golden Rule.

If we feel guilt, why do we feel it? To attempt to talk ourselves out of its existence, as many do with the existence of God, just ignores the question. I believe our conscience is for our moral survival, just as our *fight-or-flight* response is for our physical survival.

---

[41] emphasis added

Think of it this way, if what restrains me from picking your pocket is the fact that you might catch me, what will I do when you aren't looking? But if what restrains me from picking your pocket is the moral compass within my heart that tells me it's wrong; if my reason is that I don't wish to hurt the heart of the One to whom I owe thanks and praise, then my life will be a blessing to others, and I will have peace in my soul. Therefore, guilt is a blessing to humanity.

Unfortunately, all too many individuals in our society suppress their moral compass, that feeling of guilt that implies an impending judgment. If only they would allow the Moral Law to lead them to the Moral Lawgiver who put it there in the first place—for just such a purpose!

The Same God

Wow, God is a big subject! I think the best thing to do for simplicity's sake for our final test for the existence of God, is to review notable points covered in the previous sections and see how they correlate to the God of the Bible.

Since establishing the Bible as divinely inspired in chapter 2, we know we can trust it to give an accurate description of the One who provided it. This knowledge allows us to make a common sense and obvious correlation. Since we know that not only is the Bible's message consistent from Genesis to Revelation about God's redemption of humanity, but it is also consistent regarding the attributes and character of the God of the universe, of intelligent design, and the Moral Law.

The God of the Universe

There are specific attributes the God of the Bible would not only have to claim but must possess to cause the existence of the universe. A turn to the Scriptures will help us find those unique characteristics. In Exodus 3:14, God told Moses, "I AM WHO I AM." Now, while it appears to be a rather simplistic statement, God's proclamation about Himself is weighty with implications.

Notice that God did not say, "I once was..." or "Someday, I sure hope to be..." but, "I AM WHO I AM." In other words, the God of the Bible has always existed. He is eternal.

The God of the Bible brought everything into existence out of nothing. However, He did not wind it up like a watch and let it go; God also sustains what He created:

> • *Genesis 1:1*, In the beginning God created the heavens and the earth.

> • *Colossians 1:17*, He is before all things, and in Him all things hold together.

> • *Hebrews 1:3*, [He] upholds all things by the word of His power.

> • *Acts 17:25*, "He Himself gives to all people life and breath and all things."

The God of the Bible, the uncaused First Cause of the universe, never needs a nap! While we might need our three-o'clock snooze, His unlimited power never wanes or diminishes, according to Isaiah 40:28:

> Do you not know?
> Have you not heard?
> The Everlasting God, the LORD,
> the Creator of the ends of the earth
> Does not become weary or tired.

The God of the Bible is the cause of our existence as well, as stated in Isaiah 44:24-25:

> Thus says the LORD, your Redeemer, and the one who formed you from the womb,
> "I, the LORD, am the maker of all things,
> Stretching out the heavens by Myself
> And spreading out the earth all alone,
> Causing the omens of boasters to fail,
> Making fools out of diviners,
> Causing wise men to draw back
> And turning their knowledge into foolishness."

The God of Design

No doubt about it, the God of the Bible created the universe, including this planet, for a "love relationship" with the creatures He created in His image. Verses twelve and eighteen of Isaiah 45 astoundingly point to the anthropic principle:

> "It is I who made the earth, and created man upon it.
> I stretched out the heavens with My hands,
> And I ordained all their host."

> Thus says the LORD, who created the heavens (He is the God who formed the earth and made it, He established it and did not create it a waste place, but formed it to be inhabited), "I am the LORD, and there is none else."

Unlike other planets that we know are waste places through modern exploration, our humble abode is not a "waste place" as the Scriptures state.

The above is not the only nugget of truth among Scriptures that point to provable and exciting scientific facts that were written long before they became notable discoveries by learned scientists. One thought-provoking and factual nugget will direct us to the *hydrologic cycle* in the science of hydrogeology. Consider what the God of design spoke to the prophet Isaiah:

> "...the rain and the snow come down from heaven,
> And do not return there without watering the earth
> And making it bear and sprout,
> And furnishing seed to the sower and bread to the eater."[42]

Looking for a clear explanation of the hydrologic cycle, I found the following:

> The hydrologic cycle begins with the evaporation of water from the surface of the ocean. As moist air is lifted, it cools and water vapor condenses to form clouds.

---

[42] Isaiah 55:10

Moisture is transported around the globe until it returns to the surface as precipitation.

Once the water reaches the ground, one of two processes may occur; 1) some of the water may evaporate back into the atmosphere or 2) the water may penetrate the surface and become groundwater. Groundwater either seeps its way to into the oceans, rivers, and streams, or is released back into the atmosphere through transpiration.

The balance of water that remains on the earth's surface is runoff, which empties into lakes, rivers and streams and is carried back to the oceans, where the cycle begins again. Lake effect snowfall is a good example of the hydrologic cycle at work.[43]

Just as water returns to its place to form clouds, which begins the cycle all over again, it must first accomplish the work of providing for Earth and its inhabitants. So too, in verse eleven of Isaiah 55, God stated:

"So will My word be which goes forth from My mouth; It will not return to Me empty, without accomplishing what I desire, and without succeeding in the matter for which I sent it."

There we have, in two passages of Scripture, scientific fact and spiritual application allowing the creation to point us to the Intelligent Designer who created each cycle for a purpose.

Yes, the God of the Bible is the Creator of the universe and all it contains. He *upholds all things* to have a love relationship with those He created in His image. His desire is an abiding relationship with people who will respond to Him in pure love and worship, offering Him the praise that is due Him. May we all shout to our great God:

"Worthy are You, our Lord and our God, to receive glory and honor and power; for You created all things,

---

[43]http://ww2010.atmos.uiuc.edu/(Gh)/guides/mtr/hyd/smry.rxml

and because of Your will they existed, and were created."[44]

The God of the Moral Law

Yes, the God of the Bible sets a standard for morality. What we recognize intuitively as right and wrong is perfectly consistent with His standard, and there are no contradictions. The Bible reminds us that we possess an internal witness of the law; that human beings do, in fact, "show the work of the Law written in their hearts, their conscience bearing witness and their thoughts alternately accusing or else defending them."[45]

I will never forget the comments of two friends who told me what happened to them internally regarding a bit of advice I once gave them. They continued to push me for a list of dos and don'ts that they could simply follow to get right with God. I offered a little suggestion. "Whatever your question, whenever you sincerely want an answer, if you truly seek His will and want His way, simply lift it up and ask Him, 'Does this please You?' If your intentions are true to find His will in the matter, if your goal is to please Him honestly, then He will speak to your conscience." After coming to the Lord a short time later, they admitted they followed that advice, and it drove them crazy because it worked! Again, following our God-given conscience will always lead us to the throne room of grace.

The God of Prophecy

I think we can safely conclude—the God of the Bible *is* God. We learned from chapter 2 that fulfilled prophecy is an excellent piece of evidence to establish the validity of the Bible. However, God explained through His Word, that the real purpose of prophecy is to prove He is the One and only, true and living God. Since He is the God who caused this little planet's existence, and is omniscient, omnipresent, omnipotent, and eternal (a Being Who sees all things at once and not in sequential order through the time-

---

[44] Revelation 4:11
[45] Romans 2:15

space continuum that we are bound to) thus He can predict what is going to happen on it. In Isaiah 44:7-8, God declared there is no God but Himself and offered a challenge to any so-called god—His challenge stands:

Who is like Me? Let him proclaim and declare it;
Yes, let him recount it to Me in order,
From the time that I established the ancient nation.
And let them declare to them the things that are coming
And the events that are going to take place.
Do not tremble and do not be afraid;
Have I not long since announced it to you and declared it?
And you are My witnesses.
Is there any God besides Me,
Or is there any other Rock?
I know of none.

All I can say to that is—neither do I.

FINAL THOUGHTS

As I mentioned earlier, my heart certainly goes out to those who honestly struggle with the question of God's existence. Since I am sure you too can empathize with those who struggle with this subject, I will make a few suggestions. The next time you are with your honest skeptic friend who doubts the existence of God, perhaps with a nice hot cup of mint mocha you just might want to pose this question: "Do you think it is possible that the God who created us would like us to know He exists?"

If she is intellectually honest, her reply will be "Yes." The reason why she will answer "yes" is that God has placed in every human heart the recognition of His existence. Since she can agree that His existence is at least possible, you can then present to her some of the tests for His existence that I gave in this chapter. I think Romans 1:19-20 confirms and sums up the tests quite nicely:

That which is known about God is evident within them; for God made it evident to them. For since the creation of the world His invisible attributes, His eternal power and divine nature, have been clearly seen, being understood through what has been made, so that they are without excuse.

As He does for each one of us, God reveals Himself in a variety of ways so that your doubting Thomasina may know Him—no excuses. Your loving witness is just one of the many ways.

It all boils down to intellectual honesty. Remind your seeking friend of Deuteronomy 4:29, "Seek the LORD your God, and you will find Him if you search for Him with all your heart and all your soul." If your friend takes a serious approach in her quest for answers to the question of God's existence, or His will for her life, or a conviction of sin, God will surely provide the answer. That is His promise.

QUESTIONS & RESOURCES

1. What is the folly of the atheist?

2. How can we know that the universe has a Creator?

3. Can you explain the anthropic principle?

4. Is the conscience merely a matter of feelings? Explain.

5. What would the world look like or be like if everyone obeyed their God-given conscience?

6. Have you ever tried anchovies delicately wrapped around little green capers?

Mere Christianity by C.S. Lewis. HarperCollins Publishers, 2001.

The Knowledge of the Holy by A.W. Tozer, Harper San Francisco, 1998.

A Shattered Visage: The Real Face of Atheism by Ravi Zacharias, Baker Books, 1993.

CHAPTER 4 ~ *Popular Objections*

Have you ever noticed how ingrained it is in the human condition to find excuses for just about everything? Sometimes, when we have to, we can sure think quickly on our feet. Someone once sent me a humorous e-mail suggesting a variety of things an employee can say if the boss catches her sleeping on the job. Thankfully, when the kids were small and I needed a couple of winks, all I had to do was give them a quiet project, grab my snuggly blanket, and nestle in on the couch for a 15-minute power nap without the risk of being fired. Nevertheless, there they were at my disposal: excuses I could use just in case Jeff walked into my office and caught me drooling on my computer's keyboard. The suggestions ranged from, "Oh, I must have made decaf by mistake," to the employee lifting her head as she offered a solemn, "In Jesus' name, amen."

Now, if excuses abound for use in the case of an unexpected visit from the boss, how much more so for avoiding an encounter with the God and Judge of the universe? Keep this in mind if, when sharing your faith, you become frustrated because so often one objection after another can appear as though it were an excuse for holding God at arm's length. However, this is not always the case. Some concerns expressed are not excuses but are, in fact, the seeker's obstacles to belief. Our goal is to take these concerns seriously and offer sound answers to the variety of popular objections.

In this chapter, I would like to cover just a few of these objections, including the idea that Christianity is oppressive to women, the charge that hypocrites fill the church, the claim that the Christian worldview is too narrow, and a few others.

I hope that when you encounter these popular objections, you will know how to address them appropriately and lovingly—not as excuses, but as perhaps, thistle surrounding a rose bush.

Oppression

When I was twenty-one years old and lived in the desert, enduring 110° heat for two long summers, I found that oppressive. When I drove from appointment to appointment in bumper-to-bumper traffic all around the San Francisco Bay area as a corporate salesperson, I found that oppressive. When I felt I had no control over my life and carried the weight of every burden upon my shoulders—from finances to diminishing hopes of ever having a child—I found that oppressive. When I would lie in my bed at night, unable to sleep because of a nagging fear of death, I found that to be especially oppressive.

However, when I gave my life to the Lordship of Jesus Christ, I did not gain mounting oppression, but freedom, a future, and hope—and so did you. Isn't it sad that many people who look on from the outside assume that Christianity must be terribly oppressive for women? However, this is simply not the case.

Oppression is a state of mind and soul. Webster defines the word *oppression* in a couple of ways: 1) "unjust or cruel exercise of authority or power," and 2) "a sense of being weighed down in body or mind." They define the word *oppressive* as "overwhelming or depressing to the spirit or senses."[46]

Phrases like *weaker vessel* or the words *submit* and *submission*, seem to provoke a variety of false impressions for women who have never had this objection adequately addressed. Thus, as the serpent beguiled Eve, he has convinced many women in our society that a relationship with Jesus Christ means a life of oppression. They imagine Christian women as being under the cruel thumb of some male authority figure in the church, or a tyrannical husband in the home, or both. However, nothing could be further from the truth for godly men and women who genuinely love and serve the Lord according to His design.

---

[46]See: https://www.merriam-webster.com/dictionary/oppression (also see *oppressive*)

Insult or Compliment?

The phrase "weaker vessel" from 1 Peter 3:7 can conjure all sorts of adverse reactions, which is a shame. Unfortunately, many individuals remember two words from the Scriptures yet forget or have never investigated the context of their use. In today's vernacular, many women regard the term "weaker vessel" as an insult. However, the reference was not meant to imply that women are somehow inferior to men in some way—but rather, as women, we can view ourselves as 24-karat gold, which is delicate, beautiful, and valuable—unlike, say, a bar of steel reinforcement.

Regrettably, those who oppose that phrase in Peter's epistle never seem to look at the use of it in its proper context. Did the author perceive women as common, inexpensive, disposable metal, or pure gold to cherish? Peter commands:

> "Husbands likewise, live with your wives in an understanding way, as with a weaker vessel, since she is a woman; and grant her honor as a fellow heir of the grace of life, so that your prayers may not be hindered."[47]

That beautiful passage above shows our value to God and our position in the Christian faith. Perhaps this is why, at one time in our culture, it was unspoken and understood that a man would hold a door open for a woman, or pull out her chair for her, or stand when she entered a room. If you don't remember that happening or doubt that it ever did, I guess you'll have to watch the movie *Miracle on 34th Street* from 1947 to see this as an unspoken part of our culture. Just look at the scene where Maureen O'Hara's character walks into the office of "R.H. Macy" to join the meeting. Oh, the level of respect we have lost, or rather as women, have recklessly slapped back and away.

---

[47] I'm referring to the 1977 NASB version of 1 Peter 3:7 since it seems that's the one that uses the term "weaker vessel" which many are familiar with and quote. The current version, though expressing the same, reads: "You husbands in the same way, live with your wives in an understanding way, as with someone weaker, since she is a woman; and show her honor as a fellow heir of the grace of life, so that your prayers will not be hindered."

First Peter 3:7 establishes our equality with men in the kingdom since women are referred to as "*fellow heirs* of the grace of life." However, did you notice that if the husband does not grant his spouse honor as a *fellow heir*, God will not hear his prayers? It seems to me that the heat is clearly on the guys in this passage.

Chaos or Balance?

Then there's that word *submit*. With only part of the story, women can take the view that the husband's boot is firmly planted upon the wife's neck. With such a perception of Christianity, no wonder many women feel uncomfortable with the concept of submission. However, to understand this word fully, we must keep in mind that the God we serve is a God of order. One gander at creation and anyone can see this is true. The universe is not chaotic—it is, in fact, meticulously balanced and orderly. It is the same in marriage. Each member of the family must hold a particular level of authority—or headship—for harmony to be in the home. The word *submit*, as used in the Scriptures, means *to place under in an orderly fashion*. The concept has nothing to do with value, but rather with who is accountable for what. If the husband perverts this design by abusing his position or headship in the home, God will hold him responsible for it.

I believe we can agree that everyone submits to someone whether he or she follows the Scriptures or not. When I was in corporate sales, I submitted to the authority of the company president, yet it did not change my intrinsic value as a human being. When I travel, I submit to the authority of airport security. As a first-responder, I submit to my fire chief. Regardless of who I *submit* to my intrinsic value remains the same. It is the same with marriage. God, in His infinite wisdom, called the wife to submit to the authority of her husband. The husband honors the wife as a fellow heir, and the wife acknowledges the husband by submitting to his leadership. (Frankly, I found it quite handy to say on occasion, "Wait till your father gets home," when my children misbehaved.)

Honor and Blessing

Submission is not an insult to women—it is a necessity. The order was not instituted by people, but by God. Here again, we must turn to the Scriptures to understand the concept of submission in its proper context. Ephesians 5:22-25 reads,

> Wives, be subject [submit] to your own husbands, as to the Lord. For the husband is the head of the wife, as Christ also is the head of the church, He Himself being the Savior of the body. But as the church is subject to Christ, so also the wives ought to be to their husbands in everything.
>
> Husbands, love your wives, just as Christ also loved the church and gave Himself up for her.

It is a beautiful picture. When godly submission is understood and followed, there is harmony in the home. The husband expresses sacrificial love, to the point of death if need be, and the wife responds by submitting to his loving and godly leadership. If the wife is married to an unbeliever, her loving submission serves as a powerful testimony.

There are many beautiful marital transformations for women who gave their lives to Christ before their husband eventually came to the Lord. What usually happens is that, during difficulties, the husband will begin to ask his wife to pray. He sees her godly attitude. He suddenly notices that God hears and answers those prayers aligned with His will. Hubby recognizes her supernatural life change—and it cuts deep into his heart. Whether it takes the husband six months or sixty years to submit to God, as women, we can bring blessing to the home by our obedience to God and His ordered design.

How sad it is that instead of obeying God's design and plan for marriage, so many men in our culture have become passive in the home as the wife usurps authority. I don't know which came first in abandoning the God-given role—the passive, disinterested hen or the hard-boiled chicken—but our society is undoubtedly hurting as a result, particularly the children. I imagine it began in the garden since the Scriptures state that Adam was *with* Eve when she ate the fruit. It appears that, without a word, he allowed her to share with him a little forbidden fruit on the half leaf.

The truth of the matter is that we are all to submit to one another. The apostle Paul wrote in Romans 12:10 that we are literally to outdo one another in showing honor. The Scriptures clearly state the equality of every believer. Paul, who some women accused of being chauvinistic, wrote:

> There is neither Jew nor Greek, there is neither slave nor free man, there is neither male nor female; for you are all one in Christ Jesus. And if you belong to Christ, then you are Abraham's descendants, heirs according to promise.[48]

I think it is also important to note that even in the Tri-unity of the Godhead, though each Person is co-equal, there is headship. The role of the Holy Spirit is to bring glory to the Son, and the role of the Son is to bring glory to the Heavenly Father.

What is really at the heart of the personal objection to submission, whether we are conscious of it or not, is our ingrained bent toward rebellion and control. It's just that simple.

Real Women's Lib

Not long ago, I received the following e-mail from a woman who noticed I was the only female contributor in the book, *Is Your Church Ready?*[49] co-Edited by Dr. Ravi Zacharias and Dr. Norman Geisler:

> "I was looking to purchase a book that you are highlighted in from Ravi Zacharias Ministries on apologetics. It's quite refreshing to see women in ministry—in what I hope is a 'leadership' role. I am very convicted that we must lead by gifting and not let gender get in the way. Having said that what are your views on women in the church and home? Do you promote the

---

[48] Galatians 3:28-29

[49] *Is Your Church Ready? Motivating Leaders to Live an Apologetic Life*, Ravi Zacharias and Norman Geisler General Editors, Zondervan, Grand Rapids, MI, copyright © 2003.

subordination of women in the home and church? Sorry to come off crass—not my intent. I'm simply trying to be efficient."

Since I had a sense of her position by her e-mail, and because I've counseled many other women with aspirations of ministry in the male-dominated area of Christian apologetics, I thought a live phone call would be best. I was candid with her regarding my thoughts.

Unfortunately, she was shocked and insulted by my "outdated" view of women in ministry and the home, yet would not—or could not—listen to my reasoning from the Scriptures. She was rude, forceful, and insulting. She was particularly horrified when I told her my view on women as pastors; the one leadership position in the church, I believe, should not be usurped by women regardless of well we *preach*.

"Well!" she said in a huff, "I wonder if Ravi Zacharias understands and knows who he's got writing in his books?" Then, immediately following this lovely insult of Ravi, (When you think about it, that's just what it was though I don't think she'd believe so.) her volume suddenly dropped. Speaking in a near whisper, she offered a quick and timid, "Oh, I have to go now, I can't talk about this any longer, my husband is home." She then immediately got off the phone. I then thought, perhaps she should first address this topic with her husband rather than with me.

Has the sexual revolution liberated women? Or, has it subjected them to discontent and bondage? From my conversations with dear women who distort or ignore God's Word, many are left frustrated, confused, and have damaged personal relationships. To fully realize the devastating lies of radical feminism in our culture, all one has to do is consider what was witnessed and recorded during the "women's march" in Washington, D.C., on January 21, 2017. This "march" was just one day after the inauguration of the 45th President of the United States of America.

The goings-on in D.C. on that fine Saturday certainly moved the *women's movement* all right—right into the gutter. Keynote speakers were rude, foul-mouthed, and embarrassingly idiotic (the has-been pop-star Madonna, a beacon of hope for all women, I'm sure, found herself under investigation for admitting to the crowd that she had "thought an awful lot about blowing up the White House"[50]).

Many women in that January 2017 march were the same ones who bragged about how they can do anything a man can do and, therefore, should be treated as no different than a man. These same women who are always so eager to sue or ruin a man's career or life if he should make any comment that could be interpreted by them as "insensitive" or deemed—wait for it—sexist, communicated things that would make shock jock Howard Stern blush. Such hypocrisy! It was like *open-mic-night* in Washington, D.C., for filth on a grand scale.

Those poor, deceived souls who "marched" and who abide by the radical feminist thinking are miserable, living contradictions. One sign, in particular, caught my eye. It stated boldly, "WE WANT THE SAME REPRODUCTIVE RIGHTS OUR MOTHER'S HAD!" with the words "SUPPORT PLANNED PARENTHOOD" scrawled underneath. Of course, what these militant feminists don't realize (especially the one who made the sign) is that if their mothers took advantage of their "reproductive rights" when it came to them, *they wouldn't be there to hold the sign or to protest anything!* The pro-life women and groups who organizers barred from the march should thank God they were rejected and are not yoked to such an event.

The painful truth is this: The more women believe they are liberated from what is referred to as "traditional roles," the more harm they've done to themselves, their marriages, their children, and society.

Since 1993, I have worked with women in Pregnancy Resource Centers all across this country. To hear their stories and see the statistics is heartbreaking. With the legalization of abortion, many women began to view it as almost a rite of passage. Unfortunately, they now carry scars on their hearts and bodies from a *choice* too

---

[50] See:http://www.breitbart.com/big-hollywood/2017/01/22/report-secret-service-investigate-madonna-blowing-white-house-comment/

painful for me to imagine. However, God has called many of these dear women out of bondage and to emotional and spiritual healing so they can lead others to the same freedom, forgiveness, and future in Christ that they have found.[51] We saw many of them in Washington D.C. the following weekend during the historic "March for Life," which gave me hope that we can make an impact when attempting to reach women who have been or are, deceived, or simply misinformed.

True women's liberation is only found at the foot of the Cross. A perusal of the Scriptures reveals the fact that men and women, in the eyes of the Lord, are equally valuable. For instance, Jesus did not shy away from the Samaritan woman at the well, engaging her in conversation. Though it was taboo in the culture for a Jewish man to speak to a woman, let alone a Samaritan, Jesus offered her an opportunity to receive eternal life. Not only this, but He chose to reveal to her His identity, the fact that He was and is the Messiah. By her testimony, she was able to reach her community, and many Samaritan people received salvation.[52]

Remember, men were not the first to discover Jesus's empty tomb.[53] It was not a man who was first to fall at the feet of the resurrected Lord. God used the testimony of women to proclaim His glorious resurrection before the apostles did. In Acts 18:26, we see that God used Priscilla as a teacher to Apollos, alongside her husband, Aquila. In 2 Timothy 1:5, the apostle Paul credited young pastor Timothy's mother, Eunice, and grandmother, Lois, for the fact that the young man had a "sincere faith."

Value, Not Oppression

Indeed, wherever the influence of Christianity has spread, it has brought freedom and blessing to women. For example, some cultures viewed women as merely the property of her husband.

---

[51] If you have experienced a pregnancy loss due to a horrific *choice* and feel you'd like counseling and healing but don't know where to turn, please contact https://www.care-net.org/ to locate a Pregnancy Resource Center near you. Or, you can contact them and learn how to volunteer and help other women who can relate.

[52] John 4

[53] Luke 24

Before Christian missionaries came to India, a widow was burned along with her deceased husband, whether she wanted to join him in death or not. Tossing infant girls into the sea was also a common occurrence in India up until the nineteenth century when Christian missionaries were able to bring this horrific practice to a halt. Before the influence of Christianity, in Africa—as in India—wives and concubines were killed upon the death of their chieftains.

There can be no doubt that women owe a debt of gratitude to the influence of Christianity and the value it places not only on women but also on all human life. The reason for this high value is because the Christian worldview acknowledges all human beings as created in the image of a holy God.

Christianity is anything but oppressive to women, especially since its Scriptures declare all men and women co-equal before the Father as joint-heirs with the Lord Jesus Christ.

Hypocrisy

One of the more popular reasons why unbelievers tend to back away from an invitation to your fellowship's next potluck could be their feeling that they'd rather not associate with the *hypocrites*. Apparently, for those who raise this objection, the church is filled with them. I must admit this would make it a rather unpleasant place to spend a Sunday morning if that were the perception.

Usually, when presented with the objection of hypocrisy in the church, I just keep digging. I continue to ask the *why* questions. I find, with specific objections, the more I probe, eventually, a painful association crops up for the reluctant seeker. If I take the time, and the individual with whom I am attempting to share my faith knows that I genuinely care about her, she will feel safe enough to share a painful story regarding some preacher, priest, or parent who was less than Christ-like. Since I know I will never argue a person out of his or her feelings, I try my best to validate how they feel, especially since this objection can be quite delicate. Nevertheless, there is an answer.

Since many people are willing to regard Jesus as a good moral teacher, I usually ask, "Was Jesus Christ a hypocrite? Did Jesus just talk about the exemplary life but portray something else, or was His life consistent with what He taught?" I have yet to hear anyone hold to the belief that Jesus was a hypocrite. After all, even unbelieving Pilate said, "I find no guilt in this man."[54]

Jesus Christ was not a hypocrite. However, fallen individuals who profess to know Him most certainly can appear to live inconsistent with what they profess to believe.

Look to Jesus

Unfortunately, people will look at struggling Christians as their example of godly living, rather than at Jesus Christ, who is our supreme example. I think it is important to point out that everyone has areas of hypocrisy in their lives—including the folks who raise this objection. It appears to me that people who believe it is wrong to steal, have no problem pilfering supplies from the office, placing personal telephone calls on company time, or mailing their Christmas packages through the company's mailroom.

I will never forget, as a rookie sales representative many years ago, how the other sales representatives instructed me to figure my mileage for my expense reports. I think the formula went something like this: mileage x 2 + 10. It was imperative that they show me the formula. After all, how would it look if my trip to San Jose was thirty miles when everyone else's was seventy?

Again, it is essential to direct attention to Jesus as our example, not to the fallen individuals who profess to know Him. Jesus said in Matthew 7:21, "Not everyone who says to Me, 'Lord, Lord,' will enter the kingdom of heaven, *but he who does the will of My Father who is in heaven will enter.*"[55] Jesus knew false converts would call upon Him, yet their hearts would be somewhere else.

---

[54] Luke 23:4

[55] emphasis added

Remember, walking through the doors of a beauty salon does not make you a manicurist. Sitting at the little table while shaking the bottles of nail polish does not make you a manicurist. Taking money as you sit there does not make you a manicurist. You could even attempt to do someone's nails, but as soon as you tried, unless you were a manicurist, your sin would find you out. You would be a hypocrite. The word *hypocrite*, as used in the Scriptures, can quite literally be defined by the word *counterfeit*.

Therefore, some folks who walk through the doors of their local fellowship are not there because they have an abiding love for the Lord, but rather because they enjoy the social aspect. Some folks pop in on a Sunday because their family attended that church for years. Perhaps you've met people who have a network marketing business and just want to make it grow. Then, when everyone they can pitch is pitched, the family suddenly moves to a new church down the road. However, none of these scenarios has much to do with the Lord Jesus Christ and those who sincerely believe.

Since Jesus addressed the hypocritical religious leaders of His day, He will most certainly address the hypocrites of our day. A perusal of Matthew 23 will give you a good idea of what Jesus thought of counterfeits in the meeting. Since all judgments belong to the Lord, perhaps those who hold this objection should leave it with Him to separate the wheat from the chaff and then conduct some honest self-examination.

Let Sin Abound?

Sometimes, there can be a little confusion in the mind of the unbeliever about what constitutes hypocrisy. Smoking is always a good example because many unbelievers tend to have this innate feeling that the habit of smoking is a sin. When we think about it, *anything* that keeps us in bondage is a sin. Anything that controls us more than the Spirit of the Lord is a sin. However, what an unbelieving onlooker does not understand is that that woman who just put out her cigarette before walking into the church hall was recently freed from the bondage of drunkenness. What they don't know is that the Lord is currently working on her habitual lying, and with great success. However, some people look on and say, "What a hypocrite—telling me there is freedom in Christ and then lighting up her cigarette." Oh, that we would all be as perfect as those who judge unjustly! I thank the Lord we aren't, because the sad fact is, those who condemn in this manner do not see their hypocrisy; their sinful tendencies which keep them separated from a relationship with God.

The woman with the cigarette can honestly proclaim freedom in Christ. How wonderful it is that the Lord is patient with us. Now, what *would* make the professing Christian a hypocrite is if she rebuked the smoker for smoking, then sneaked behind the bushes to light up her own in the hope that no one would notice.

However, the fact remains that we all sin. Each one of us falls short of God's holy standard. The good news is that we don't have to carry the shame, the guilt, or the penalty of our sins. Yes, we do suffer the consequences of our sin, but isn't it wonderful that when we confess, He is faithful and just to cleanse us of all unrighteousness?[56] Now, this does not mean we can sin with reckless abandon in one moment and then turn around and confess in the next, only to start the cycle all over again willfully. God will not tolerate constant, willful sin. Since true believers are children of God, He will discipline them. After all, the following goes for daughters too:

> You have forgotten the exhortation which is addressed to you as sons, "My son, do not regard lightly the discipline of the Lord, nor faint when you are reproved by Him; for those whom the Lord loves He disciplines, and He scourges every son whom He receives."[57]

As believers, we can't get away with much, can we? Our heart grieves when we grieve the heart of God. Our confession is a product of sorrow over the transgression, not a means of getting the slate clean only to dirty it again willfully.

---

[56] 1 John 1:9

[57] Hebrews 12:5-6

Here Today, Gone Tomorrow

Under the umbrella of *hypocrisy* is the objection that many followers of the Lord Jesus Christ eventually fall away from the faith. *If Christianity is so freeing and great, promising a new life, why do some fall away?*

I think this is best answered by 1 John 2:19:

> They went out from us, but they were not really of us; for if they had been of us, they would have remained with us; but they went out, so that it would be shown that they all are not of us.

If folks fall away from the faith, the faith they had was not genuine in the first place. The fact that they left is proof positive they never were regenerated in Christ; they never were new creations, or truly born again. Jesus' parable in Luke 8:11-15 regarding the different ways individuals hear the Word and react is a perfect picture of how some people can look good at first, but wither away in short order. Some fall away due to their lusts, their fears, the grudges they harbor, life's pleasures, or any other enticing temptation, while others grow and are fruitful for the kingdom.

Unfortunately, there will always be wolves among the sheep. Oh, how folks love to remind us of those who have had to confess of some horrible transgression publicly. How quick the unbeliever is to use these examples as proof that *Christianity doesn't work because if it did, these things would never happen.*

Yes, we must grant that there are indeed wolves among the sheep, but we can also point out that many more individuals haven't fallen from grace as those public figures have. Many more perform selfless acts for those who are suffering and are in need. For example, we have close missionary friends who minister in China, in El Salvador, South Africa, and we have others in Sudan, whose newsletter every month brings me to the point of tears. There are much more genuinely faithful Christians who open hospitals and schools, feed the hungry and house the homeless, clothe the naked, and care for the orphan and widow.

These faithful believers far outnumber those who begrudgingly confess to some scandalous transgression. They bear fruit, and their fruit remains. We know them by the fruit they produce. Again, you cannot look to the individual as an example of how we ought to be, because we are bound to our flesh until the Lord takes us to glory. Our only example should be the Lord Jesus Christ and, as the Scriptures state, "He who believes in Him will not be disappointed."[58]

Environment

Some people believe that the only reason we follow Christ is that we were born into a Christian home. Their thinking is that our faith only goes as deep as our generations. They assume that because a parent believed, we simply followed in their belief like a herd of cattle.

However, when talking with many professing Christians, I find that their backgrounds are quite varied. Not all believers come to Christ from homes that trusted and believed in the Lord. For example, I know a woman who grew up in the Jewish tradition, converted to Catholicism, but unwittingly embraced the occult. She married a man who was raised and educated in the Roman Catholic system. He later rejected Catholicism, embraced a pantheistic worldview for much of his adult years, then came to Christ at the end of his life. Though they raised three children in the Roman Catholic tradition, they were weaned spiritually on the occult. Their children were introduced to and dabbled in everything from the Ouija board, to tarot cards, to visiting fortune-tellers. Of those three, each rejected Catholicism, and two radically gave their lives to the Lord Jesus Christ later in life. The third child continues to dabble in the occult, but as she puts it, "just for fun."

The point is that individuals come to Christ for much more compelling reasons than upbringing or environment. Otherwise, we would surely have a hard time explaining the growing number of radical Muslims all around the world who come to a saving knowledge of the Lord Jesus Christ, as reported by our missionary

---

[58] 1 Peter 2:6

friends. We would also have a hard time explaining the growth of Christianity in places like China or the former Soviet Union. One cannot solely base a relationship with Christ upon a professing believer's upbringing or environment.

Even so, this does not invalidate the faith of my children simply because they grew up in a Christian environment and continue to live and express their passion for the Lord. My parents taught me well that if I did not look both ways before crossing the street, I would become part of the pavement. As an adult, I did not dismiss this claim because I found it to be a valid one. It is not that we believe because our parents would be displeased if we rejected the faith, or that we are somehow conditioned or brainwashed into believing. The reason why we believe is that we have found the claims of Christ to be valid.

People are not born Christians. To be sure, they could have been born into a Christian home or environment, but Christianity is a decision. It is a conscious choice made by an individual who understands the consequences of accepting or rejecting Jesus Christ. Quite simply, Christianity is a decision of the will, not a result of pressure from parents. Otherwise, you'd probably see what I addressed in the previous section entitled "Here Today, Gone Tomorrow."

Born That Way

One of the most significant obstacles to conversion is the thinking that God *grades on the curve*. I cannot even begin to write about how many people I share the Lord with who believe their particular sin will keep them out of heaven. Then, of course, some people want to know what list of sins they need to avoid so they can make it into heaven because they've steered clear of the *terrible ten* or the *sinful seven*. Other folks look at individuals who are bound by a particular behavior or who have committed a specific act, and they believe that because of this, those folks will never gain entrance into heaven. The challenge with that thinking is that it assumes, like that generous teacher who takes pity on the class that's failing algebra, God grades on the curve. The good news is, He doesn't.

Years ago, I shared Christ with a couple bound by same-sex attraction and the behavior that follows. Continually they attempted to get me to state that their conduct was one of the *deadly dozen*. I never brought up the subject of same-sex attraction during our conversations because I realized it was simply a symptom of their greater lost condition; that they did not have a relationship with the living God. What I needed to do was answer their questions regarding the person and work of Jesus Christ, His death, burial, and resurrection. I needed to establish with them the validity of the Bible and the existence of a loving God.

One day, as I sat conversing with them in their living room, my Bible in hand, they began yelling at me that I didn't understand, I didn't know what it was like for them, that it wasn't their fault, that they were "born that way." Again, I never brought up the subject. Their conviction always did.

After they had finished their loud rebuke, my response in like manner and with similar passion was, "Well, I have a news flash for you... I, too, was born *that way!*" They looked as though they were about to fall off the couch. Their stunned expressions screamed of *NOT THE CHURCH LADY!!!* as they would affectionately call me.

After allowing that proclamation to hang over the room for a few minutes and while their mouths were still agape at my confession, I added, "And I was born with the capacity to steal, and cheat, and lie, and murder, and commit every other depravity known to mankind. Welcome to humanity—we are all born *that way!*"

Neither one of them made a peep as I then began to read Roman's 1 aloud. I could see in their faces shock and horror. As I read, I also continued to interject, "No one has ever shared this with you before, have they?" They both simply shook their heads *no*. I then stated, lovingly, "Isn't good we know it now?" And yes, after three years of loving on them and answering their questions, both came to faith in the Lord Jesus Christ.

Without a doubt, there is no grading on the curve for sin; there is only Christ granting forgiveness from the cross. It strikes me funny how we believe that somehow God thinks like us. When in reality, if we want a list all we need to do is peruse Proverbs 6:16-19:

> There are six things which the LORD hates,
> Yes, seven which are an abomination to Him:
> Haughty eyes, a lying tongue,
> And hands that shed innocent blood,
> A heart that devises wicked plans,
> Feet that run rapidly to evil,
> A false witness who utters lies,
> And one who spreads strife among brothers.

When you look at the list above, all sin falls into one category or another. Since we have all, at one time or another, found ourselves on that list, this means every single one of us is guilty of those behaviors that *the LORD hates* and are *abominations* to Him. I am so thankful He made provision to grant us forgiveness for and freedom from this conduct!

Too Narrow *is the Gate?*

Imagine for a moment that it's Christmastime. The delightful aroma of fudge is in the air. You decide to surprise the kiddies by making chocolate–marshmallow Turtles. Upon opening your cookbook, you suddenly feel indignant. *Surely, there must be a better way of making these turtles—this recipe is entirely too narrow*, you think.

Instead of using the narrow suggestion of two cups of semisweet chocolate chips, you decide to use four-and-a-half cups of mint and butterscotch chips. Instead of the narrow suggestion of two tablespoons of vegetable shortening, you decide (because, after all, you want to keep your girlish figure) that one teaspoon of shortening should be just fine. Moreover, because the children enjoy them so much, you are going to use thirty mini-marshmallows instead of the narrow suggestion of twelve large ones. Also, as far as that cup of pecan halves goes, you feel pretzel sticks are far better. Now, following this type of thinking, how do you think your "Turtles" will turn out? Can you refer to them as "Turtles" after doing your *own thing* with the authentic recipe?

If there are hazards when we reject a recipe because it seems too narrow, how much more so when rejecting the biblical formula regarding spiritual matters? Obviously, the question isn't one of narrowness but of reasonableness to believe. Narrowness does not govern whether something is right or wrong. Narrowness can't be a way to determine what is true. If, by following the prescribed method, we arrive at the correct conclusion, who cares if the method is narrow?

Still, this is a trendy objection. Christianity seems too narrow. I think many feel this way because the Christian proclaims that Jesus is the only way to salvation. However, the misunderstanding comes when folks think we declare this out of our imagination. Indeed Christianity is narrow, but not because the Christian proclaims it—but rather because Jesus Christ did. In Matthew 7:13, Jesus said:

> "Enter through the narrow gate; for the gate is wide and the way is broad that leads to destruction, and many are those who enter through it. For the gate is small and the way is narrow that leads to life, and there are few who find it."

Those Who Haven't Heard

Then we face the global concern, *What about the gal on the deserted island who never read a Bible or heard about Jesus? Is there no salvation for her?* I think it is terrific when an unbeliever suddenly has the heart for people who have never heard the gospel. All right, perhaps I am a bit sarcastic—because we know this objection has little to do with a desire to see others come to faith in Christ. Instead, it has everything to do with a false view of God. The unbeliever's basis for rejecting Christianity is the idea that God will send people to Hell because they haven't had a chance to believe and receive, and therefore God is unjust. How can God send people to Hell simply because they haven't heard? However, the fact is, He doesn't.

Thankfully, God holds us accountable only for what we do know, not what we *do not*. If anyone on this planet, no matter where he or she is, truly seek to have a relationship with the living God based upon the light God gave him or her, He will reveal Himself through the light of that knowledge no matter how primitive. He will not reject them.

If your doubting Thomasina raises this objection, simply remind her of this wonderful truth: God has ordained that she lives in a land where access to the gospel is abundant through Christian fellowships, bookstores, television, the internet, and even radio. Suggest that because she has such access, perhaps the Lord will use her to communicate the gospel to other people groups since her heart is so tender toward them. In all honesty, the question is not about folks in other lands. Instead, with such an abundance of knowledge in *her* land, the question you might want to ask is why *she* still rejects.

A Piece of the Whole

Imagine, for a moment, that you are bobbing about in the ocean and are about to drown when suddenly a large Styrofoam boat floats in front of you. The captain reaches out his hand to draw you into the vessel, but you reply, "No, thank you. I will not come into the boat and be saved because, in another land, there is an individual drowning which has not yet heard about this boat of salvation." Little did you realize that while you drowned, the person you were so concerned about in the other land was saved by a piece of Styrofoam given to her by the same captain who attempted to save you! Though it was not the entire vessel, she found salvation by a portion of it nonetheless. The same captain who could have saved you with the whole boat has saved the foreigner by way of the small piece she accepted, while you, through your rejection, chose to drown.

Hellfire, Brimstone—and a Party?

Finally, I would like to address a rather popular objection that makes the hair on the back of my neck stand on end whenever I encounter it. I have friends—perhaps you do, too—who think they'd rather not go to heaven because they'll miss the party with their friends in Hell. I find this attitude particularly frightening because it is obvious they have no clue about the reality of eternal torment.

I think it is important to remember that since God is holy, every sin is a violation against Him. God is also just and cannot allow sin to go unpunished. Since all human beings sin because of our fallen nature, we are all justly condemned to Hell. However, since God is also a God of infinite love and mercy, He sent His Son to take the penalty for our sin onto Himself. We, therefore, have an opportunity to receive eternal life with God rather than eternal judgment in Hell. Jesus Christ made a way of escape through faith, trust, and belief in Him and His work on the cross, alone.

Thus, God does not *send* anyone to Hell—instead, we are condemned to Hell by the fact that we are born with a terminal disease called sin. Anyone who finds himself or herself in Hell is there because he or she chose to reject God's method of salvation. God has provided every opportunity to help humanity avoid making that choice. He has made Himself known through the light of creation, the light of conscience, the light of Himself by coming into a lost world, and the light of His Word—*so that we are without excuse.*[59]

When speaking of Hell, Jesus often referred to it as *Gehenna*, a real place that was familiar to those with whom He spoke. I imagine He referred to Hell as Gehenna so the people listening to Him would have some frame of reference. I appreciate Ralph Muncaster's explanation of Gehenna:

> Gehenna is an actual place in the Hinnom Valley just southwest of Jerusalem. Solomon, in his later years, turned the valley from a natural paradise into a place where the idols of his wives' pagan gods were worshiped. Infants were sacrificed into terrifying flames. The valley later became the city cesspool where refuse, dead animals, and bodies of criminals were dumped and

---

[59] See Romans 1.

burned. Worms ate into dead flesh until they were consumed by the blaze. The fires never ceased. The foul stench never stopped. To the Jews, Gehenna was absolute hell.[60]

Hell, created for Satan and his minions, is far from a wild party where a bunch of pagans happily thumb their noses at God. Revelation 19:20 speaks of it as a "lake of fire which burns with brimstone [sulfurous flames]." Now, if you've ever smelled rotten eggs, you've had a whiff of the scent of brimstone.

In Matthew 8:12, we find a description of Hell as a place of "outer darkness." When I think of "outer darkness," I imagine the lava caves beneath the ground near Mount Saint Helens, not far from my home. When you hike through the caves, guides strongly suggest you have at least two light sources. Youth pastors will take groups of teens into the caves. They hike as far as they can go—then the entire group will turn off all flashlights and lanterns. The goal is to give the young people a sense of Hell's outer darkness. After just a few seconds, most of the teens complain of feeling disoriented, paranoid—and yes, very frightened. Their lights don't stay out for long.

However, the outer darkness of Hell is complete and eternal. Hell is also a place of abject loneliness since, in outer darkness, you cannot see a compassionate face, and therefore your "friends" cannot comfort you. Neither will you ever experience the loving presence of the God you flatly rejected.

Matthew 8:12 also speaks of Hell as a place of "weeping and gnashing of teeth." Have you ever been in so much pain that you gnashed your teeth? I have. When I was in my early 20s, I accidentally, while quickly removing my contact lenses, tore the corneas in both eyes. It was horrible. I cannot imagine that kind of pain for all eternity.

According to Mark 9:48, Hell is also a place where the "worm does not die, and the fire is not quenched." If the worm, as small

---

[60] Ralph O. Muncaster, *What Really Happens When You Die?* (Eugene, OR: Harvest House Publishers, 2000), p. 32

and as fragile as it is, can not die, the beings who, by their rejection of God, chose to go there do not die either.

Hell is a horror. It is a place of eternal torment with Satan, demons, and worms. It is an unspeakable terror with weeping and gnashing of teeth. What awaits is disorienting and frightening darkness and unquenchable fire that reeks of rotten eggs. However, the greatest horror of Hell is total separation from not only loved ones and friends but from God for all eternity—remembering forever the willful rejection of the light that God gave them. Some party, huh?

FINAL THOUGHTS

At the beginning of this chapter, I suggested we refrain from misinterpreting seeker's objections as simple excuses to avoid deciding for Christ. Instead, with love and patience, we should address each one of their objections. However, it is indeed possible that some unbelievers will continue to pose objection after objection simply to avoid the pure heart of the matter for them. I call these "encounters with a 'yeah, but.'" If you work in a counseling type ministry, you've probably met a "yeah, but." No matter how many objections you satisfactorily answer, the reply is, "Yeah, but what about...," and off they go with yet another objection. I'd like to suggest a handy way of getting around the perpetual "yeah, but" challenge.

If you sense the objection could be an excuse to stave off touching on the real issue at hand, posing a direct question can help. Ask, "Other than your concern that Christianity seems oppressive to women, is there anything else you can think of that would prevent you from placing your trust and faith in Jesus Christ right now?"

Honestly, no objection needs answering for someone to come to know the Lord. Salvation comes by an act of the will prompted by the Holy Spirit, not by answering objections. However, offering answers to popular objections does help remove obstacles to belief or to help ground believers in their faith. Helping to remove obstacles is the ministry of Christian apologetics. My prayer for you is that, after understanding these answers to some of the more prevalent concerns, you will feel better equipped when chatting with a seeker you would love to see in the kingdom.

QUESTIONS & RESOURCES

1. How would you address the perception that Christianity is oppressive to women?

2. How would you address the concern that Christianity is too narrow?

3. How did I respond to the *born that way* challenge?

4. What should you do to eliminate areas of hypocrisy in your life?

5. Who was it that said the way to salvation is narrow?

6. What is the worst aspect of Hell?

How Should We Then Live? by Francis A. Schaeffer, Crossway Books, 1983.

How Christianity Changed the Word by Alvin J. Schmidt, Zondervan, 2004.

The Gay Gospel: How Pro-Gay Advocates Misread the Bible by Joe Dallas, Harvest House Publishers, 2007

CHAPTER 5 ~ *Truth Matters*

I hope you will grant me a little license to describe a familiar scene from chapter 18 of John's Gospel. Here is what I picture: I imagine it a somber moment. Pilate was in a pickle. He knew that the Person standing before him was completely innocent, then again, there was the crowd to please. Frustrated, Pilate almost pleads with Jesus to tell him of His crime, so that he can have a reason to sentence to death this Man the Jewish leaders brought before him.

Pilate had asked the Jewish leaders, "What accusation do you bring against this Man?" Did they give a clear-cut list of offenses? Were the supposed crimes so outrageous that Jesus was deserving of death? Their response to Pilate was weak and vague: "If this Man were not an evildoer, we would not have delivered Him to you." In other words, "Surely you can't possibly imagine that we, the religious leaders and pillars of the community, would deliver up to you an innocent man."

After a short dialogue, Pilate asked Jesus, with dire exasperation in his voice, "What have You done?" Jesus proceeded to tell him of His kingdom. Pilate then blurted out, "So You are a king?"

Jesus responded calmly and directly. "You say correctly that I am a king. For this I have been born, and for this I have come into the world, to testify to the truth. Everyone who is of the truth hears My voice."

Pilate, knowing the Man before him was innocent, yet also knowing there would be consequences if he did not keep the political situation favorable, in an almost depressed state muttered, "What is truth?" and then turned away to speak to the crowd. Pilate never bothered to wait for an answer to his question of questions.

What a missed opportunity. There Pilate stood—before the embodiment of truth, before the One who could give him that life-changing answer, yet Pilate wasn't patient enough to wait for our Lord's reply.

Pilate had searched for the truth: "What accusation do you bring against this Man?" "What have You done?" "So You are a king?" To each of these questions, he waited for an answer, yet when he finally asked the most important one, he chose to answer it himself and only with another question.

I think there are many individuals right under our nose who, like Pilate, mutter to themselves, *What is truth?* Though they desperately desire the answer, believing in their heart, there is no such reality as truth they attempt to develop their own. However, for whatever reason, God has chosen to reveal the truth to you and me. On what basis God chose us, only He knows, but for what purpose, we surely know.

God did not reveal truth to us so that we could keep it a secret. It was revealed to us so that we might share it with others. Unfortunately, in today's climate, that certainly can be a challenge. Because of this difficulty, I thought a discussion on truth—what it is, what it isn't, how we can spot it and test it, and why it matters—just might help further ground you in the truth, and hopefully, help you lead many others to the Truth as well.

What Is Truth?

Let's take a moment to look at two basic types of truth: 1) *subjective* truth, and 2) *objective* truth.

Referring to the Subject

Subjective truth claims refer to the subject, namely the person who is making that claim. For example, if a young woman told you that olive green is the most beautiful color, or that brisk autumn mornings feel better than warm summer evenings, or that Cheez Doodles always taste great with peanut butter on them, you can consider all of these to be subjective truth claims. Subjective-truth claims are an internal kind of truth.

You really can't test the validity of a subjective truth claim other than by the claim itself—and by the fact that you might witness the woman who made the above claim wearing olive green as she took a stroll every brisk autumn morning, smiling away, munching on Cheez Doodles dipped in peanut butter. Now, you might trust her claim, but your proof from observing her dress and actions might also be mistaken. She might dislike the color olive green but had no time to launder something else. Autumn mornings could be the only time she has an opportunity to go for a stroll. As for her unusual snack, she just might be pregnant!

Referring to the Object

Objective truth claims are quite a bit different from subjective truth claims. Objective truth is true whether anyone wishes to believe it true or not. One truth claim has to do with personal preference, taste, or opinion (that's why you really can't test the validity of subjective truth). The other truth claim concerns an object apart from the individual.

For instance, imagine that you and I are sitting in my dining room enjoying a spot of tea together. You notice my matryoshka dolls—nesting dolls—in my curio cabinet. You ask where I purchased them, and I tell you I bought them while in Russia. Suddenly you begin to eyeball me because you're not quite sure you want to accept my claim that I visited Russia. (Now, I know you're not really like this. You know I wouldn't lie to you—but let's just say, for example.)

Because my truth claim alone hasn't convinced you, I then present evidence that I was, in fact, in Russia. I might show you photographs or a video taken of me while I was there. I might also produce my passport or the stub of my plane ticket—destination, Khabarovsk. I just might call upon other individuals who were also on that trip as witnesses that I was indeed in Russia. The point is, I can prove I was there. Now, you might still be skeptical—but the fact remains, whether you wish to believe the evidence or not, I did go on a missionary trip, which after a very long train ride, landed me at my final destination of Blagoveshchensk. That is objectively true—true whether you wish to accept the claim and the evidence or not.

A chair is a chair, and while I might like to express my subjective opinion by calling it a table, my opinion is not rooted and grounded in objective truth. I can call it whatever I want or believe whatever I wish, but the fact remains, it's still a chair.

Unfortunately, what has happened in our culture—and others—is that in the mind of many individuals, objective truth no longer exists. For them, all truth falls into the realm of the subjective, especially in moral or spiritual matters. The truth is simply relative to an individual's taste or opinion.

However, what seems to have escaped the notice of those who hold to a worldview where there is no objective truth, is that this worldview still assumes one very foundational truth; that one truth is the truth that there is no truth to know. In other words, to say, "There is no truth," *is* a truth claim about truth—which those who hold to this position say no one can know. Oops! Their argument against truth is self-refuting, which is to say, their claim against truth breaks down as soon as they make the claim. If there is no truth, their position or claim cannot be true either.

Nobility in Neutrality?

Many individuals, who hold to a relativistic moral and spiritual worldview, actually feel that this is a neutral position—because, for them, every person's worldview is just as valid as the next. As the thinking goes, since all individuals should accept everyone's brand of faith as equally valid, moral relativists can view themselves as "nobly neutral." Therefore, it only makes sense to rebuke Christians for "pushing" their morality or spirituality on others since to the relativist, spirituality, morality, and truth are simply matters of personal taste or opinion. In other words, "How dare Christians suggest their view is superior or more accurate than anyone else's considering our truth that all views are equally valid? Obviously, neutrality is king!"

However, since when is it noble to be neutral concerning what is intuitively right or wrong? Would neutrality be virtuous in our attitude regarding terrorist attacks all around the world? Would it be noble regarding the increase in ambushes of law enforcement in the United States? Was neutrality noble in Hitler's Germany?

If the goal of moral and spiritual relativism is to silence the gospel, it seems to be working. Many of us are now less apt to share our faith because, after all, who wants an accusation of "pushing" or "imposing" morality, or a particular worldview, on others? What many Christians, in this predicament, do not realize is that a worldview has been "pushed" and "imposed" upon them. The worldview that is pushed on the Christian is that it is wrong for us to actively communicate and support morality and share a formula for a healthy spiritual life, or the embracing of a biblical worldview, with others. Therefore, the imposition is upon Christians—to remain silent. Telling Christians they should not share the gospel is a worldview that encourages them to *hush-up*. I believe the best thing we can do is lovingly and gently draw the relativist's attention to the inconsistencies in this worldview, and show her that it is anything but neutral.

Are Christians Relativists?

Considering the variety of denominations within Christianity, we can almost understand how folks can hold to the false assumption that Christians are the relativists. However, as we in Christendom know, while we might disagree on non-essential issues, on the essentials of the faith, *united we stand*!

When it comes to the basics, we believe the same things regarding the nature and the character of God; humanity's fallen state and our original sin condition, the virgin birth of Jesus Christ, and His sinless life and atonement for our sins on the cross. All those who hold to a Christian worldview believe in His bodily resurrection, and His imminent return. Christians also agree on other essentials of the faith, as stated in the major creeds of Christendom. Therefore, our disagreement over nonessentials such as the style of worship and music, the use of wine or grape juice, matzo, or pita bread during communion, or if we should sprinkle or dunk them during baptism, does not make Christianity somehow just another flavor of relativism.

Also, when professing Christians have some level of disagreement among themselves, this does not mean that there is no objective truth within Christianity. The differences do not prove that one can never arrive at the truth. The first question should be, *What is the nature of our disagreement?* Is it whether or not Jesus Christ was indeed God in the flesh (God incarnate), or is it over whether the preacher should wear a robe, jacket, and tie, or a floral Hawaiian shirt?

Healthy disagreements are good things because, through them, we arrive at objective truth. We can arrive at truth by working through the most logical and best-supported arguments. Unfortunately, the nobly neutral relativists have many people convinced that to *argue* (I did not say *quarrel*) is bad and that those who engage in argumentation are simply divisive and annoying. This view is why, if you attempt to participate in a constructive dispute that leads to truth, inside or outside of the church, you just might be accused of violating the Rodney King axiom: "Can't we all get along?" However, disagreement does not always lead to disaffection.

Not long ago, I conducted a women's retreat in one of the most beautiful places on Earth (yes, my subjective view), Leavenworth, Washington. My daughter, Nicole, was with me as we enjoyed an extended stay for a bit of shopping in the quaint Bavarian-style village when we happened upon a fundraiser. Stretched out before us all along the sidewalks were tables upon tables of old books selling for five dollars or less. How fun! There was every topic under the sun. Nicole was ecstatic to obtain, among other things, a rustic copy of Shakespeare's *The Taming of the Shrew*, and I was excited to find Edward J. Cornell's *An Introduction to Christian Apologetics*, which I had never read. In it was the following "say it like it is" little gem, which relates to our particular topic:

> Truth is worth defending. Moses defended it, as did the prophets and apostles after him. Christ disputed with the doctors in the temple over the Law of Moses. Tolerance of everything is a mark of an empty head, not a mark of *agape* love. Theological pacifism is the death

of theology. It is neither Scriptural nor logical to refrain from intelligent controversy.

The perfect pattern of argumentation is set in 1 Peter 3:15. *The preparation:* "In your hearts reverence Christ as Lord." *The assignment:* "Always be prepared to make a defense to anyone who calls you to account for the hope that is in you." *The mood:* "Yet do it with gentleness and reverence."

Nor are we much impressed by those who think that defenders of a system are on the 'defensive' and are fearful that they are wrong. Rather, it is the firm conviction that Christianity *is* true which goads men [and women] on to propagate it with aggressive arguments.[61]

All Roads to a Heavenly Home?

Imagine you are traveling by car. You have a particular destination in mind and a chatty traveling companion to keep you company. Just then, you happen upon a fork in the road. You stop for a moment, and as you try to figure out which route to choose, your driving companion suggests, "It doesn't matter which one you take—they all lead to our destination." Though you are a bit suspicious of that claim, her confident air prompts you to comply. After noticing one road is a bit prettier than the other is, to the right you veer and continue on your journey. Suddenly, the smooth pavement dissolves as you find your car is hitting pothole after pothole until you reach another fork in the road. Concerned, you timidly suggest to your traveling companion, "Perhaps I should just look at the map."

"What for?" she states, confidently and carefree. "As I said, all these roads lead to our destination. Just pick the one that you want to follow." Again, you obey her advice, but this time, the ride gets bouncier, and you find you are traveling over very rough terrain. Thank goodness you recently put new tires on your Smart Car.

---

[61] *An Introduction to Christian Apologetics* by Edward J. Cornell, copyright ©1948 by Wm. B. Eerdmans Publishing Company, page 85. Insertion mine.

Whoops, another unforeseen fork in the road lies before you. By now, your peace is gone, and outright panic is setting in. "This road can't be right," you say to your blissful companion. "Perhaps I should go back. Or perhaps I need to check the map."

"It wouldn't make any difference. Whatever road we take will lead to our destination. Go ahead and pick the one that feels right to you and press on." Her self-assuredness once again affords you a bit of comfort. After idling there for quite some time, you finally choose a path based on your feelings and not on the map. Aghast, you find that the road you decided has led you to a sheer cliff. As you slowly and carefully attempt to back your car out of this predicament, you notice a sign that reads, "KEEP MOVING FORWARD. DO NOT BACK UP. SEVERE TIRE DAMAGE!"

The moral of the story? All roads do not lead to the same destination in the material world or the spiritual. Neither are all religions the same, leading everyone to a heavenly home—as some might like to suggest. For example, some world religions are polytheistic. Polytheists worship many different gods, while Christians believe that there is only one true and living God. Some believe in cyclic rebirth or reincarnation, but the Bible states in Hebrews 9:27 that, "It is appointed for men to die once and after this comes judgment." Though members of other world religions feel that their good works or deeds will save them, the message of the gospel is that we are saved by grace alone as a gift from God.[62] Because religions of the world contradict each other in some rather significant ways, any world religion of our choosing cannot lead us to the Father.

Frankly, we aren't the only people of faith who claim a particular spiritual expression is true or the correct path to take. Members of most world religions believe that their religion is *the* one true road to salvation. After all, the reason why homicide bombers or Christian missionaries are willing to lose their lives is that they both hold that what they believe is true. However, if worldviews contradict, the thing to do is not judge them as equally valid simply because their adherents hold the view or are willing to

---

[62] Romans 6:23

die for it. What makes *sense* is to test the validity of the claims—to examine them and ask which worldview or system of belief is more reasonable to believe.

Testing the claims of other worldviews is crucial since the Scriptures call us to "Test *and* prove all things [until you can recognize] what is good; [to that] hold fast."[63] The fact that Scripture instructs us to test means that there is a correct answer. Through rigorous testing by comparison and evidence, we can find truth and reality regarding spiritual matters.

Sincerely Wrong

Sincerity and passion are superb; however, if they are misguided, the result can lead us off a cliff—or at the very least, to severe tire damage. Many people today sincerely believe that, as long as you are sincere in what you believe, what you believe is sincerely true *for you*. I'm sure you know as well as I that, again, sincerity absent objective truth can be rather costly. For example, there was once a seemingly innocuous little cult that called itself "Heaven's Gate." Certainly, this was an extremely sincere group of adherents regarding what they believed. So genuine, that some members felt it necessary to return an expensive telescope, claiming it was defective. The shopkeeper looked over the completely functional telescope, then, offering a puzzled look at the cult members, he asked, "Why is it defective?"

Their reply: "One cannot see the UFO [flying behind the Hale-Bopp comet] with it." How tragic that, not long after that head-shaking encounter in March 1997, thirty-nine cult members were found dead, sincerely believing they had to commit suicide to board a UFO that no one could see with *any* telescope. Now, while their sincere intentions were to reach heaven, their method was tragically false.

---

63 1 Thessalonians 5:21 AMP. Brackets and italics in original.

Following Your Imagination

If ever a proverb were fitting for a worldview that dismisses objective truth, it has to be Proverbs 16:25, which reads:

> There is a way which seems right to a man,
> But its end is the way of death.

At first blush, moral relativism does seem somewhat good, fair, and noble. That's why so many individuals inside and outside the church are taken in by it. Nevertheless, its end is not only intellectual but also spiritual death. The sad reality is that this thinking has subtly permeated just about every area of our society, and it is currently being foisted upon our children.

The foisting of moral relativism upon our children is not new. The enticing allure to bring young parents to buy into it for their children isn't new either. Consider a not so subtle example from an article that goes back to when I was a young mommy. It was in the September 1998 edition of the *Portland Parent*. My then 5-year-old daughter, Nicole, spied the rather aloof-looking child on the magazine cover in a doctor's office with the title and byline above his head, "*Nurturing a Child's Spirituality* by Gail E. Hudson." As it turned out, the Lord used this article for a precious teaching moment with my daughter as I read it aloud to her over a burger and fries. I never made it very far along before it was time to ask once again, "Nicole, does that make sense?" At five years old, she knew it didn't. The following is just an excerpt:

> Once on a walk with my 4-year-old daughter, she turned to me and asked, "What do you think God looks like?"
>
> I pointed to the tufts of grass growing in the cracks of the sidewalk, the towering cedar trees, and the silvery, overcast sky. "I believe all of this is the face of God," I said reverently.
>
> "Not me," she replied matter-of-factly. "I think God is a woman with brown hair, a polka-dot dress, and red, bouncy earrings."
>
> Although nothing in my teachings or beliefs had presented God as a flashy-dressing female, I was soothed

by my daughter's vision. It told me that she felt free to follow her own imagination and create a personal relationship with God. And more importantly, she was uninhibited by my own or anyone else's spiritual images and mandates. As a parent trying to nurture my young daughter's innate spirituality, I figured that I must have been doing something right.

First of all, don't you just want to hug that little girl? How precious that, though distorted, she is thinking about God! It's funny, isn't it, that this sweet little girl attempted to make the case to her mother about what God looks like, and very "matter-of-factly," I might add.

However, I don't know about you, but I'm not so sure the little girl's description would *soothe* me. Personally, my immediate question would be to ask my little girl why on earth she envisioned God in such a way in the first place.

God as a "Flashy Dressing Female"?

The author clearly believed that truth concerning spiritual matters is purely subjective. Mamma thinks it is perfectly fine—and is, in fact, soothed by her daughter's image of God as a flashy-dressing female, while she can see the face of God in tufts of grass, towering trees, and an overcast sky. No matter, to Mamma both views are equally valid. Thus, Mamma sincerely believes that she must be doing something right. To leave her daughter with an image of God as a flashy dressing female is right, to persuade her daughter by sharing her view of God is wrong.

Since Mamma holds the worldview that it is wrong to inhibit her child by *imposing* her spiritual image or mandate upon her, she does have some measure of what is right and wrong, or what is true or untrue, concerning spirituality. Obviously, for Mamma, it is virtuous to allow your child to feel free to follow her *own* imagination concerning her view of God, and it is wrong to correct her. Apparently, the best way to nurture the innate spirituality in our children is to leave them to themselves. Yet I wonder what Mamma's reaction would be if her daughter came home and said,

"I know what God looks like—He looks like Jesus Christ because I have come to believe that 'in Him, all the fullness of Deity dwells in bodily form.'"[64] We can only hope and pray!

Isn't it just like the enemy of our soul to try to convince us that the worst thing we can do for our children is to pass on to them our spiritual torch? That to correct a distorted view of God is to inhibit them by imposing a spiritual mandate or image upon them? However, one thing this loving mother did get right. Indeed her daughter does have an innate spirituality. The reason why she does is that the God who is real and knowable put it there for the very purpose of wooing her into a personal relationship, not with tufts of grass, or trees, or the sky, but with Himself.

Proof of Truth

Can we follow our imagination concerning reality? Or, do we all intuitively recognize that objective and absolute truth exists? Everyone can agree, whether we wish to admit it or not, that there is objective truth in a variety of areas of reality.

Law is one such area. If perhaps, while at a department store, I decide to slip a fancy piece of costume jewelry into my pocket, no doubt, I'll feel a tap on my shoulder from security upon my hasty departure from the store. Now, I can talk until I am blue in the face about how shocked I am that the jewelry was found upon my person. Nevertheless, the security camera truthfully caught me snatch and conceal the goods. The truth, in this case, will not set me free but will send me off to the county jail.

Mathematics is another area where objective truth is a reality. For example, my wonderful husband, Jeff, spent quite a few years as a builder. Imagine for a moment that he applied a relativistic worldview to his measurements while building a home. Can you just see the face of the homeowner as she asks, "What happened to my twelve-foot walls? These are only three feet tall!" To which my

---

[64] Colossians 2:9

husband, the relativist builder, would reply, "Well, what is twelve to you is three to me!"

Medicine might get a bit sticky for a patient in a world lacking objective truth. Perhaps you thought you were going to the hospital for an appendectomy, but upon awakening in the recovery room, you find that your incision seems to be in an odd place. When you question your doctor, she shares her subjective feeling that, for her, the appendix and gallbladder are the same things. And, don't you dare try to impose your worldview on her!

What if my hairdresser, for example—oh, I don't even want to go there. I think you get a general idea. In actuality, the relativist can say whatever she likes about her opinion that objective truth does not exist—however, her language and behavior prove otherwise. She approaches her checkbook, the products she buys, the doctors she visits, and the lawyers she retains with the notion that words have a particular meaning and that some critical things in life are just objectively true.

Truth in Morality: It Exists, and It Matters

As you can just imagine, the painful and natural outcome for a society that dismisses the reality of objective truth, and especially in moral absolutes, is adherence to the idea of doing what is right in our own eyes. After all, who can say anything is wrong? Since many professing Christians are uncomfortable when faced with an opportunity to make a difference and turn the tide with the politically correct crowd, their silence has allowed this thinking to catch on like wildfire. It is Habakkuk 1:7 right here in our nation: "They are dreaded and feared. Their justice and authority originate with themselves."

Just to show you how pervasive the worldview of moral relativism is, consider for a moment what the United States Supreme Court stated in 1992 in *Planned Parenthood vs. Casey.* What the U.S. Supreme Court essentially did, in this case, was to grant credence to the "follow your own imagination" philosophy in some of the most fundamental matters. For the Supreme Court to arrive at such a conclusion on the nature of truth and meaning, the groundwork was in place long beforehand. Here is just a snippet of the court's opinion:

> Our law affords constitutional protection to personal decisions relating to marriage, procreation, contraception, family relationships, child rearing and education.

The justices then cited a couple of cases and went on:

> These matters, involving the most intimate of personal choices a person may make in a lifetime, choices central to personal dignity and autonomy, are central to the liberty protected by the Fourteenth Amendment. At the heart of liberty is *the right to define one's own concept* of existence, of meaning, of the universe, and the mystery of human life.[65]

There it is—Moral Relativism 101, right from the pen of the U.S. Supreme Court. The court's opinion in 1992 was that we no longer need to burden ourselves with the objective truth that personhood affords protection under the Fourteenth Amendment of our Constitution. *Planned Parenthood vs. Casey* spoke of pre-born children, but the door is open to deprive other individuals of "personhood" as well.

No longer need we concern ourselves with being endowed by our Creator with certain inalienable rights. In fact, we can dismiss Him altogether because we, the autonomous individual, can define our own concept of existence, of meaning, of the universe, and human life. And apparently, we can determine what value we place on human life if we happen to place any value on it at all. Since our value judgment of the pre-born can be fluid, we can call them babies if we want to keep them alive in the womb, "products of conception" if we don't. It's our choice. Semantics makes all the difference.

Now, while you might refer to it as murder, the Nazis called it the Final Solution. While you might call it mayhem and horror, ISIS called it religious liberty. Do you see how a department of justice

---

[65] As cited in Francis J. Beckwith's excellent book *Politically Correct Death: Answering the Arguments for Abortion Rights* (Grand Rapids, MI: Baker Books, 1994) page 188, emphasis added

or police force almost makes no sense in this sort of world—after all, how dare we impose our morality on others? Frightening, isn't it? However, there is hope, wisdom, and freedom. Don't despair—the good news is that you are not in the dark about moral relativism, and the great news is neither is God.

The Truth Will Set You Free

I know this might seem bold, but it *is* possible to arrive at truth in spiritual matters and thus possess a right view of God and His method of salvation. Thankfully, God has indeed said something about Himself and the way we are to view and approach Him. He has not left our pursuit of Him up to a simple matter of taste or opinion, as you might select your favorite brand of salad dressing.

That He is, *who* He is, and *how* we draw near to Him, are matters of objective truth, truth whether or not anyone wishes to accept or acknowledge it as such. God in His love, and mercy, and grace never meant for those He created in His image to have a subjective expression of spirituality. Now, I don't know about you, but I praise God for the truth and simplicity of the gospel. "There is salvation in no one else; for there is no other name under heaven that has been given among men by which we must be saved."[66] And that name is Jesus. God the Father, being the perfect heavenly Parent, did not leave His children to themselves—instead, He went to great lengths that they might know Truth.

How many of us can attest to the fact that in our fallen, rebellious state, we desire to do our own thing, and especially in the area of spiritual expression and standards of morality? Romans 1:18 states that our natural inclination is to "suppress the truth in unrighteousness."

Unfortunately, our fallen nature has put us at enmity with God. Our fallen state has left us with the desire to worship because we are spiritual beings, but in our depravity, we seek to replace the truth with a counterfeit. If it were not for the gracious beckoning

---

[66] Acts 4:12

of the Spirit of God that prompts our response, we would each be left in the pitiable state described in Romans 1:21-23:

> Even though they knew God, they did not honor Him as God or give thanks; but they became futile in their speculations [opinions] and their foolish heart was darkened. Professing to be wise, they became fools, and exchanged the glory of the incorruptible God for an image in the form of corruptible man and of birds and four-footed animals and crawling creatures.

Our blessed Lord requires that we pursue truth in our approach to and worship of Him. Jesus expressed God's heart and desire for His image-bearers beautifully in His conversation with the Samaritan woman at the well:

> "An hour is coming, and now is, when the true worshipers will worship the Father in spirit and truth; for such people the Father seeks to be His worshipers. God is spirit, and those who worship Him must worship in spirit and truth."
>
> The woman said to Him, "I know that Messiah is coming (He who is called Christ); when that One comes, He will declare all things to us."
>
> Jesus said to her, "I who speak to you am He."[67]

The Way, Truth, and Life—Truly!

Have you visited your local bookstore lately? If not, pop into one and peruse the books located in the section marked "Spirituality." It's quite an eye-opener. I remembered doing this in preparation for my talk at a youth rally some time ago and purchased a little book that immediately caught my eye. (I managed to get the last one. I'm sure they ordered more since sales of the author's works are in the millions.) The book was *Conversations with God for Teens* by Neale Donald Walsch. In this little book, geared toward young people, "God" is supposedly answering a teenager's questions. I thought you might like to know

---

[67] John 4:23-26

what "God" is saying to our young people. The following excerpts are just a taste:

> It may be a surprise for most humans to learn that there is no such thing as right and wrong. There is only what works and what doesn't work, given what it is that you are trying to do.
>
> Absolute Right and Absolute Wrong do not exist. A thing is "wrong" only because you say it is wrong, and a thing is "right" for the same reason.
>
> Right and wrong, therefore, do not exist as absolutes, but only as momentary assessments of What Works and What Doesn't Work. You make these assessments yourself as individuals and as a society, given what you are wishing to experience and how you see yourself in relationship to everything else that is.
>
> In the book *Friendship with God*, I brought the human race a new gospel that would heal the world in two sentences: *We are all one. Ours is not a better way, ours is merely another way.*[68]

Now, you're probably thinking, *Where did he get this stuff to tell our kids?* Well, it didn't start with the United States Supreme Court in 1992, and it didn't start with the New Agers or the postmodernists of today, or even with Neale Donald Walsch. Its source is pretty apparent—simply put, it comes straight from that old snake in the grass. Of him, Jesus warned:

> "He was a murderer from the beginning, and does not stand in the truth, because there is no truth in him. Whenever he speaks a lie, he speaks from his own nature, for he is a liar and the father of lies."[69]

Misquoting The Truth

Well, the father of lies is at it again. The serpent of old who is called Satan and the devil doesn't own one original thought, and

---

[68] Neale Donald Walsch, *Conversations with God for Teens* (Charlottesville, VA: Hampton Roads Publishing Company, Inc., 2001), pp. 88, 89, 91, 97-98

[69] John 8:44

he often quotes, then twists Scripture or its context to prove his case. How sad, though, that many people still fall for it. On page 85 of *Conversations with God for Teens*, a teen questioner, who is astonished to learn that "God" does not judge because nothing is "bad," asks Walsch's caricature of God the following question. Below it, you will find "God's" answer:

> God does not make judgments? I thought that's what God did.

> Well, the human race has been thinking that for a long time, but it's not true. It's one of those misunderstandings I've been talking about. It's an illusion. The illusion of judgment. Followed by the illusion of condemnation. It has been written: Judge not, and neither condemn.[70]

Interesting, isn't it, how quickly the very people who wish to reject the heart of Jesus' message are always first to quote Him (or rather, misquote Him)? They quote, "Judge not lest you be judged," as a tool to persuade us to keep silent on the moral ills of our day. They quote, "Love your neighbor as yourself," which, of course, they believe they have satisfied because they once lent their neighbor a lawnmower. They remind you that Jesus hobnobbed with tax collectors and sinners—as if His presence with them meant he condoned their sinful behavior. By taking His words or actions out of context, it's easy to make it seem as if Jesus were just this freewheeling kind of guy who wouldn't think twice about someone *doing their own thing.*

However, Matthew 7:1-5 states that we are not to judge *hypocritically*—not that we should always avoid making moral judgments. If I warn someone that it is wrong to steal while I am pilfering at Nordstrom, that would be a clear indication that I had better get the log out of my eye before I chastise you over the speck of dust in yours. Also, Walsch's young questioner had a right to be astonished at the idea that impending judgment by a holy God is imaginary. I believe that at the very core of our being, we intuitively know Revelation 19:11 is an imminent reality: "I saw heaven opened, and behold, a white horse, and He who sat on it

---

[70] Walsch, p. 85

is called Faithful and True, and in righteousness He judges and wages war."

Concerning "love your neighbor as yourself," those who quote it always seem to neglect the first and more important part of Jesus' words. In Matthew 22:36, a lawyer asked Jesus which commandment of the Law was the greatest. We find His response in verses 37-40.

> [Jesus] said to [the lawyer], "'YOU SHALL LOVE THE LORD YOUR GOD WITH ALL YOUR HEART, AND WITH ALL YOUR SOUL, AND WITH ALL YOUR MIND.' This is the great and foremost commandment. The second is like it, 'YOU SHALL LOVE YOUR NEIGHBOR AS YOURSELF.' On these two commandments depend the whole Law and the Prophets."

According to Jesus, we cannot have the second absent the first. We are to love God with all our heart, soul, and mind, first and foremost—which then gives us the ability to love our neighbor as ourselves.

Additionally, as far as Jesus' associating with those of questionable character, He certainly wasn't condoning their sinful behavior. He commented that the reason why He was with them was that they were spiritually and morally sick and needed a physician. He recognized that it was necessary to sit among them to bring them the truth and freedom from their spiritual and moral illnesses because Jesus has always been and still is in the business of radical life change.

Set Free by The Truth

All the above is to say that the subjective views people hold of Jesus are a bit off the mark. Jesus, who is God (qualifying Him as the only One with the correct answers on spiritual and moral matters), believed in the reality of objective truth. After all, that's who He was and is. Jesus Christ is Truth. When we deny the truth, we deny Jesus Christ. Consider the following passages referring to the reality and importance of truth:

• *John 1:17*, "The Law was given through Moses; grace and truth were realized through Jesus Christ."

• *John 8:31-32*, "So Jesus was saying to those Jews who had believed Him, 'If you continue in My word, then you are truly disciples of Mine; and you will know the truth, and the truth will make you free.'"

• *John 14:6*, "Jesus said to him, 'I am the way, and the truth, and the life; no one comes to the Father but through Me.'"

• *John 15:26*, "When the Helper comes, whom I will send to you from the Father, that is the Spirit of truth who proceeds from the Father, He will testify about Me."

• *John 17:17* [Jesus, in His high-priestly prayer to the Father said], "Sanctify them in truth; Your word is truth."

Truth matters. It sets us free; it sets us apart; it is not vague or elusive. Truth, according to Jesus in the above passages, is something we can and will recognize. The reality of the Christian faith is not "your truth" or "my truth." Praise God that by His beckoning, it is truth that *we came to*, not that we invented.

Moreover, morality is not a collection of ideas we create and change according to tradition or our momentary whim. Moral absolutes are the same yesterday, today, and forever because they are rooted and grounded in the Truth—the very nature and character of the God who said, "I, the LORD, do not change."[71] Jesus brought us out of the bondage of deception to the truth and freedom we enjoy in Him.

FINAL THOUGHTS

For many of us, I know it is hard to believe that we must produce evidence for the existence of absolute truth. There was a time when this wasn't the case. I think, though, that times can change yet again. I think the time just might be on the horizon for us to penetrate an invisible wall and reach those who have abandoned truth. Perhaps God will use you. I know He would like

---

[71] Malachi 3:6

to. Since this is the case, I want to take a moment and offer some tools that you might find helpful.

It is imperative to open the lines of communication. When someone tells you that your truth is true for you alone, it really can shut the whole conversation down unless you ask a straightforward question. When chatting with someone who claims that truth is subjective, that there are no moral absolutes, or that all types of spiritual expression are equally valid, simply ask, "How do you know?" One of two things will happen.

One: Your acquaintance will attempt to defend her claim. The minute she begins an attempt to prove her position is correct, you can lovingly point out her inconsistency in claiming there is no truth while claiming that her claim about truth is true. By doing this, you might just help her realize the bankruptcy of her position—and thus open the door for you to share the Good News lovingly and enthusiastically.

Or two: Your acquaintance will not attempt to defend her claim because, if she is intellectually honest with you and herself, she will realize she has no idea why she believes what she believes.

If you notice irritation in her tone, it could simply be a result of a misunderstanding regarding what you believe. She assumes everyone holds the view that you can select any brand of religious expression because, to her, this is a matter of taste or opinion. Therefore, in essence, she thinks that what you're saying is, "You will be separated from God forever if you don't like my brand of salad dressing."

Remember, the truths of your faith are what you came to realize, not what you invented. Begin with what's intuitive. Be patient. Since the subjective approach is prevalent and, on the surface, sounds so appealing, it's going to take prayer, patience, time, and truth to breach the strongholds. Just as God was and still is patient with you and me, let's try our best to be patient with our seeking family and friends. "The Lord is not slow about His promise, as some count slowness, but is patient toward you, not wishing for any to perish but for all to come to repentance."[72]

---

[72] 2 Peter 3:9

QUESTIONS & RESOURCES

1. What is the difference between subjective and objective truth?

2. How would you respond to someone who makes the statement, "Well, that's true for *you*," after you shared the gospel?

3. What are some differences between other world religions and Christianity?

4. Why do you believe that objective truth and moral absolutes matter? Is your answer solely your opinion? How do you know?

5. Where did the thinking originate that nothing is right or wrong? Who told us?

Relativism: Feet Firmly Planted in Mid-Air by Francis J. Beckwith and Gregory Koukl, Baker Books, 1998.

The Death of Truth, general editor, Dennis McCallum, Bethany House Publishers, 1996.

The Universe Next Door: A Basic World View Catalog, third edition by James Sire, InterVarsity Press, 1997.

CHAPTER 6 ~ *Of Monkeys and Men*

"The reason why humans no longer have fur is that they started wearing clothes."

"If Jesus had come at an earlier time during our evolutionary change, He probably would have come as a monkey."

The subject of evolution sure tends to lend itself to some rather curious speculations. The above statements, for instance, were serious thoughts offered by two highly successful professional women during a conversation we had regarding their position that macro-evolution[73] is a fact, and intelligent design is a religion. While this is a popular position, popularity should not be the basis by which we gauge the position's accuracy.

I must confess that, for many years, I thought macro-evolution made some sense. I mean, hey, the lecturer in the white lab coat wearing reading glasses perched precariously on the tip of her nose, said it was so. Who was I to disagree with a learned scientist? However, my nagging question remained—why are there still monkeys?

For me, things quickly changed. Once I gave my life to the lordship of Jesus Christ, I simply adjusted the mechanism of evolution in my mind. Thus, I believed God used it to bring about the existence of human beings—mystery solved. My reason for holding that position, I now admit, was a rather poor one. I believed that to keep to a literal creation account—God created everything in six days, and it was all very good—and to believe in

---

[73] When using the term *macro*-evolution, I mean one *kind* evolving into another *kind*. For example, a monkey evolving into a man, rather than *micro*evolution, which are smaller variations, such as the differences between a Chihuahua and a wolf, yet remain part of the same canine family or kind.

a worldwide flesh-flushing flood was a bit too anti-intellectual for a sharp gal like me. (Some brat, huh?)

It wasn't long before I realized that if I were going to believe the Bible as the inspired Word of God, I would have to take another look at the Genesis accounts of both creation and the flood. I recognized that what I needed to do was to stop blaming God for a weak theory and consider the evidence. I needed to do the work of investigation that substantiated the biblical accounts. My time delving into various materials was worth every minute, and I am delighted to have an opportunity to share with you what has become one of my favorite subjects. (I guess it's one of my favorites because the theory of macro-evolution is perfect fodder for someone who enjoys taking the *reductio ad absurdum*— reducing to the absurd—approach when facing challenges to belief.)

With that in mind, I'd like to offer a short review of the theory for macro-evolution and its implications. Then I'll briefly address the fossil record to see if we can find any validity to the macro-evolutionary claim. Afterward, a consideration of biblical accounts of creation and the flood will be made. I'll do this because there is a connection between the flood and the fossils. What I think just might happen is that, by the end of this chapter, you'll see the theory of macro-evolution not as science, but as an atheistic worldview that indeed requires enormous faith to believe.

In the Beginning, "Nothing" Exploded

Perhaps you learned as I did during my years in grade school, the same particularly fantastic story about humankind's humble and rather insignificant emergence. The story went something like this: In the beginning (or, *once upon an eon*), there was nothing— and by chance, it exploded. This explosion caused dust, gas, and radiation to whirl everywhere. Sprinkled with a little gravity, planets, and stars formed from the particles of the original explosion, or *Big Bang*. For millions of years on our humble abode (Earth), lightning flashed through an atmosphere of methane and ammonia. Then suddenly, for no reason, and quite by *chance*, a group of molecules came together in a primordial broth, reproduced, and life began.

By *chance*, these new organisms grew and mutated. Because of their strong survival instinct, which they got just by *chance*, the stronger survived over the weaker. Through *chance* mutations and the death of more vulnerable and less fortunate species, all creatures evolved into what we see today, including you and me. Therefore, to sum it all up, an explosion—disorder, that is—and *chance* occurrences brought forth order, intricate design, and *Homo sapiens*.

Confidence in the Big Bang theory has not waned, as was proven to me by a recent article that caught my eye entitled, *What Was Our Universe Like Before the Big Bang?* The article only proved one thing. That, since so many people are thoroughly convinced, "scientists" can now stretch credulity to its extreme. If you rely on the title alone, you would assume they knew *what our universe was like before the Big Bang*—until you take the time to read the article, which most people don't.

To be perfectly clear, we can't definitively answer this question—but we can speculate wildly...

"As of yet, these aren't established as laws of physics we understand or have checked in any way," said (theoretical physicist Sean) Carroll.

The article's conclusion:

"It's important to simultaneously let people know that we don't know what we're talking about," said Carroll. "These are speculative ideas that are just beginning to be taken seriously, but there is hope! I think we can actually figure it out if we keep it up."[74]

Yes, as long as the grant money flows, just-so stories are endless. We can pose any theory, and chase it as if it made sense, but pose God as a necessary Being, and we're unscientific and anti-intellectual. Amazing!

---

[74]https://gizmodo.com/what-was-our-universe-like-before-the-big-bang-1791889926

From Theory to Assumed Fact

Since the Big Bang theory does present itself to many as a rather compelling story, you would imagine there must be some concrete evidence to support it. Especially because—and I'm not quite sure when it happened—somehow, the *theory* of macro-evolution has become an assumed and accepted fact. Consider the matter-of-fact tone of a *Time* magazine article entitled "How Man Began."[75] In ever-so-small writing, beneath a rendering of our supposed above-average ancient ancestor, who is running through the forest wearing nothing but a worried expression on his face, is this little tidbit of information concerning this *Homo erectus*:

Accomplished ancestor: *Homo erectus* might not look like much, but he was the first creature to use fire, fashion advanced tools and leave mankind's African home.

Apparently, the guy was brilliant. Perhaps the picture is of one *Homo erectus* in particular, the creature better known as Java man. They might have called him that because he was discovered on the island of Java, but I'd like to think that he simply enjoyed hanging out at the local Starbucks of his day. Perhaps, since he was so advanced, they should have at least drawn him with a hot cup of joe in one hand and a briefcase in the other!

Fantastic stories regarding our supposed ancient ancestors don't end with the popular magazines or television shows of today. Simply take your children on a little outing. I'm sure you'll notice if you haven't already, the evolutionary philosophy alluded to, or downright blatant, just about everywhere you go. It sure seems to me that the dogma is everywhere, from the aquarium to the zoo.

Even at my backyard volcano, we cannot escape indoctrination when we visit what is affectionately known as the "blast zone." This dramatic landscape is located on the north side of Mount St. Helens in Washington State. Just to give you a bit of background, during the nine-hour eruption on May 18, 1980,

---

[75] Michael D. Lemonick, *How Man Began, Time* magazine, March 14, 1994, p. 81

Mount St. Helens released the energy equivalent to a blast from 400 million tons of TNT. Now that's what I'd call a *big bang*. From the power of that eruption, some areas were scraped down to the bedrock. Since what goes up must come down, debris and ash accumulated hundreds of feet thick on the landscape around the volcano. Ecologists in the area believed it would take a hundred years before life would return to the mountain, a landscape devastated.

However, to the amazement of all, especially the ecologists, it turns out that foliage can grow quite plentiful upon the new landscape. Within two years of the eruption, 90 percent of all the original plant and wildlife had returned to Mount St. Helens.

At the visitors' center, after receiving this fascinating information on the return of plant and wildlife, we were asked the following question during one guide's impassioned presentation: "Do you know who the real hero is for the return of the plants and animals to Mount St. Helens?"

Perhaps you and I just might be thinking of the same Person, but not the guide at the visitors' center. Placing a gopher puppet on her hand, she proclaimed, "The gopher! You see, he burrowed into the ground before the eruption, and when it was over, on his way out, he kicked up soil and seeds. Once the rains came, the seeds germinated, and other animals who eat those plants returned. Since the gopher couldn't find food, he eventually died, but his body became a meal for another animal. So even in death, the gopher was the real hero."

Now, you might be wondering how this is an example of the theory of evolution. I share this experience because it demonstrates that glory is repeatedly given to the creature, not the Creator, which also seems to be an underlying theme of the theory.

The Rise of Monkey Business

The theory of macro-evolution is not a new worldview. It dates back to the ancient Greeks. However, its popularity took off when Charles Darwin published his book *On the Origin of the Species* in 1859. In 1871, in *The Descent of Man*, Darwin posed the idea that human beings had evolved from lower life-forms. Darwin's writings offered, in the mind of many of his adherents, a sensible mechanism to explain away the Creator. Darwin thus paved the way for the ridiculing of Bible-believing Christians that followed. The most famous (or I should say, infamous) example would be what took place during the July 1925 Scopes "monkey trial."

Briefly, what happened was that the American Civil Liberties Union (ACLU) decided to solicit a teacher to challenge the Butler Act. This law forbade teachers to teach evolution in Tennessee public schools. In their quest to locate a willing candidate, they were able to persuade a physical-education teacher named John Scopes to become the defendant. For him to truthfully testify that he had, in fact, taught evolution, he instructed two students in the back seat of a taxi. (As it turned out, Scopes never took the witness stand—and after the trial, he wasn't sure he had ever even taught evolution.)

The famous criminal lawyer, and atheist, Clarence Darrow defended Scopes. Former presidential candidate, and Christian, William Jennings Bryan represented the state. By the fifth day of the trial, a shift took place. The issue was no longer whether Scopes had violated the law, but whether creation or evolution was correct. The court found Scopes guilty of violating the Butler Act and was fined $100, which Darrow promptly paid.

During the trial, however, reporters flocked to Tennessee, and the media began to ridicule Christians for believing the Bible and the creation account. Because of the ridicule, Christians began to back away from the creation model. With the emergence of German higher theological criticism of the Bible in the universities and churches across America, added to that the decline of the nation's moral foundation, it became easy for macro-evolution to rise to the popular platform we see today.

Unfortunately, what most people picture when they think of the Scopes "monkey trial" is the movie *Inherit the Wind*, a popular fictional account of the events in Tennessee during the summer of

1925.[76] Less famous is the fact that many of the "proofs" of evolution used in the *Scopes* trial were debunked through modern scientific study. Concerning the supposed "ape-men" that were cited as evidence, one turned out to be a hoax, one an ape, two fully human, and another merely an extinct pig.

The Implications

"No single essential difference separates human beings from other animals." Quite a statement, wouldn't you say? That is the first line of the *Time* magazine article I mentioned earlier. In other words, there is no essential difference between a human being and a dog. Since the evolutionary position claims that humans are merely products of random chance, there was no pristine creation, no Creator to whom we are accountable, no fall from a state of innocence, and thus there is no need for the cross.

Think of it this way. If, for example, there is no intelligence behind the design, then there is no design—no meaning to what we behold. If all things from the stars to microorganisms are simply products of random chance, then no Creator has a plan and purpose for His creation or our lives. Once we can dismiss the Creator, nothing restrains us from doing what is right in our own eyes, because neither is there a Moral Law.

With this backdrop and understanding, I believe we can now begin to tie in some of what I went over in previous chapters and understand how we can so quickly feel it perfectly fine to reject the existence of God and objective truth entirely.

When society dismisses the Moral Law and Lawgiver, the survival of the fittest dictates, therefore, if you happen to be weak or sick, or you're in pain and are suffering. If you are viewed merely as a financial burden to those around you, then it makes perfect sense to put you to sleep "compassionately"—like the old, unwanted house pet that has overstayed its welcome.

---

[76] *Inherit the Wind*, produced and directed by Stanley Kramer, 1960, starring Spencer Tracy, Fredric March, and Gene Kelly, adapted from the stage play *Inherit the Wind*, written by Jerome Lawrence and Robert Edwin Lee.

The implications are staggering, frightening, and as plain as what we see and hear in the news daily as to what a purposeless, random-chance worldview produces. The good news is, we do not base our belief in a Creator God upon the frightening logical implications of not believing in Him. We believe, as His Word states, because of the "convincing proofs,"[77] one of which is His handiwork that we behold "day to day… and night to night."[78]

Let's Look at the Record

Now and again, late, during those warmer-than-usual summer nights, I enjoy lounging around on my back deck to stargaze. The best time is during the new moon. It is pitch black out there at night in the forest, with no sign of city lights. I don't know if you've ever noticed it, but the longer you stare at the sky, the more stars you can see. Oh, I know, I know—it's just my eyes adjusting to the light (or lack of it, I should say), but it is still magnificent to behold. I have to tell you that it simply amazes me how anyone can gaze upon the heavenly bodies and remain thoroughly convinced that the existence of those bodies, as well as their own, were simply the result of random chance occurrences.

Chance—if you read the little plaques at your local zoo and listen to the evolutionary dogma long enough, you'll realize there is no end to what *chance* can do. Thus, for the average evolutionist, this thing called *chance* is the perfect replacement for God, a fantastic mechanism to explain away a personal Creator. After all, *chance* is powerful, *chance* has creative ability, and *chance* even improves upon what it creates! Unfortunately for those who cling tenaciously to this (which requires greater faith than belief in a personal Creator), as any mathematician can prove, *chance* can never be spelled with a capital *c*. The reason is simple— *chance* is nothing but a mathematical probability.

Though I regretfully confess that I genuinely did waste much of my time in grade school utilizing my desk as a headrest (that dear

---

[77] Acts 1:3
[78] Psalm 19:2

science teacher was more accurate than she knew), I do recall the mantra, "What chance creates, chance destroys."

Imagine for a moment that my husband, Jeff, and I are going to play a game of Scrabble. Imagine Jeff placing a handful of tiles in the cup, shakes them vigorously, and then spills them onto the board. The tiny plastic squares, by random chance, then drop out of the container and form the words *JEFF LOVES JUDY*. Would those words, in that case, have any meaning or purpose? The answer is no. Why? Because after Jeff and I have a good laugh about it, as quickly as he can scoop up those letters and spill them out again order will become disorder, or *what chance creates, chance destroys*, and the letters will probably read something like *JLU FEDJ YVFE OS.*

Now, imagine that instead of spilling the tiles onto the playing board, Jeff handpicks the tiles one by one from the cup as I sit there, probably batting my eyes at him. He then carefully spells out the words *JEFF LOVES JUDY*, suddenly those letters have meaning and purpose. The meaning is that he loves me, and the purpose is his desire to communicate that message to me. The difference between the first scenario and the second is that there is an intelligence behind the design. (Exactly like the *God* billboard I spoke of in Chapter 3.)

Again, what chance creates, chance destroys. This basic principle is entirely contrary to the theory of evolution. Evolution proposes that we should see advancement, or betterment, of creatures through *chance* mutations as time goes on. In reality, we do not see that at all. What we do witness is an increase of disease, deformity, and death, and in many cases, extinction.

Cyclops and Breathing Fish

That a critter mutates is not a sign that macro-evolution is a fact. A mutation is like decay—the carcass has to exist before rot can set in. A creature had to live at one time in a pure, perfect state for it to mutate. Therefore the question remains: How did the animal get here in the first place? To throw in the idea of mutation doesn't answer the question—it only creates a new one. Again, since nothing mutates for the better, random chance mutations usually do not help a critter—they hinder its existence.

Perhaps you're like me in that you never forget a face. I will especially never forget one face in particular. I saw it when I was just eighteen years old as I was walking through the halls of Cornell University in Ithaca, New York. There it was, floating in a jar of formaldehyde—the head of a lamb with cyclopean malformation. With only one eye in the center, it was a miniature Cyclops! Just in case you are curious, here is how this condition occurs. If by chance, a pregnant ewe, on her fourteenth day of gestation, eats the herb *Veratrum californicum*, toxic alkaloids in the plant affect the preborn sheep, causing the cyclopean malformation—or, as the condition is more affectionately known, *monkey face.*[79] Trust me— it doesn't look anything like a monkey. Now, are we to believe that random chance processes are positive and helpful to the creature? Are we to assume that, given enough time, the little Cyclops will adjust to its malformation and thus improve and survive as an addition to the sheep species? Unfortunately, this malformation/mutation, since it is apart from the Creator's ideal and original design, results in its death.

However, for a moment, let's grant the evolutionist the premise of random chance mutations as a mechanism for the arrival of all the creatures we see today. Perhaps the lungfish, a fascinating creature I met at the Oregon Zoo, could help explain just how it arrived at its unique survival mechanism. Here is a fish that lives in drought-prone areas. When riverbeds completely dry up, the fish will burrow into the bottom mud and form a mucusy cocoon around itself. Because it possesses lungs, it can breathe, and thus it can survive in its cocoon for quite some time. When the rains return, the river fills up, and the lungfish emerges from its long siesta.

Now, granting the evolutionary premise, did the lungfish call a meeting and say to its fishy friends and family, "You know, I've been thinking, every year when the drought comes, we all die.

[79] Just in case I've piqued your curiosity and you would like to do further research on cyclopian malformation, please see Cleon V. Kimberling, *Jensen and Swift's Diseases of Sheep* (Philadelphia: Lippincott Williams & Wilkins, 1987).

Next year, why don't we develop some lungs, then create little cocoons and curl up in them for a few months until the rains return? What do you say we give it a whirl and see how it goes?" That's pretty silly, huh? Obviously, unless on the very first go-round they had *figured it out*, they would all be dead!

I can only imagine just how many other organs in the lungfish would have had to "mutate" right along with its intentionally evolved, perfectly working lungs. With its new lungs would also have to be the development of the necessary apparatus to give it the ability to construct its mucusy cocoon. (By the way, if the creature can *figure it out*, what room is there for *random chance?*)

Obvious Monkey Business

Despite the mounting evidence against the macro-evolutionary hypothesis, the proponents of this worldview seem to become more creative every day. I once happened upon a rather humorous little item in my local newspaper about what some hail as a possible link from beast to man. The article was entitled "Tall and Meaty, Bigfoot Lumbers Around."[80] Included was a drawing of a large, powerful-looking, furry creature.

Point by point, the creature was meticulously described: its eating habits, demeanor, height, weight, strength, movement, eyesight, hearing, sense of smell, noises it made, and of course, its foot size. The punchline summed up the whole matter quite nicely, including a factoid that began, "Generally accepted scientific evidence of the species." It was answered with one word. Can you guess what that one word was to describe the "generally accepted scientific evidence"? Here it is— "none." (Why was this *news?*)

The best part of the article was noted off to the side with an icon of a telephone above it. It read, "Bigfoot Unplugged—what does a Bigfoot sound like? To listen to some strange sounds that researchers claim may be Bigfoot caught on tape, call the Info-line." I called the number supplied, and all I heard was banjo music. Apparently, Bigfoot was either truly "unplugged" or had

---

[80] Phiet Luong, *Tall and Meaty, Bigfoot Lumbers Around*, *The Columbian* (Vancouver, Washington), Fall 1996.

evolved with hidden talents that even the learned scientists had neglected to mention.

Since my humorous Bigfoot article was quite some time ago, I decided to get an update on the latest in the ape-men–monkey mystery. Therefore, I e-mailed Frank Sherwin, professor and zoologist with the Institute for Creation Research and international creation-science lecturer and debater, to get the latest scoop on *who is hot* and *who is not*. The following was his summation:

> The case for "human evolution" continues to be mired in controversy. The secular community states the best link between man and his alleged apelike ancestor is *Australopithecus*—which means *southern ape*. Creation scientists maintain that's exactly what the shattered fossil remains show—an extinct ape. Everything about this creature was apelike. Even evolutionist Meg Rudolph called *Australopithecus* a "hodge-podge genus" (*Geotimes*, May 2001)!
>
> Daniel Lieberman is an expert on "human evolution" and admitted in *Nature* magazine (March 2001) that "the evolutionary history of humans is complex and unresolved."
>
> Henry Gee, again in *Nature* (one of the most well-established science publications in the world), said, "Fossil evidence of human evolutionary history is fragmentary and open to various interpretations" (July 2001).
>
> Is this why "human evolution" should be taught as fact in taxpayer-funded public schools? Since our public educational domain is supposedly the free marketplace of ideas, would it not be refreshing to have quotes like the above free and open to American public school children?

As a mother and grandmother, I think Professor Sherwin makes a pretty valid point.

The Missing "Missing Link"

Now, I hate to throw another Bogart classic film at you, but have you ever watched *The Cain Mutiny?* Humphrey Bogart played a shell-shocked, overworked, hard-driving, paranoid World War II ship captain. During a voyage, a gallon of strawberries mysteriously vanished.

Even though Bogart's character was informed that a couple of sailors had confessed to eating the strawberries, the captain was determined to find a missing, duplicate key which he, using "geometric logic," theorized someone had created and used to break into a cabinet containing the coveted strawberries. His thinking was that if he found the duplicate key, it would lead him straight to the strawberry thief. The captain was so confident his theory was correct that in the middle of the night, he had the entire ship turned upside down to find a key, though deep down inside, he knew only existed in his mind. Quite bizarre behavior, wouldn't you agree?

Nevertheless, like the ship captain in *The Cain Mutiny*, who was looking for the missing, duplicate key to substantiate his theory, so too are the macro-evolutionists looking for the missing link to substantiate theirs. The truth is, the missing link, as well as the key on the *Cain*, are not missing—because neither exists. However, to call it "missing" assumes its existence. They use the term "missing" because it seems pretty silly to search for something that you only imagine exists—or that you know, deep down inside, couldn't possibly exist. The evolutionist approaches the subject with a colossal presupposition. That there is a link to miss— Big Foot or small—to substantiate the theory.

Of course, those who hold to intelligent design and special creation also approach the subject of origins with a presupposition: that there is a Creator God. The difference is, when you sincerely search for the Creator, you find Him because, as the Apostle Paul stated in Acts 17, "He is not far from each one of us," in addition to the fact that He actually does exist!

Of the millions of fossils in museums around the globe, not one proves any animal has ever evolved into another. There simply are no transitional forms. Neither have they found any "missing link" between man and any other animal. Every skull, jaw, tooth, and bone fragment has proved to be a hoax, fully human, or entirely animal. The following is a list of what some of the most popular finds, that still live on in children's public school textbooks, have turned out to be:

- Java man: an ape

- "Lucy": a chimpanzee

- Neanderthal: fully human

- Nebraska man: a wild pig

- Peking man: no physical evidence for its existence

- Piltdown man: a human skull and an ape's jaw

- Ramapithicus: an orangutan

- Ardi (discovered in 1993): a toe, found 10 miles away from the rest of the incomplete fossil, was the primary 'evidence' for this creature's supposed uprightness.

- "Toumai" (found in the spring of 2002): a skull, "badly disfigured and needed reconstructive surgery, leading to criticisms that any interpretations were subjective."[81]

The "finds" never stop! Another impressive headline from 2017 read, *Scientists Find 'Oldest Human Ancestor.'* Ladies, close your science textbooks we're done, this is it—evidence for sure! After all, the first line in the article reads, "Researchers have discovered the earliest known ancestor of humans." Unfortunately, for these zealous folks, what they *found* actually points us to a common Creator and not a common ancestor.

Upon reading the article, *Scientists Find 'Oldest Human Ancestor,'* you realize it displays yet another brutally deceiving title as the item is filled with vague language and *just-so* conclusions.

---

[81]http://crev.info/2005/04/gorilla_or_hominidnbsp_touma239_controversy_continue/

Saccorhytus was about a millimetre in size, and *is thought to* have lived between grains of sand on the sea bed.

"We *think* that as an early deuterostome this *may* represent the primitive beginnings of a very diverse range of species, including ourselves. All deuterostomes had a common ancestor, and we *think* that is what we are looking at here."

Also interesting are the conical structures on its body. These, the scientists *suggest, might* have allowed the water that it swallowed to escape and so *might* have been a very early version of gills.[82]

The quaint imaginations supported by an awful lot of ambiguous language make it clear that scientists haven't found our *oldest human ancestor* at all!

For the Birds!

In another imaginative attempt to support the evolutionary hypothesis, some scientists proposed what they referred to as the "protein clock" theory. This theory was supposed to "pin down with great precision" when humans branched off into mammals. Unfortunately for the evolutionists, after they tested the hypothesis, it turned out that humans were more closely related to chickens than they were to mammals, including the apes. Can you just imagine the names they would have assigned to our supposed ancient ancestors? *Australopithecus* would be *Australochickenus* or *Bock-Bockosithicus*, or maybe *Paleobird-brainenus*, or perhaps even *Neanderclaws!* If it weren't so sad, it would be funny.

Once again, Professor Frank Sherwin lends his insights:

Investigating the record of rocks (the fossils) for physical validation of the Darwinian process has revealed... nothing. One of the ironies of Darwin's infamous book, *On the Origin of the Species*, is that he never addressed the origin of species! In the 21st Century,

---

[82] http://www.bbc.com/news/science-environment-38800987 emphasis mine

the secular community is still investigating the origin of species. Ironically, Dr. A.G. Fisher, in the 2002 edition of the prestigious *Grolier Multimedia Encyclopedia*, stated, "Both the origin of life and the origin of the major groups of animals remains unknown." Unknown, ever since Darwin—but they're still looking. Meanwhile, the Christian has a Book that very clearly describes the origin (and destiny!) of the species.

Amen to that! Admissions for the weaknesses in the theory abounds, and not just in *Grolier's Multimedia Encyclopedia*. The tide is shifting, and some researchers, realizing the bankruptcy of the evolutionary hypothesis, are bold enough to admit it. Consider what Sir Fred Hoyle and Chandra Wickramasinghe once wrote:

> The likelihood of the spontaneous formation of life from inanimate matter is one to a number with 40,000 noughts [zeroes] after it... It is big enough to bury Darwin and the whole theory of evolution. There was no primeval soup, neither on this planet or any other, and if the beginnings of life were not random, they must therefore have been the product of purposeful intelligence. [83]

Somehow, I am reminded of 1 Corinthians 1:20. "Where is the wise man? Where is the scribe? Where is the debater of this age? Has not God made foolish the wisdom of the world?"

A Turn to the Word

Macro-evolution certainly does seem to require quite a bit of faith. However, since we place our faith in a Divine Creator, we'll turn to the Scriptures to look at further reasons for having that faith. Taking your time to absorb the text, read Genesis 1:1–2:3. As you read, you just might want to underline the phrase, "and there was evening, and there was morning," and circle every occurrence of the phrases "after their kind" and "after its kind."

---

[83] Sir Fred Hoyle and Chandra Wickramasinghe, *Evolution from Space* (New York: Simon & Schuster, 1984), p. 148.

The Days

The text shows that modifying "day" with "evening" and "morning" each day represents 24 hours. There seems to be no ambiguity in the text regarding the length of each day. Not only is each day modified with "evening" and "morning," but the text also includes the number of each day. There is no reason to imagine that these were indeterminate periods, longer or shorter than twenty-four hours. I point this out because, as I stated earlier, I once believed God used evolution as the mechanism for the creative process. Therefore, each day had to, I thought, represent long periods. However, the text refuted me flatly.

With recent discoveries of carbon-14 (^{14}C) in diamonds,[84] which has a half-life of only 5,730 years, and in dinosaur bones purported to be millions of years old, along with soft tissue which decays rather quickly, it is time to re-think the millions, upon millions of years claim.[85]

I think what could be more of a puzzle is why God would take as long as six days to create. Why would it take a God who can create *ex nihilo* (out of nothing) six days to accomplish the task? Surely, He could have done the whole thing in an instant. Perhaps He, being our perfect and supreme Parent, was setting an example for His children. God commanded us to work six days and rest on the seventh.

> Remember the sabbath day, to keep it holy. For in six days the LORD made the heavens and the earth, the sea and all that is in them, and rested on the seventh day; therefore the LORD blessed the sabbath day and made it holy.[86]

On the seventh day, God rested from His work. Now, I would have to agree with others who suggest that God, Who does not need to rest, was simply alluding to the end of His creation

---

[84] https://answersingenesis.org/geology/carbon-14/radiocarbon-in-diamonds-confirmed/

[85] http://crev.info/2015/06/c14-dinosaur-bone/
also see, http://www.icr.org/article/5587/365

[86] Exodus 20:8, 11

process. After the sixth day, it seems that no new life forms were created. That is certainly consistent with what we see in nature. No new life forms emerge—instead, many have died away or are dying away. Also, simply because naturalists and scientists will discover what they refer to as "new" creatures, that does not mean they are new to this planet.

"After their Kind"

All right, count them up—did you arrive at ten? Did you notice that the phrases "after their kind" or "after its kind" appear ten times in the first chapter of the book of Genesis, indicating how living things reproduce? Again, God's Word is on target scientifically, this time pointing our attention to gene structure. Indeed, all living things reproduce "after their kind." Living things, over the years, do not mutate into entirely different species. They can't because DNA (deoxyribonucleic acid) makes that impossible.

Charles Darwin, who was not a scientist but earned a degree in theology from Cambridge University, knew nothing about DNA since it was a discovery that came after his publication. Had Darwin known about the genetic code, which is preprogrammed into every living thing determining what it will be and do, perhaps he would have abandoned his theory before publication since the genetic code is what makes evolution, as Darwin suggested it, impossible.

I guess the best way to explain the genetic code is through a simple illustration. Just suppose, as I was sitting at my computer typing away, I boasted, "My computer is so smart that whenever I misspell a word, it figures out what I've done wrong—and to save me from embarrassment, it corrects the mistakes all on its own!" Would that statement be accurate?

What if I decided to leave my computer on for eons with the *Microsoft Word* program open, with the hope that it would someday evolve into the *Mavis Beacon Teaches Typing* program? Would that be a good idea? Would *Word* eventually become *Mavis*, or would I simply be left with an enormous electric bill?

My boasts about my computer being smart would not be accurate, and neither would it be a good idea to run up my electric bill. The reason is this: my computer isn't smart—the intelligent computer programmer is. It took an intelligence independent of the computer system to create the initial program to make it work the way it does. For this same reason, no matter how much time I add to the equation, *Word* can never evolve into *Mavis*.

Consider that when the same computer has glitches or a virus, I have to call in a professional who will log on to it for an inside look so the technician can fix them. With DNA, a phone call is never necessary. God already put something fascinating in place that does constant repairs.

There are sub-microscopic bits of protein called *repair enzymes*, which are ultra-tiny molecular machines that, at every moment, go up and down DNA strands looking for, finding, and repairing mistakes, lesions, or pesky mutations. There are whole families of these utterly amazing molecular machines. This little bit of protein is *programmed*, like my computer, so that it can tell the difference between damaged and undamaged DNA—and then it aids in the repair of sections, if necessary, with other enzymes that are programmed to handle the repair. How did all that evolve through time, chance, and natural processes? Obviously, it couldn't have.

Just as my computer did not create its computer programs, likewise, plants, parasites, pets, and people did not create their genetic codes. Each genetic code was preprogrammed by our intelligent Creator independent, or apart, from the system. This preprogramming is why lungfish can survive underneath riverbeds and why, regardless of how much time you add to the equation, monkeys cannot turn into men.

Creation Groans

God called His creation "very good." Random chance and mutations do not result in what one would consider "very good." All you have to do is consider cyclopean malformation to know that's true. By Genesis 3, the entire creation was suffering because of the sin of Adam and Eve. When I think of that poor creature, that little lamb born with no hope for survival, I think of Romans 8:20-22:

> The creation was subjected to futility, not willingly, but because of Him who subjected it, in hope that the creation itself also will be set free from its slavery to corruption into the freedom of the glory of the children of God. For we know that the whole creation groans and suffers the pains of childbirth together until now.

Water, Water, Everywhere

I have always wondered how long it was between the creation and the fall. The Scripture seems to be silent about that. However, we do know that after the fall, human morality deteriorated rather quickly. Within just the first generation, the first murder was committed. After a time, the world became so corrupt that "every intent of the thoughts of his [humanity's] heart was only evil continually."[87] What a horrible place. As recorded in Genesis 6, God was "grieved in His heart" and intended to judge the earth by water.

Thankfully, though it must have seemed a crazy thing to do at the time, faithful Noah responded to God's command to build an ark, along with his three sons. The ark, or barge, was one of enormous capacity at 450-feet long, 75-feet wide, and 45-feet high—certainly large enough to house the animals the Lord would draw into it. As it turned out, the barge would be a vessel of salvation for just eight persons and a variety of animals. "Essence of Ark"—it must have been quite odiferous, yet better to be inside than outside.

Since many people picture the flood account as depicted in cartoon drawings, as merely an easy-does-it boat ride with the animals smiling away at Noah in the open air on deck, let's look at the actual account:

---

[87] Genesis 6:5

> The flood came upon the earth for forty days, and the water increased and lifted up the ark, so that it rose above the earth. The water prevailed and increased greatly upon the earth, and the ark floated on the surface of the water.
>
> The water prevailed more and more upon the earth, so that all the high mountains everywhere under the heavens were covered. The water prevailed fifteen cubits [22½ feet] higher, and the mountains were covered. All flesh that moved on the earth perished, birds and cattle and beasts and every swarming thing that swarms upon the earth, and all mankind; of all that was on the dry land, all in whose nostrils was the breath of the spirit of life, died.
>
> Thus He blotted out every living thing that was upon the face of the land, from man to animals to creeping things and to birds of the sky, and they were blotted out from the earth; only Noah was left, together with those that were with him in the ark. The water prevailed upon the earth one hundred and fifty days.[88]

A pretty dramatic picture, wouldn't you say? In Genesis 7:11, the text states that "all the fountains of the great deep burst open, and the floodgates of the sky were opened." Therefore, it wasn't just a gentle, light, steady rain, as some might think. There was dramatic tectonic activity on the earth that made "all," not just some, but rather, "all the fountains of the great deep" to burst open. Incredible.

Today's Consistent Evidence

When I read the biblical account, I must admit that I find it difficult to accept, as some people have suggested, that the flood of Noah was simply a local event. That thinking seems to be refuted by logic, the geological evidence, and the text itself. After all, how could the water cover the highest local mountain without running downhill into another region? (Is it possible that someone else

---

[88] Genesis 7:17-24

could have erected a wall around the locale of the flood higher than the highest mountain?)

Further, if the flood were a local event, you would think that God could have done something simpler than have Noah construct a massive vessel. After all, God simply sent angels to lead Lot and his family away from one local event—the destruction of the cities of Sodom and Gomorrah. Surely, within 120 years, He could have brought Noah and his family quite a distance away from a "local" flood. Why bother with building an ark? Why bother bringing a vast array of animals to that ark, rather than just leading them out of the region of Mesopotamia?

However, there's overwhelming evidence for a worldwide flood all around us. Globally, there are mass graves of fully formed fossils in muddy sediments that were rapidly laid down by water. That is only way fossils can form, by a swift burial or catastrophically—they cannot develop over millions of years because decay would erode any trace of them. Since there are no "transitional" forms in these sediments, some evolutionists use the term "abrupt appearance" to explain away the existence of fully formed creatures, catastrophically preserved for all to see.

It amazes me just how incredibly powerful water is and what sort of damage it can inflict in a short amount of time. If you visit the north side of Mount St. Helens, you will observe a small-scale "Grand Canyon," not formed over millions of years by the gentle movement of Spirit Lake as it was before the eruption took place, but catastrophically in a matter of hours on May 18, 1980.

Another fascinating piece of evidence for a global flood is that approximately 270 people groups around the world, who are isolated from each other, speak of an event in their history when the world as a whole was destroyed by a flood—including man, and beast. They also tell of a vessel of safety provided for a small group of survivors. The commonality of this tradition among these unrelated people groups would make sense from global cultures, which were once one happy family around Babel and then dispersed. Unfortunately, without good Jewish scribes in their camps, the stories were not preserved accurately through time and thus had variations. However, the core of the accounts remains the same.

There also exist rather compelling eyewitness testimonies of a massive vessel in the mountains of Ararat. Though individuals have offered their testimony at differing times and without contact with each other, their accounts seem to be entirely consistent. They all seem to report seeing a vessel in the biblical location and size, partly covered, partly exposed—with a stair-step topography leading up to it.

God did indeed overwhelmed planet Earth with water, and by His love and mercy, He then set a bow in the sky as a promise that He would never again judge the world in that manner. However, as the sin of Cain intensifies, and evil and debauchery increase, we must remember that He also promised He would judge the world once again before He completely restores it, but the next time, by fire.

What we observe today on Earth and throughout our universe is consistent with what we should see if the biblical accounts of creation are accurate. I haven't even touched upon concerns regarding the flaws and inaccuracy of current dating methods used on rocks and fossils. However, I think there was enough evidence in this chapter to prove that God's Word, once again, is trustworthy.

FINAL THOUGHTS

When I think of what God has done with my life in the time since I submitted it to Him, it amazes me. You would never recognize Judy B.C. with Judy A.D. I certainly praise and thank Him for that—it's just another piece of evidence that God can make something of nothing.

> I will give thanks to the LORD with all my heart;
> I will tell of all Your wonders.
> I will be glad and exult in You;
> I will sing praise to Your name, O Most High.[89]

---

[89] Psalm 9:1

Therefore, serve the LORD with gladness;
Come before Him with joyful singing.
Know that the LORD Himself is God; it is He who has made us, and not we ourselves.
We are His people and the sheep of His pasture.[90]

Yes, He is the One who has made us and "not we ourselves." This is one reason why I think God created us last. Perhaps God wanted to prove to humankind that He didn't need our help, advice, or ingenuity during the creation process. If we could, surely we would somehow attempt to take credit for what "God hath wrought." I think we all know unbelieving individuals who boldly proclaim, "If it were me, I would have created it this way... " Wouldn't it be fun, at just such a moment, to hear the Lord of all creation thunderously respond from the heavenlies:

Now gird up your loins like a man,
And I will ask you, and you instruct Me!
Where were you when I laid the foundation of the earth?
Tell Me, if you have understanding.[91]

With Job, I can imagine their response in chorus, would be: "Behold, I am insignificant; what can I reply to You? I lay my hand on my mouth."[92] Sometimes, isn't that just the perfect place for it?

---

[90] Psalm 100:2-3
[91] Job 38:3
[92] Job 40:4

QUESTIONS & RESOURCES

1. Can you name three reasons why evolution requires enormous faith?

2. What is it about every living thing that negates the possibility of one species evolving into another?

3. What phrase in the Word of God tells us just how all living things reproduce?

4. What are some of the implications of believing we are simply products of random chance?

5. Have you ever seen the movie *Inherit the Wind* and then compared it to the facts of the actual events?

Creation Scientists Answer Their Critics by Duane T. Gish, Ph.D. Institute for Creation Research, 1993.

The Illustrated Origins Answer Book by Paul S. Taylor Eden Publications, 1992.

The Human Body: An Intelligent Design, by Alan L. Gillen, Frank J. Sherwin III, Alan C. Knowles, Creation Research Society, 2001.

The Remarkable Record of Job by Henry M. Morris, Baker Books, 1988.

For a list of great resources and articles, see icr.org.

CHAPTER 7 ~ *Evil and Human Suffering*

" **L**ook, Mommy, isn't she so pretty? She's an angel! I want to hold her, Mommy!" I stopped loading my groceries onto the conveyer belt at the checkout stand to see what had so charmed my then three-year-old daughter, Nicole's tender heart. She pointed excitedly as my eyes fixed upon the "angel" in question. She was dressed in an exquisite costume with soft, fluffy, white feathers surrounding her beautiful form. It was none other than Jon Benet Ramsey, pictured on the cover of a tabloid magazine.

Encircling the photo of this precious and lovely little girl were words describing her tragic death. The contrast of utter innocence (Nicole's sweet response and that darling child's picture) and total evil (the murder of that beautiful little girl) took my breath away. I was thankful that at three, Nicole had not mastered reading yet, as it would have broken her heart to know the truth.

"Sweetheart, she really is an angel, isn't she?" was my sorrowful response. After that experience, as a parent, I just kept wondering how I would ever explain to my children just how evil the human heart can be. Yet only God knows its depths.

We see it on the news, we read it on the internet, we see it in our lives and in the lives of family and friends around us and the questions abound. With the rise of violent attacks on innocent people, I'm sure I'm not the only one who receives countless telephone calls and messages questioning God's role in humanity's inhumanity and the existence of pure evil. Therefore, now is the time to answer.

While there are several facets to what we would consider "evil," I think the most common concerns are human suffering and the evil acts committed by others. With that in mind, first, we will consider the problem of evil in the world from our perspective. Then we will look at who is to blame for its existence. Afterward, I will show you that, though we don't have all the answers, while God does indeed work all things together for good, His definition and ours might be a bit different, as you'll soon see. Finally, since I think it is essential to address the subject on a fiercely practical level, I will discuss ways in which you can minister to individuals who face a crisis of belief because of a particular facet of this issue in their lives.

Our Myopic Perspective

Whenever the topic of evil and suffering arises, I cannot help but remember a brief conversation I once had with an older gentleman. He dismissed God wholly based on this objection. His anger toward God was evident as he swore and then bitterly proclaimed, "There is no God." That gentleman's passion and mine prompted me to ask him how he had arrived at his conclusion. He replied, "Listen, I was in World War II, and I saw what went on in those concentration camps. And I can assure you, with the horror that went on there, there can be no God."

How telling his response was. That faithful veteran, and others like him, intuitively know something about the character of God. That if God exists, He would be good, and just, and loving—and possessing these attributes, He would certainly not allow evil to occur. The veteran's conclusion, I think, is a reasonable one. For many people like him, the following questions remain:

1. If God is all-good and created everything very good, why is there such a thing as evil in the world?

2. Why did God allow evil to creep into His very good creation, and why doesn't He wipe it out of existence?

3. If God created all things, did He also create evil?

4. How can perfect creatures of God produce evil?

One cannot address these tough questions with trite answers. Though there are no easy answers, I think *a solution* can lie in exposing some common perceptions or misconceptions.

Just Desserts?

Often, when something horrible happens to someone "really nice," the reaction is, "They didn't deserve something like that to happen to *them!*" Why is this the first assumption? The answer is because most people believe that if you are a *good person*, all of life should be one long blissful joy. The reason why they should never have had *bad* things happen is that, of course, *good* things should happen to *good* people. On the flip side of that buffalo nickel, if you are a *not-so-nice person* and *bad* things happened to you, you simply deserved it.

Therefore, if life does not measure up to this basic rule of our imagination, we call it "injustice"—and begin to blame God. Immediately, we lose all proper eternal perspective, and the creature starts to accuse the Creator. Yet, shall the pot say to the Potter, "What's up with that?"

When we play the God blame game instead of leaning on His divine sovereignty, we mistakenly stand as His accuser. The thinking, *How can such an awful thing happen to a nice person like me?* can perhaps come from a faulty notion that God created us simply to make us happy. Therefore, when pain enters our lives, or when we suffer a loss, we tend to question His goodness, His power, and finally, His very existence. We think, *How can this awful thing be the will of a good God who supposedly loves me?*

Perhaps the first question we should ask is, *If God did not create us simply to make us happy, what is our ultimate purpose?* I think the old *Westminster Shorter Catechism*[93] sums this up the best. Appropriately, the first question reads, "What is the chief end of man?" Perhaps some folks would answer it this way: "Man's chief end is to glorify his things, and to enjoy himself forever." However, as you and I know, that certainly is not the answer. The answer to question one of the Catechism is, "Man's chief end is to glorify *God*, and to enjoy *Him* forever."

---

[93] If you would like to share the *Westminster Shorter Catechism* with your children you can find the Westminster Shorter Catechism Project at: http://shortercatechism.com/, emphasis added

In light of that, there must be more to suffering than what our emotions tell us. Our emotions can sometimes make us believe that our suffering is to no end or no useful purpose. Therefore, when we experience pain or loss or suffering, our temporal perspective kicks in, and we lose our eternal perspective. Again, the primary problem is in our perception—a perception that is skewed by our fallen nature and by our propensity to focus only on the here and now instead of the hereafter. It is skewed by the fact that our fallen nature distorts our view of God. Therefore, some individuals, instead of trusting in His sovereignty, accuse Him—as if evil were somehow His fault because He hasn't wiped it out.

What? Who? Me?

So here we are back at square one. As the accusation goes, if God is all-good and all-powerful, He can and should wipe out all evil, and thus He, therefore, is cruel and unjust for not annihilating all evil. Now, while we must grant the premise that it is undoubtedly true that God, at any moment, could easily wipe out all evil, a notion folks seem to grasp intuitively—believers and unbelievers alike—there is a severe challenge with that. If God annihilated all evil, then *all* evil—both actual and potential—would be destroyed. Absent the cross that would have to include you and me as well. He would have to wipe us out based on the actual evil we have committed and our future, or potential, evil as well.

If perhaps you are thinking, as others do, that you would be exempt from such a broad-brush evil eradication, let me make a suggestion. What if, at your next women's "Mug and Muffin" fellowship time, everyone brings their favorite coffee mug and some fresh-baked pastries while you provide a video of the past twenty-four hours of your thought life? Now, close your eyes and think about what we'd all get to see. Do you think anyone would want to sit next to you the following Sunday? (Don't worry—my video wouldn't fare much better.)

My dear sister, not one of us are above committing the crimes we read about or the evil we vigorously oppose. Heaven help us if we ever think we are. Jesus said that if you even look at someone with contempt in your heart, it is equivalent to murder, and therefore it must be dealt with before the throne of grace. We all violate God's holy character, both in thought and in deeds done or neglected.

Since the problem of evil directs us to the character of God, I have to ask these questions: What is more merciful? What is more loving? For God to annihilate those made in His image, who have abused their gift of free choice and still abuse that gift—or to have made provision for it through the cross of Jesus Christ? Would it be better for Him to eradicate us immediately from the world He created—or to use sin, sickness, and suffering for a higher purpose? Which is of greater virtue?

Indeed, the greater virtue is that He can use our miserable temporary circumstances for His higher and eternal purposes. Again, if God were to wipe out all evil, He would be the only one left. That act would defeat the very purpose for which He created us: genuine, honest, freewill, non-robotic fellowship with Him, our Creator.

The good news is that God ultimately *will* defeat and overcome evil and restore His creation once again to "very good" status. What we have is the best possible world operating under a cloud of the fall. How thankful I am for His mercy in not annihilating all evil but working His will despite it. By His grace, since He has not yet defeated evil, everyone has an opportunity to come to trust and believe in Him.

Does "All-Power" Mean Anything Goes?

Even so, challenges abound. Many people argue that if God is all-powerful and benevolent, He will destroy all evil. If God doesn't destroy all evil, perhaps He is omnipotent and not benevolent, but malevolent—because how can a good God bear to see His creatures suffer from evil? Or, maybe He is benevolent but not all-powerful—therefore, He cannot destroy all evil, which if that is the case, and God is not omnipotent, for them it logically follows that there is perhaps no God at all.

However, each premise contains a misunderstanding of what it means that God possesses omnipotence or all-power. Omnipotence does not mean that God can do absolutely anything. There are things He cannot do. He cannot do anything that would violate His other attributes—this is why He cannot lie. And no, He cannot make a rock so big He can't move it, as some philosophers like to pose, because—as it's been well said—"God doesn't do dumb things." However, aside from that, He will not make something so big that He cannot control it. God cannot do anything that is actually impossible, and it is actually impossible to destroy evil without destroying free choice—and free choice is necessary to a moral universe.

Since God cannot do what is contrary to His nature, He cannot be blamed for that which He cannot do. He cannot give human beings free choice sometimes and not at other times. He cannot create beings as free moral agents, then snap His fingers and make them robots whenever they stray from His will. God cannot create beings with free choice and then force them to make the right choices. If that were the case, they would not be free moral agents who have the responsibility and capacity to choose to bless or curse Him.

Evil's Source

My mom is an artist. You name it she's done it—in just about every medium. She is also extraordinarily crafty but in a good way. Walking through her house is a lot of fun because you will notice creative little things and ask, "Where did you get this?"

My mother's usual response is, "Oh, they wanted thirty bucks for it, so I decided to make it myself for a dollar." It's a family joke. For years I kidded her, saying I was sure she made her huge oriental rugs as she rode to work on the number thirteen bus. She once taught herself how to paint in watercolor—and then proceeded to win an award for what was to her simply an attempt at the medium.

Now, have you ever witnessed an artist at work? They place the smallest brushstroke on the canvas, then lean back in their chair to observe. Again, and again: minor stroke, lean back, and observe, correct, change, add, observe, and on it goes until they are satisfied with their work.

When I think of Genesis 1:31, I picture an artist. Only this Artist leaned back to observe His work of creation only once. "God saw all that He had made, and behold. It was very good." In the beginning, our Creator, the only appropriate One to judge creation, completed and then beheld His handiwork. Just as an artist places one last stroke upon canvas with her brush and then leans back to observe, so too, God beheld His creation and deemed it very good. Since the very core of God's nature is goodness, everything He does is "very good," including His creation, as described in Genesis 1 and 2.

Evil is *not* "very good." I know, I know—"Duh!" Nevertheless, hang in there with me. First, we must realize that God did not create this world the way we see it today. The Creator of our first parents bestowed upon them as part of being image-bearers, the very good gift, and the power of free choice. With their free choice, our first parents chose evil, abusing their gift by rebelling against God.

What we now experience are the results of the abuse of a very good gift our perfect Heavenly Parent bestowed upon those He created in His image—namely, the freedom and power to make choices for good or for evil. While in their state of innocence, Adam and Eve abused God's gift of free choice and chose to rebel against His sole restriction upon them.

Although God did make evil possible, individual human beings alone are responsible for actually carrying it out by the choices they make. It's just like what my mom-in-law says about dieting: "It's all about choices." That goes for carrot sticks or carrot cake, love or hate, good or evil, praising God or shaking our fist at Him. Nevertheless, the fact that humanity would choose evil was the risk God was willing to take to enjoy a free-will fellowship with us.

We might wonder why God would even put that tempting tree of *The Knowledge of Good and Evil* in the Garden. We might well reason, *If it weren't for that stinkin' tree, we wouldn't be in the mess we are in right now.* However, without the tree, our first parents really wouldn't have had free choice. To illustrate this concept, say, for example, that I have asked you to come for a visit to my home, and I've told you that you could travel on any road you desired to reach me. With your free choice, you look at a map to select which route you wish to take, only to find that only one leads over-the-river-and-through-the-woods to Grammy's house.

Now, was it true that you could take any road you desired? No, it wasn't. You did not have an opportunity to exercise your free choice since there was only one path that would reach my home. It is the same as the tree. Without a chance to choose to obey and not eat, or to choose to disobey and eat, the creature does not have free choice or free will at all.

Didn't He Create—Everything?

God was not the creator of evil. What He created was a perfect universe without sin, without suffering, and without evil. Evil came into this world by a willful act of disobedience toward a loving Heavenly Father, Who knew the consequences for it would be tremendous and warned our first parents of it.

Keep in mind that God created all substances. Evil, however, is not a thing or substance. Evil is just like mutation (see chapter 6). The creature has to first exist for the mutation to corrupt it. Therefore, evil is the corruption of God's very good creation that was here before it was sullied. Just like rust, moth holes, or mold, the original state before the corruption was pure and whole.

Whine, Whine, Whine, Whine, Whine!

Some people might object and say, "Why do I have to suffer for the sins of the Adam's family?" Think of it this way. If perfectly innocent human beings living in a gloriously beautiful environment where they would never know want—people who enjoyed such purity of fellowship with God and each other that in their nakedness they did not experience shame—would choose evil, how much more would we make that same choice in our current fallen condition? Because God is good, and just, and loving, His remedy for sin and evil is for everyone. I am so thankful that "choose for yourselves today whom you will serve"[94] is still a decision we can make for the exercise of our free will and by the drawing of the Holy Spirit.

Romans 8:28—Not Just Something to Quote!

At the intellectual level, and perhaps the spiritual, what I've shared just might suffice in addressing the problem of evil and human suffering. However, I think it is vitally important to discuss this subject on the fiercely practical level. After all, that is where we live. To do this, I thought I would share with you the circumstances surrounding a baby boy who made a significant impact on not only a tiny mountain community but on friends and family members across this country, and—who knows—from this writing, perhaps eventually the world.

I must tell you that, as far as births are concerned, I have never seen a baby more anticipated by an entire community than little Kenneth Hubbell, due May 20, 2001. The number of people at Carol Hubbell's shower was indeed a blessing. It included many individuals, male and female, who I never met before. It was great fun sitting in a large circle in our fellowship hall, passing gift after gift around the room that Carol excitedly received and unwrapped. The gifts included beautiful handmade bedding and clothes; baby toys, cartons of diapers and baby wipes; and everything else you could imagine that an expectant mom would need.

Kenneth was child number six, with the older siblings ranging from age 10 to age 17. For 42-year-old Carol, he was little Mr. Surprise, Surprise! With finances extremely tight, she was very grateful for the baby shower, viewing it as the blessing of a lifetime.

On May 11, I received an urgent phone call from our prayer-warrior chain. Carol was in the hospital. She hadn't felt the baby move that morning and became concerned. Fervent prayers rang out throughout our little valley and from friends and family

---

[94] Joshua 24:15

members across the country that, by God's grace, Kenneth and Carol would be okay.

I have, as I'm sure you have as well, fervently prayed for many pre-born little ones who faced some unexpected complication. I will tell you, I have never had this experience before, but as I fervently prayed for this child's life, I strangely felt the Spirit of the Lord say, "No." My heart sank as I attempted to petition the Lord for this child's life, yet when I did, I somehow felt as if the phone line was severed. I cannot explain it but, knowing the answer was a supernatural *no*, I started praising God for what He was going to do in all of our lives with the loss of this child, and I simply asked Him to grant strength and grace to the Hubbell family, Carol in particular. At that moment, I felt as if the phone line was suddenly reconnected.

On May 12, which happened to be my wedding anniversary, Kenneth was delivered. A perfectly beautiful baby boy with a cherub face, chubby cheeks, and all—yet he was lifeless. The cord had wrapped around his neck while in the womb, and little Kenneth had already been delivered into the Everlasting Arms.

Yes, we grieved. We grieved for a family as a family. Many of us who attended that beautiful shower just a week before now mourned with a hurting family at Kenneth's tiny grave. Some days after the funeral, when the Hubbell children were back to school, Carol's husband was back at work, and her extended family and friends flew back home, another sister in the Lord, and I popped over for a visit.

There I sat in her living room in utter amazement at how graciously Carol was handling every expectant mother's worst nightmare. She was communicative about her feelings and her loss. We sometimes cried, and sometimes we even laughed. Amazingly, she talked naturally and openly about her emotional pain, and oddly, how thankful she was to feel it. I will never forget her words: "The pain makes me know I'm alive."

As I listened, I thought of how, in so many situations in my life, I had stuffed my emotional pain—with the result that, before giving my life to Jesus Christ, I had become a hollow, angry shell.

Sadly, I had mastered the art of keeping everyone at arm's length, especially when I needed him or her the most. It suddenly dawned on me that the woman I had come to minister to, had unwittingly ministered to me. She had struck a nerve, deep and thick, and I sat in awe of my God and this woman of pure, simple faith.

"Why?"

How do we make sense out of what seems to be senseless? How do we make sense of the loss of a precious baby boy? We cannot help but ask, "Why?" Why was it that this baby came so close to the threshold of birth, only to never have the opportunity of drawing his first breath? Why? We turn to one another and ask, "Why?" Also, knowing we will not get very far with human wisdom, we turn to God and ask, "Why?"

As parents, don't we sometimes respond, "I'm the parent—that's why," or "Everything is under control—go back to sleep," or simply, "Just because."

However, have you noticed that our heavenly Parent sometimes gives us the same answer? Fortunately, He does it in a much more loving manner. He tenderly replies, "Be still and know that I am God."[95] Honestly, as difficult as that might seem, that is all we need to know.

When we think of pain and suffering and seemingly purposeless loss, we immediately think of the Book of Job. Throughout its pages, we find Job and his friends attempting to reason through or explain his loss and suffering. Then finally, when God spoke, He posed to Job question after question relating to His creation. God said in essence, "All right, Job, do you want to know it all? Here it is since you are reasoning about what you don't understand. Go ahead, Job, contemplate, and give an answer to My questions if you can!" Job was so overwhelmed with what God set before him that he realized his folly in questioning the all-wise, all-powerful, sovereign Lord of creation.

---

[95] Psalm 46:10 NKJV

It was as if God told Job, "Job, this is huge, this is bigger than you. It has to do with My eternal plan. You're temporal, Job, and you think that way. I am infinite, you are finite—and if I began to explain it to you, you still couldn't handle it, Job. I am not going to give you every answer, but know this—not a sparrow falls to the ground without My notice. So how much more do you think I am concerned about those who bear My image?"

Yes, when Job lost his children, in essence, God told him what He would say to you and me: "This is not *illogical*, what I allow— it is *alogical*. It is not in the realm of your logic. It is beyond your ability to comprehend. Therefore, be still and know that I am God."

That is where Job came to have peace: trusting in the total sovereignty of Almighty God. What a powerful thing it is to arrive at the place of complete trust, trust without question. May we link arms with Job as we too proclaim, "Though He slay me, I will hope in Him."[96]

His Will, His Way

Perhaps your fellowship is like ours. We offer baby dedications for new babies and their parents. It's not an elaborate thing, just a simple opportunity to proclaim that the parents will intend to train up the child toward a loving relationship with God and that the congregation will support them in that goal. Before praying for the family, the pastor will ask several essential questions of the parents. A few years after the passing of little Kenneth, I asked Carol Hubbell if she and her husband would have had a dedication ceremony. Carol's quick response was, "Oh, absolutely!"

One of the first questions the pastor poses for the dedication is, "Are you fully willing to accept God's will for this child, no matter what?" I have yet to hear any parent say, "No," when asked this. However, when God reminds us that He can take us up on that, that He can take what is rightfully His, many grieving parents ask, "How can a loving God allow such a thing to occur? Surely He could have intervened!"

---

[96] Job 13:15

The fact is, in general, human beings do whatever they can to avoid pain. We seem to want everything on our terms. "Lord, teach me this lesson this way, and I promise I'll learn it." "Lord, if you get me out of this situation, I promise I'll..." "If you give me this job..." "If you heal my illness..." In other words, "I will only carry the thorn on my terms."

In avoiding pain, we do not allow room for growth and maturity. Isn't it always a great blessing and encouragement to know people who have lived through horrible circumstances and then share about the powerful lessons learned, faith strengthened, families bonded, and commitments made to the Lord on account of a particular tragedy they suffered? Indeed, the valley of suffering can be a blessing—because it just might be what it takes to make us stop everything and reevaluate our lives, its value, and our priorities. Pain and suffering cause us to seek answers to hard questions.

Simply because we in our finitude do not have the answer to the *why* question, just because we do not see the purpose for suffering, does not mean an infinite God has no purpose for it. I truly believe that God uses human frailty, pain, and sickness to allow humanity to rise to the occasion to bring out the best in those who bear His image. In all this, He grants us the opportunity to reach out and love our neighbor as ourselves, and receive blessings that can only be perceived and appreciated through the eyes of the Holy Spirit.

If you have ever been close to those who suffer in Christ, you will find they teach everyone around them that they can indeed have *a peace that passes all understanding* in their suffering. They are living testimonies that show us that His grace is sufficient to take us through our pain and trials. God redeems the circumstances that go along with living in a fallen world. Then He grants us an eternal perspective and an opportunity to lean on His sovereignty, to trust that He is merciful.

Yes—surely God could have intervened in the death of tiny Kenneth Hubbell. However, He had a higher purpose. Isaiah 55:8 tells us:

"My thoughts are not your thoughts,
Neither are your ways My ways," declares the LORD.
"For as the heavens are higher than the earth,
So are My ways higher than your ways
And My thoughts than your thoughts."

Did Carol and her family shake their fists at God during that difficult time? Not once. Like the rest of us in our little fellowship and community, they watched blessing after blessing come out of that painful loss. Human suffering does cause us to ask why a loving God would allow it. However, I know that God can and does bring about good. Again, in our finitude, we do not see His whole purpose. But when we rest in Him and His attributes, we can rely on the truthfulness of Romans 8:28:

We know that God causes all things to work together for good to those who love God, to those who are called according to His purpose.

Keep Probing and Listen Well

Perhaps you know someone who feels they simply cannot put their trust in God because they agree with some of the challenges presented in this chapter. It has been my experience, as I chat with folks hither and yon regarding spiritual matters, that at the heart of the problem of evil (sin, sickness, and suffering), is not so much an intellectual challenge as an emotional one. Thus, as women, I feel we can make headway in addressing this challenge. The reason why I believe this is true is that the topic takes an enormous amount of compassion and patience.

Playing intellectual games in an attempt to win an argument will lose *any* witnessing opportunity. Still, with an objection such as evil and human suffering in the world, the damage we might do can go much deeper. We can pound the table all we want with erudition, but unless we take the time to discover what is at the heart of the objection, we won't get very far in guiding the hurting seeker to the appropriate answer.

I find that when I take the time to delve into the reasons behind the objection, a heart-wrenching story usually follows. The key is to grant individuals the opportunity to feel loved and safe enough to express their pain and anger in a non-combative environment. When I spoke with that angry World War II veteran, I reminded him of how gracious God was to send him over to liberate those prisoners whom sick, sinful humanity had treated so horribly. After a short discussion, he acknowledged that, at the very least, there must be a God. He understood that the horror he witnessed was not God's doing. God's doing was to send him there to rescue the people He loved. It was marvelous to see his attitude toward God—and his countenance—change, but first, I had to take the time to discover the *why* behind his anger. It was certainly worth it.

FINAL THOUGHTS

That we would have joy in this life at all is an amazing thing, isn't it? That we can feel God's presence as we walk among the thorns and thistle life seems to put in our paths is genuinely an incredible mystery. Hopefully, as your seeking friends and family, who watch you react to your less-than-ideal circumstances, or whatever comes your way, will ask, "How can you have such peace? I know how I would react. What do you have that I don't?"

God redeems our suffering. In the midst of it, we fulfill God's purpose for our lives. By His grace, and when we know we are in His will, at the very point of our suffering, we can have strength, and wisdom, and peace—and yes, even joy. If, no matter what, we can have this joy here and now walking in His will, can you just imagine how much beyond joy it will be when we fulfill our eternal purpose and finally see Him face-to-face, enjoying Him forever?

Yes, today we stand on this side of time, and ask, and wonder, "Why?" However, when He takes us from this life into the next, I imagine that our Lord will point to those who have been drawn to Him through tragic events and by His lovingkindness, He'll say, "Him, and her, and them, and all because of. . . " The Scriptures reveal that there are "things which eye has not seen and ear has not heard, And which have not entered the heart of man, All that God has prepared for those who love Him."[97]

While it would be helpful to know the answer, somehow, I think the pain we endured, the loss we suffered, the horrors we witness will be faint memories as we stand in the presence of the Lord and those in Christ whom we love and have gone before us. Thus, why I believe, as flight or fight is for our physical survival, and the Moral Law for our moral survival, the desire for an answer to the *why* question is for our spiritual survival directing us to the only One who can address it.

Until we are with Him in Glory, we must live today, the day the Lord has made, no matter what it holds. We must live in a world where evil abounds, so what is the best way to cope? We not only cope but also press on toward the prize through:

• Support of our brothers and sisters in Christ.

• The reading of the Word of God to cleanse us deep inside, which keeps everything in a proper perspective and gives us the wisdom we so desperately need.

• Casting our cares at the feet of our Sovereign Lord through prayer because He hears and responds, even if it isn't as we think that response should be.

• Reaching out to others and not fretting over our circumstances because God already knows all about them.

Along these lines, please consider the truth and beauty in what Arthur Pink wrote in his book *The Attributes of God*.

"Seeing that He is clothed with omnipotence, no prayer is too hard for Him to answer, no need too great for Him to supply, no passion too strong for Him to subdue; no temptation too powerful for Him to deliver from, no misery too deep for Him to relieve."[98]

---

[97] 1 Corinthians 2:9

[98] Arthur W. Pink, *The Attributes of God* (Grand Rapids, MI: Baker Books, 1975), p. 51

QUESTIONS & RESOURCES

1. How did evil creep into God's *very good* creation?

2. What is the best way to help someone who is struggling with the problem of evil and human suffering?

3. What circumstances can you share that show how God brought good out of a bad situation?

4. What is humankind's usual response to pain and suffering? Why?

5. Reflect on how you responded to suffering in your life. What did you teach people around you regarding your walk with the Lord as a result?

The Case for Faith by Lee Strobel, Zondervan Publishing House, 2000.

The Problem of Pain by C.S. Lewis, Harper San Francisco, 2001.

The Attributes of God by Arthur W. Pink, Baker Books, 1977.

CHAPTER 8 ~ *Jesus The "I AM"*

Have you ever noticed how, at any given time, some passages of Scripture seem to captivate your mind more than others do? It might be a passage that never really jumped out at you when you've perused it in the past. And then one day, for some strange reason, it almost seems as if you are transported to that place and time as you meditate on the text. I've recently had this experience, and I thought I just might share it with you.

Now, picture if you will an exquisite chariot moving gracefully along an ancient road. The chariot, ornate and stately, offers a display of wealth and splendor. Its primary occupant is a man of significant influence and authority—he is a royal court official, to be exact. The man, with beautiful ebony skin and a booming voice, is seated quite comfortably as he reads the Scriptures aloud, perhaps to occupy the minds of his charioteers as well. He is the Ethiopian eunuch of Acts 8:27-39. Suddenly, Philip, a disciple of the Lord, was brought by the Spirit of God to the man's chariot and found him reading from the book of Isaiah:

> He was led as a sheep to slaughter;
> And as a lamb before its shearer is silent,
> So He does not open His mouth.
> In humiliation His judgment was taken away;
> Who will relate His generation?
> For His life is removed from the earth.[99]

This proselyte to Judaism, who spent time in Jerusalem worshiping God, was prompted by this compelling passage to ask Philip the one question every believer, who has a heart for the lost, desires to answer. "Please tell me, of whom does the prophet say this? Of himself or of someone else?" The answer led the Ethiopian eunuch to immediate conversion, baptism, and rejoicing as he

---

[99] As cited in Acts 8:32-33.

traveled home to influence his country with the knowledge and identity of the *Suffering Servant* of Isaiah 53.

Now, while Acts 8:27-39 might not jump off the pages for everyone, surely Isaiah 53 immediately grabs the attention of almost every reader. Something is compelling regarding the prophecy in Isaiah 53, just as something is compelling about the One who fulfilled it.

The Most Critical Question

Jesus asked the question, "Who do you say that I am?" For a long time, especially during my youth, my response might just have been that He was Mary's son, who, for some strange reason I didn't quite understand, was crucified under the authority of Pontius Pilate. That Jesus had fulfilled any prophecies, I was completely unaware. As far as ascribing deity to Him, according to my uneducated opinion, no one could ever know a thing like that for sure.

Then, at the age of eighteen, I had what I usually refer to as an "emotional experience in a church hall." The hellfire-and-brimstone message got me out of my seat and in front of an altar, desiring a ticket to heaven. *Repeat a prayer? If that is all there is to it, why, I can do that!* Two weeks after my lickety-split baptism, I asked the pastor a question after being challenged by a couple of unbelievers regarding my "conversion." (The unbelievers' goal was to show me just how much I didn't know. It worked.)

Now, my question to the pastor was simple. However, I never expected the answer I received. Undoubtedly, the pastor would confirm my suspicion that no one could know a thing like this absolutely, so I asked, almost flippantly, "Was Jesus God?" Thinking back on this, I wish I had had a camera to capture the somewhat pained and puzzled expression on the pastor's face as he slowly nodded in affirmation as he stammered, "Y–Yes, we believe Jesus *is* God." When I truly gave my life to the lordship of Jesus Christ ten years later, the question of who He was and is was wholly and finally settled in my heart, mind, and soul.

No matter how one frames the question, no matter what prompts it, it is the most important question anyone can ask, for the answer indeed holds eternal implications. Who was Jesus of Nazareth? Since He is the central figure of our faith, let's take a look at the person of Jesus, humanly speaking and spiritually speaking. Let's also take a look at what Jesus said of Himself and why He is to be believed—and especially why, at His name, *every knee will bow, and every tongue will confess that Jesus Christ is Lord to the glory of God the Father.*[100]

Humanly Speaking, Why the Fame?

Who was this Jesus? Who was this man who impacted human history more than any man who has ever walked the face of this planet? What was it about Him that His name should still spark such debate and passion over 2000 years after His death? After all, even before His birth, the deck seemed stacked against Him regarding worldly fame and success since even His conception appeared to be questionable.

Jesus' place of birth wasn't a famed city such as Rome, nor some grand palace—neither was His cradle a glorious bassinet trimmed in gold. Quite the contrary—He was born in a cave among rank farm animals—His crib, a feeding trough. And, putting the lie to the depictions of a handsome Jesus with blonde hair, blue eyes, and European features, the Scriptures state that He had "no stately form or majesty that we should look upon Him, nor appearance that we should be attracted to Him."[101]

Jesus was not a famous conqueror of armies or nations, especially since He never traveled more than a hundred miles from His birthplace. He never attempted to achieve the office of governor, or mayor, let alone Caesar. As far as His teachings were concerned, many of the fundamentals that He taught regarding how to live life as it ought to be lived could be found in not only the Jewish tradition but among the ancient philosophers as well.

---

[100] Philippians 2:10-11, paraphrased.
[101] Isaiah 53:2

Unlike Paul, Jesus was not a student trained under scholarly Gamaliel. Neither was Jesus a Pharisee of Pharisees among the religious leaders of His day, which would have afforded Him a platform for immediate success had that been His desire. Instead, He was a humble carpenter, plying His stepfather's trade—His spiritual forerunner was His fiery cousin, John. To some, I'm sure Cousin John seemed a madman—bellowing a message of repentance and baptism to all who'd listen, living in the wilderness clothed in animal skins, and surviving on a steady diet of locusts and wild honey. If you were to seek some high position in the community, you would not pick Cousin John as your campaign manager lest you offend the very people whose vote you'd hope to gain.

Jesus, I'm sure, would have had no use at all for Dale Carnegie books like *How to Win Friends and Influence People* since His uncompromising words revealed the right intentions and heart of those who confronted Him. At times, His bold proclamations about Himself were difficult for even His followers to accept, since "as a result many of His disciples withdrew and were not walking with Him anymore."[102] The core of His message did not tickle the ears since it was not the wondrous glories of heaven that Jesus spoke of the most, but the torment of Hell and the horror of judgment.

Jesus' siblings did not take Him seriously, and they even seemed sarcastically resentful of His growing popularity.[103] He did not take 20 years to establish Himself, building His fame through Madison Avenue sales-and-marketing techniques as he attempted to memorize *The Art of the Deal*. He did not enlist the biggest and brightest Oxford scholars, nor did He call upon the likes of Anthony Robbins to afford His followers a you-can-do, coal walkin' attitude.

Rather, Jesus' ministry lasted only three short years. Of His companions, a motley crew of 12 chosen men, one stole from the money bag and later betrayed Him, one denied Him three times, and all abandoned Him in His greatest hour of agony. In one

---

[102] John 6:66
[103] John 7:3-5

week, Jesus heard the same crowd's shouts of "Hosanna! Blessed is the King who comes in the name of the Lord," turn to cries of "Crucify Him! Crucify Him!" And that they did.

Today, the utterance of Jesus' name incites more passion than any other ever uttered by believers or unbelievers alike. I will never forget a conversation I had years ago with a co-worker. She seemed to go out of her way to use Jesus' name as disrespectfully as you can imagine. Not knowing what else to say, I finally remarked, "I thought you didn't believe in Jesus."

"I don't," she replied.

With a grin on my face and an ironic tone in my voice, I asked, "Then why do you constantly call upon Him?"

She hotly declared, "I use His name that way because I hate everything He represents." The level of her anger took me quite by surprise. Once again, at the time, I was ill-equipped with an answer. Oh, what I wouldn't give for a do-over of that same conversation today.

Consider the Big Three

So what is it about the person of Jesus that incites such passion either for or against Him? First, let's consider three rather essential points that set Him apart from any other leader, religious or otherwise:

1. Jesus always spoke the truth.

2. Jesus lived entirely consistent with God's high moral standards—not man's compromising, rule-bending standards.

3. Jesus said He was God.

Point number one and point number two made Jesus believable, so when He proclaimed point number three, all honest observers were forced to take a serious look. When you trust someone, you usually do not have to question his or her claims. I could cite several good examples of this principle, but a humorous one, in particular, comes to mind. It has to do with a somewhat

148 | P a g e

puzzling mystery that we thought involved our daughter, who was seven-years-old at the time and was not in the habit of lying to her mommy and daddy.

One morning, as I was preparing for the day, upon opening the bottom drawer of my vanity, I noticed Q-Tips strewn throughout it with the cotton missing off the tips, this seemed like something strange for my husband to do. Perhaps I had been snoring, and for lack of cotton balls, he chose the Q-Tip *tips*. I showed them to Jeff, and after being as dumbstruck as I, we sat down with Nicole for the interrogation. In the past, if she was involved in some mischief, her confession was usually immediate. It simply never entered her mind to lie about her misdemeanors.

This time she was emphatic. We sat stunned as this child told us, with a straight face, that she had not been playing in that drawer and that she was completely ignorant as to why I found the Q-Tips in such a state. Jeff and I then asked, "Oh, so maybe Mikael did it?"

"No," came her quick reply—as if to say, *How stupid can these people be? They know he's just an infant!* Then, at just about the same moment, my husband and I noticed something funny about the opening to the box. It was quite frayed. After setting several mousetraps (welcome to the woods), we offered our humble apologies to our daughter, who maintained her integrity to the end. Knowing Nicole's track record of honesty had brought credibility to her claim of innocence, yet from our perspective, the circumstances had made her claim hard for us to believe. We were wrong.

Again, when we consider Jesus' complete truthfulness and integrity (points one and two), His claims of deity must cause us to stop short and take careful notice.

God, Great Moral Teacher, or Both?

Whenever I read the Scriptures and reflect on what Jesus said concerning Himself, and then imagine anyone else making the same types of bold proclamations He made, I'm sure they would be fitted for a straitjacket without delay. It's just that simple. I don't care how brilliant they are; authorities would promptly escort him or her to their very own padded room. Consider the chat Jesus had with the high priest at His mock trial:

> The high priest was questioning Him, and saying to Him, "Are You the Christ [Messiah], the Son of the Blessed One?"
> And Jesus said, "I am; and you shall see the Son of Man sitting at the right hand of power, and coming with the clouds of heaven."[104]

See what I mean? Now, I'm sure you've talked with folks who seem very reverent about Jesus as a good teacher, citing the Sermon on the Mount as an example. Indeed, they esteem Him as the greatest, most moral man who ever lived. However, when push comes to shove, they stop short of calling Him Lord and God. However, Jesus could not be a good teacher if He was not who He claimed to be. Good teachers are not delusional—and Jesus would have to have been delusional if He were not God yet believed He was. On the other hand, if Jesus were not God and knew He was not God, then He would not be a good teacher, but a deceiver. Those would be the only two choices—delusional or deceiver—if Jesus were not the divine Deliverer.

No one expressed this premise better than the great Christian apologist and thinker C.S. Lewis:

> I am trying here to prevent anyone saying the really foolish thing that people often say about Him: "I'm ready to accept Jesus as a great moral teacher, but I don't accept His claim to be God." That is the one thing we must not say. A man who was merely a man and said the sort of things Jesus said would not be a great moral teacher. He would either be a lunatic—on the level with a man who says he is a poached egg—or else he would be the Devil of Hell. You must make your choice. Either this man was, and is, the Son of God: or else a madman or something worse.

---

[104] Mark 14:61-62

You can shut Him up for a fool, you can spit at Him and kill Him as a demon; or you can fall at His feet and call Him Lord and God. But let us not come with any patronizing nonsense about His being a great human teacher. He has not left that open to us. He did not intend to.[105]

Perhaps We Misheard Him

Have you ever had discussions with folks who deny that Jesus ever made any claims to His deity? I have met many individuals who have asserted, "Jesus never said He was God." Now, not only would this come as a shock to Jesus, but also the religious leaders of His day. After all, the authorities crucified Him for blasphemy.

Anyone who assumes Jesus never claimed to be God must stop and think carefully after reading John 8:58-59 (AMP):

Jesus replied, "I assure you, most solemnly I tell you, before Abraham was born, I AM." So they took up stones to throw at Him, but Jesus, by mixing with the crowd, concealed Himself and went out of the temple.

Think for a moment. Why would the Jewish leaders of His day want to stone Him? Was it because He suggested that He was a good moral teacher? Perhaps there was simply gross confusion regarding His claims. Maybe the Gospel writers and the religious leaders of His day only *thought* He had referred to Himself as God—meaning His crucifixion was simply a misunderstanding.

Let's seriously consider this for a moment. What did Jesus mean when He referred to Himself as God? Did He mean He was a Mormon—that He had become a god, and that we can too? Did He mean that He was one of among many gods? Did He mean, as the pantheists believe, that everything is God, and therefore so was He? Did He mean that through cyclic rebirth (reincarnation) He had finally paid for deeds done in His past lives and had reached a perfect state, but had simply arrived a bit quicker than the rest of

---

[105] C.S. Lewis, *Mere Christianity* (New York: MacMillan Publishing Company, 1943, 1945, 1952), pp. 55-56

us? Did He stand on a beach and yell, "I am God," as actress and activist Shirley McClain did, and that's why He thought He had attained deity?

I don't think so. Everyone, from the Gospel writers to the Pharisees, to the Roman soldier at the foot of His cross, understood what Jesus meant when He identified Himself. Most certainly, the Jewish leaders of His day knew that Jesus was equating Himself with the *I AM* of Exodus 3:14:

> God said to Moses, "I AM WHO I AM"; and He said, "Thus you shall say to the sons of Israel, 'I AM has sent me to you.'"

The fact that Jesus equated Himself with God was why they wanted to stone Him, and again, that is why He was crucified for blaspheming.

John 8:58-59 is not the only passage where we find Jesus referring to His Divine nature. In John 14:8-9, Jesus said that when we see Him, we see the Father. His comment in John 10:30, "I and the Father are one," meant that in their very essence, they are one unity.

Jesus was emphatic regarding the importance of belief in Him as He truly is, as in John 8:24: "I said to you that you will die in your sins; for unless you believe that I am *He*, you will die in your sins." He spoke very plainly there, did He not?

Additionally, in one of my favorite passages, Jesus disclosed who He was to one of the most unlikely people. It is a true Cinderella story of a waif who is met by, in this case, the Prince of Peace. Of course, I am referring to the Samaritan woman in John 4. How many of us women who made miserable choices apart from God, can identify with the woman at the well? However, in her state of sin, and loss, and poor choices, the Wonderful Counselor reached out to her and revealed His true identity:

> The woman said to Him, 'I know that Messiah is coming (He who is called Christ); when that One comes, He will declare all things to us.'

Jesus said to her, 'I who speak to you am He.'"[106]

I could go on citing more passages, but I think the Scriptures above have made the point. Jesus claimed to be God. Therefore, what we have thus far is a sinless life, a perfectly truth-filled life, and claims of deity. Let's take a moment to substantiate those claims further.

Can't Deny the Miraculous

It is quite a shame today that so many ordinary acts, as fantastic as they are, are often referred to as "miraculous." Childbirth, for example, is not a miracle—it is not a unique, unrepeatable event. That lazy Joe got off the couch and finally got a job is not a miracle; it was a decision. That I finally got rid of that extra Christmas-fudge poundage from the holidays was not a miracle; it was sweat.

However, everything about Jesus was *genuinely* miraculous, from His conception to His ministry to His death and bodily resurrection. His life embodied the supernatural. Even His enemies could not deny His miracles, attributing them to "Beelzebul," or Satan.[107] Non-biblical writers of His time, such as the famous Jewish historian Flavius Josephus, wrote of Jesus as a miracle-worker. That He performed the miraculous is attested to in rabbinical writings as well.

There can be no doubt among the intellectually honest that Jesus performed miracles: bona fide, authentic miracles. He did not perform miracles solely to wow the crowd, as did Simon in Acts 8. Jesus performed miracles to attest to who He was and is. His miraculous acts confirmed He possessed God's authority over both the physical and spiritual realms, as shown by these accounts:

1. Jesus displayed His miracle-working divine authority over the elements:

He got up and rebuked the wind and said to the sea, "Hush, be still." And the wind died down and it became

---

[106] John 4:25-26
[107] Matthew 12:24

perfectly calm. They [the disciples] became very much afraid and said to one another, "Who then is this, that even the wind and sea obey Him?"[108]

2. Jesus displayed His authority over physical laws, defying them when He walked upon the stormy water:

When the disciples saw Him walking on the sea, they were terrified, and said, "It is a ghost!" And they cried out for fear. But immediately Jesus spoke to them, saying, "Take courage, it is I; do not be afraid."[109]

3. Jesus displayed His authority over infirmities when He touched and healed the untouchable:

When Jesus came into Peter's home, He saw his mother-in-law lying sick in bed with a fever. He touched her hand, and the fever left her; and she got up and waited on Him. When evening came, they brought to Him many who were demon-possessed; and He cast out the spirits with a word, and healed all who were ill. This was to fulfill what was spoken through Isaiah the prophet: "HE HIMSELF TOOK OUR INFIRMITIES AND CARRIED AWAY OUR DISEASES."[110]

4. Jesus displayed His authority over the spiritual realm. As was not the case with the seven sons of Sceva spoken of in Acts 19, the demonic beings knew who Jesus was:

Seeing Jesus from a distance, he [the demonized man] ran up and bowed down before Him; and shouting out with a loud voice, he said, "What business do we have with each other, Jesus, Son of the Most High God? I implore You by God, do not torment me!"[111]

When Jesus asked, "What is your name?"

---

[108] Mark 4:39, 41

[109] Matthew 14:26-27

[110] Matthew 8:14-17

[111] Mark 5:6-7

The man then answered, "My name is Legion; for we are many."[112]

When the demonic spirits asked Jesus if they could go into a nearby herd of swine, the Scripture states that Jesus permitted them. Why did they need His permission? Obviously, because they knew, since Jesus is God, they were subject to His command, power, and authority.

5. Jesus proved His authority over life and death by bringing the widow's son, Lazarus, and Jairus's daughter back from the dead.[113]

6. By the resurrection of His body on the third day (which we will look at in more detail in the next chapter), Jesus displayed the ultimate in power and authority:

> "For this reason the Father loves Me, because I lay down My life so that I may take it again. No one has taken it away from Me, but I lay it down on My own initiative. I have authority to lay it down, and I have authority to take it up again. This commandment I received from My Father."[114]

Jesus—The God of Abraham, Isaac, and Jacob

Indeed Jesus performed miracles. He displayed the attributes of Deity. However, does this necessarily mean that He is the God of the Old Testament? Are there any comparisons that would prove He is indeed the same God of Abraham, Isaac, and Jacob? As my friend, Suzanne, would say in her very Minnesotan accent, "Oh, you betcha!"

As we know from our chapter on the existence of God, the God of the Old Covenant is omniscient, or all-knowing, "for the eyes of the LORD move to and fro throughout the earth."[115] Jesus, in His divine nature, is all-knowing since "He is the image of the

---

[112] Mark 5:9
[113] Luke 7:11-17; John 11:1-45; Mark 5:35-43
[114] John 10:17-18
[115] 2 Chronicles 16:9

invisible God."[116] "There is no creature hidden from His sight, but all things are open and laid bare to the eyes of Him with whom we have to do."[117]

Though He was not present with him, Jesus *saw* Nathanael under the fig tree. A stunned Nathanael announced:

"Rabbi, You are the Son of God; You are the King of Israel."

Jesus replied, "Because I said to you that I saw you under the fig tree, do you believe? You shall see greater things than these."[118]

Jesus was also aware of the multiple, improper relationships of the Samaritan woman at the well. So amazed was she at His knowledge of her five previous *husbands* that she left her water-pot where she stood and ran back to her city, urging the men to "come, see a man who told me all the things that I have done."[119] Now I call that conviction!

Supreme Spiritual Authority

Jesus displayed His power and authority to perform miraculous deeds as we saw earlier, but He also possesses the power and authority to judge and forgive sins. Only God can pass eternal judgment and forgive sins, as stated in Deuteronomy 32:35 and Joel 3:12. After Jesus healed the paralyzed man, He said to him, "Son, your sins are forgiven."[120]

Notice the reaction of the religious leaders after Christ extended forgiveness:

When the scribes heard what Jesus said to the man they were angry and thought in their hearts, "Why does

---

[116] Colossians 1:15
[117] Hebrews 4:13
[118] John 1:49,50
[119] John 4:29
[120] Mark 2:5

this man speak that way? He is blaspheming; who can forgive sins but God alone?"[121]

After reading their reaction, I can only shake my head. Here they completely ignore the fact that this poor soul can finally walk—that a miracle occurred right before their eyes. Rather, they rebuke Jesus for forgiving the man's sins. Talk about missing the point! However, Jesus, knowing their thoughts (displaying His omniscience), responded:

> "Why are you reasoning about these things in your hearts? Which is easier, to say to the paralytic, 'Your sins are forgiven'; or to say, 'Get up, and pick up your pallet and walk'? But so that you may know that the Son of Man has authority on earth to forgive sins"—He said to the paralytic—"I say to you, get up, pick up your pallet and go home."[122]

In Isaiah 42:8, God declared, "I am the LORD, that is My name; I will not give My glory to another." In John 17:5, Jesus not only speaks of His pre-existence but also states that He shares glory with the Father:

> "Father, glorify Me together with Yourself, with the glory which I had with You before the world was."

Further, Jesus stated very plainly in John 5:22:

> "Not even the Father judges anyone, but He has given all judgment to the Son, so that all may honor the Son even as they honor the Father. He who does not honor the Son does not honor the Father who sent Him."

We are to worship God and serve Him alone; this is why it is appropriate for Jesus to accept worship, unlike angels in a variety of passages or the apostles in the book of Acts. For example, after Thomas saw the resurrected Jesus in the upper room, he said to Him, "My Lord and my God!"

---

[121] Mark 2:7
[122] Mark 2:8-11

To this, Jesus responded, "Because you have seen Me, have you believed? Blessed are they who did not see, and yet believe."[123] Jesus did not rebuke Him—"No, no, Tom—you're breaking the first commandment—worship God alone,"—He accepted Thomas' worship.

A few more quick comparisons:

• Psalm 23 tells us that the Lord is our shepherd, and Jesus is as well, as He said in John 10:11: "I am the good shepherd; the good shepherd lays down His life for the sheep."

• Psalm 27:1 declares, "The LORD is my light and my salvation," just as Jesus declared that He is the "Light of the world" in John 8:12.

• Only God can raise the dead as stated in 1 Samuel 2:6, yet we know that Jesus raised not only others but also Himself.

Finally, I will share a few passages I always share with Jehovah's Witnesses. Isaiah 44:6 reads, "I am the first and I am the last, And there is no God besides Me." I will then compare this verse with Jesus' words in Revelation 22:12-13:

"Behold, I am coming quickly, and My reward is with Me, to render to every man according to what he has done. I am the Alpha and the Omega, the first and the last, the beginning and the end."

I will then direct the cultist's attention to what Jesus said to a terrified apostle John:

"Do not be afraid; I am the first and the last, and the living One; and I was dead, and behold, I am alive forevermore, and I have the keys of death and of Hades."[124]

Questioning the Jehovah's Witnesses, I then ask, "So, are there two 'firsts' and two 'lasts'? Or is one of the two lying? Or is the God of Isaiah 44:6 the same One who is speaking in Revelation 22:12 (as well as in Revelation 1:17-18)?" Since Jehovah's Witnesses

---

[123] John 20:28-29
[124] Revelation 1:17b-18

are not polytheists (they would not acknowledge two "firsts" and two "lasts" which would be an acceptance of multiple gods), and since they do not believe that Jesus was a liar, they must then conclude that His use of the same designation in both passages means that Jesus is God.

After sharing those passages, that is about the time when they say, "Since you are going to believe what you believe and I am going to believe what I believe, it was nice talking with you—have a nice day." Because Jehovah's Witnesses cannot refute this proof of the deity of Christ from the Scriptures, as with many people, who cannot, evasion and escape are their only course of action. Sure, it can seem as if I've just shot a BB at Mount Everest, but because I've given them the Word of God, I know it must be like an atomic bomb to an anthill. I never buy the facade. God's Word is indeed *sharper than any two-edged sword*,[125] especially when it comes to the deity of our Lord Jesus Christ.

Prophecy Packs a Powerful Punch!

As I sit here writing, I can't help but wonder if you are as excited as I am about how rock-solid our faith in Jesus should be. I have more to share regarding why we believe Jesus is who He claimed to be. I cannot end this chapter without looking at one of my favorite areas of evidence for the fact that He is the long-awaited Messiah. In chapter 2 of this guide, we saw how predictive prophecy substantiated the validity of the Bible. Well, it also confirms our faith and belief that Jesus is the fulfillment of every Messianic prophecy of the Old Covenant Scriptures.

There are two powerful passages that I can immediately turn to in the Old Testament:

- Psalm 22, which depicted the crucifixion in detail hundreds of years before crucifixion was ever used as a method of execution.

- Isaiah 53, which is a detailed description of the Suffering Servant who would atone for sin.

---

[125] Hebrews 4:12

For now, we will review other prophetic passages and leave Psalm 22 for the chapter on the resurrection (chapter 9) and Isaiah 53 for our section regarding the Gospel (chapter 10).

I think you will find the time prophecy in the book of Daniel just as exciting as the above two passages. Personally, each time I read the following passage, I cannot help but ponder the question, *How could they have missed Him? How could Israel have missed the time of their visitation?* Unfortunately, the Jewish people did miss that time. Not long before His death, Jesus lamented, brokenhearted:

> "O Jerusalem, Jerusalem, who kills the prophets and stones those who are sent to her! How often I wanted to gather your children together, the way a hen gathers her chicks under her wings, and you were unwilling."[126]

Jesus sorrowfully warned in Luke 19:43-44:

> "The days shall come upon you when your enemies will throw up a barricade against you, and surround you and hem you in on every side, and they will level you to the ground and your children within you, and they will not leave in you one stone upon another, because you did not recognize the time of your visitation."

A tragic prophecy fulfilled in 70 A.D. However, whenever I shake my head over Israel, I think of myself as well. Do we not all have stories of missing His *visitation* in our lives?

Daniel's Time Prophecy

The prophet Daniel foretold precisely when the Messiah would come, in chapter 9 of his book. Now you can see why it is hard for me to believe that the Jewish leaders, who knew the Scriptures, would have missed their long-awaited Messiah. This is also a fulfillment of prophecy. The apostle Paul explained this in Romans 11:7:

---

[126] Matthew 23:37

What Israel is seeking, it has not obtained, but those who were chosen obtained it, and the rest were hardened; just as it is written, "GOD GAVE THEM A SPIRIT OF STUPOR, EYES TO SEE NOT AND EARS TO HEAR NOT, DOWN TO THIS VERY DAY."[127]

Daniel 9:25 begins, "You are to know and discern that from the issuing of a decree to restore and rebuild Jerusalem until Messiah the Prince, there will be seven weeks and sixty-two weeks." Breaking down this prophecy is going to take a little explaining, but bear with me—it will be worth it!

The context of Daniel 9:25 indicates that Daniel was referring to years, and one "week" in the vernacular of the day referred to one group of seven. After we *do the math*, we arrive at 483 years from the time of an issuing of a decree to restore and rebuild Jerusalem until the Messiah would come. Now the obvious question to ask is, do we know what year the decree was issued?

We sure do! As the Bible reveals and archaeology confirms, King Artaxerxes in 444 B.C. gave Nehemiah such a decree (as recorded in Nehemiah 2). If you subtract 444 years from the 483-year prophecy and make the proper adjustment for the difference between the Hebrew calendar and today's calendar, we arrive at A.D. 33. We also arrive at not just the year or the week, but the very day Jesus came into Jerusalem on a donkey, which also fulfilled Zechariah 9:9:

> Behold, your king is coming to you; He is just and endowed with salvation, Humble, and mounted on a donkey, Even on a colt, the foal of a donkey.

Daniel's prophecy also stated that the Messiah would be "cut off"—die. One week after His triumphal entry into Jerusalem, Jesus, who is Messiah the Prince, was crucified, making atonement for the iniquity of us all.

Jesus fulfilled hundreds of other prophecies concerning the Messiah. No mere human could manipulate circumstances to fulfill a wide variety of events. The statistical probability for just 48 of

---

[127] Paul was quoting Deuteronomy 29:4.

these prophecies fulfilled in one person would be one chance in one with 158 zeroes after it. That is a number that is almost impossible for the human mind to grasp. However, by age 33, Jesus had fulfilled all prophecies recorded in the Old Testament regarding the Messiah of Israel through His resurrection.

Prophecies by the Prophesied One

Jesus is not only the long-awaited Messiah prophesied in the Old Testament, but also the sovereign God of the universe, Who made specific prophecies concerning individuals, events, and Himself. He predicted that Peter would deny Him three times before the rooster crowed.[128] In Matthew 24:2, as I mentioned earlier, He foresaw the destruction of the Jewish temple. Again, the destruction of the temple happened in A.D. 70, and when the dust settled, truly not one stone stood upon another. Jesus also predicted His death and resurrection as He stated:

> "Behold, we are going up to Jerusalem; and the Son of Man will be delivered to the chief priests and scribes, and they will condemn Him to death, and will hand Him over to the Gentiles to mock and scourge and crucify Him, and on the third day He will be raised up."[129]

Through His omniscience, Jesus proclaimed the prophecies, and by His omnipotence, He fulfilled them. Allowing the Scriptures to make the summation:

> God, after He spoke long ago to the fathers in the prophets in many portions and in many ways, in these last days has spoken to us in His Son, whom He appointed heir of all things, through whom also He made the world. And He is the radiance of His glory and the exact representation of His nature, and upholds all things by the word of His power. When He had made

---

[128] Matthew 26:34, 75
[129] Matthew 20:18-19

purification of sins, He sat down at the right hand of the Majesty on high.[130]

A Mystery: Two Natures—One Person

I think it is necessary to clarify something mentioned in this chapter. Several times, I wrote, "Jesus, in His deity..." This brings us to another prophecy that I think needs clarification, which will help us when we're sharing our faith with others who find this fundamental Christian doctrine of Jesus' dual natures challenging to comprehend. Isaiah 9:6 deals with a mystery and glorious truth, yet it is another difficult concept for our finite mind to grasp:

> A child will be born to us, a son will be given to us; And the government will rest on His shoulders; And His name will be called Wonderful Counselor, Mighty God, Eternal Father, Prince of Peace.

Now, how can one person have two natures? Nevertheless, there it is, "A child will be born," speaking of His humanity—but this child will be regarded as "Mighty God." He will be born, yet He is the "Eternal Father,"—meaning that He is eternal, preeminent over eternity.

This passage points us to the incarnation. God the Son, the second person of the Tri-unity, literally took on human flesh, human form. God became a man.[131] Man cannot become God or evolve into a god. However, from the moment of the incarnation, Jesus was, and is, fully God and fully man. Peter Kreeft, a well-known Roman Catholic apologist, put it this way:

> It is a mystery rather than a contradiction to say that He is one person with two natures, even if those two natures are opposites.[132]

---

[130] Hebrews 1:1-3

[131] For passages that reveal the Trinity, or tri-unity of God, check out Isaiah 44:6; 48:16-17; Psalm 2:7.

[132] Norman L. Geisler and Paul K. Huffman, eds., *Why I Am a Christian: Leading Thinkers Explain Why They Believe* (Grand Rapids, MI: Baker Books, 2001), p. 224

However, we just might be able to grasp this when we consider that humans consist of body and soul, essentially two natures in one being. Jesus often spoke from the perspective of His humanity, referring to Himself as the Son of Man. He also spoke from the standpoint of His deity as the Son of God. In His humanity, He was born in Bethlehem. In His divinity, "He is before all things, and in Him all things hold together."[133]

In His humanity, Jesus asked Mary, the sister of Lazarus, where her brother's body had been laid to rest. In His deity, He raised Lazarus from the dead with a single command, "Lazarus, come forth."[134]

Jesus is one Person with two natures; one of the doctrinal mysteries we believe by faith—and once again, we must take off our shoes for we stand on hallowed ground.

You might wonder, *Why is the incarnation an essential doctrine for the Christian to accept?* Simply put, if Jesus was not who He said He was, then He was a blind guide and a deceiver. We are back to C.S. Lewis's "poached egg" comment. If Jesus is not God, He cannot be Lord of all. If Jesus is not fully human, He could not have atoned for our sins—He could not have been the substitutionary atoning One spoken of by Isaiah the prophet. And therefore, we would be without hope. It's just that simple.

Jesus in His Humanity

Jesus, as a man, is how humanity is meant to be. Jesus was consistently obedient to the will of His Father. He was consumed with a burning zeal to maintain the holiness of His Father's house, as shown when He drove the moneychangers out of the temple. His love for humanity was unconditional. He laid down His life for the sins of the world. He possessed the heart of a servant, setting the example by wrapping a towel around His waist and washing the feet of His disciples, Judas included.[135] Jesus was morally pure—

---

[133] Colossians 1:17
[134] John 11:34, 43
[135] John 13:3-4

even Pilate said, "I find no guilt in this man."[136] He was filled with compassion for the sick, needy, and poor, and along with those who mourned, Jesus wept.[137]

Jesus Christ: fully God, fully man. Through His Divine authority, He will ultimately judge the world—through His humanity, He is the perfect Intercessor and Mediator for us before the Father. Since He is the One who created us and is the One who became one of us, there is no one more appropriate and better able to speak on our behalf.

> Since we have a great high priest who has passed through the heavens, Jesus the Son of God, let us hold fast our confession. For we do not have a high priest who cannot sympathize with our weaknesses, but One who has been tempted in all things as we are, yet without sin. Therefore let us draw near with confidence to the throne of grace, so that we may receive mercy and find grace to help in time of need.[138]

FINAL THOUGHTS

When imprisoned, John the Baptist sent his disciples to Jesus to find out if He was indeed the "Expected One," the long-awaited Messiah and Savior of all humanity. Perhaps this account has been as much of a puzzle to you at times as it was to me. After all, it was John who proclaimed, upon seeing Jesus:

> "Behold, the Lamb of God who takes away the sin of the world! This is He on behalf of whom I said, 'After me comes a Man who has a higher rank than I, for He existed before me.'"[139]

How could John proclaim His identity so boldly and then send his disciples to question if Jesus was indeed the "Expected One"?[140]

---

[136] Luke 23:4
[137] John 11:35
[138] Hebrews 4:14-16
[139] John 1:29-30
[140] Matthew 11:2-6

I think we can answer that question in light of John's imprisonment. Perhaps he was thinking, *How could this have happened to me? How could my situation be so hopeless when I put my faith and trust in the One who has finally come?* Don't we all have our moments of doubt? Don't we, too, need the same confirmation as John when facing our moments of imprisonment, whether they are physical, financial, or emotional? At those moments, I genuinely think our one desire is to receive a reminder, a little something to grasp. Jesus gave John just that—a reminder supported by evidence, as I hope I have done for you in this chapter.

Jesus told John's disciples to report to John all the signs He had performed, signs that attested to who He was. Then—and I just love the Amplified Bible's version of what Jesus said in Matthew 11:6—He reminded them:

> "...blessed (happy, fortunate and to be envied) is he who takes no offense at Me *and* finds no cause for stumbling in *or* through Me *and* is not hindered from seeing the Truth."

Were there more prophecies fulfilled than I've mentioned here? Yes. Were there more miracles? Yes. Were there more displays of God's mighty attributes? You bet. Therefore, I conclude with the words of the other John:

> Many other signs therefore Jesus also performed in the presence of the disciples, which are not written in this book; but these have been written that you may believe that Jesus is the Christ, the Son of God; and that believing you may have life in His name.

> And there are also many other things which Jesus did, which if they were written in detail, I suppose that even the world itself would not contain the books which were written.[141]

---

[141] John 20:30; 21:25

QUESTIONS & RESOURCES

1. What two points made Jesus's claims believable?

2. Can you explain what the term "incarnation" means?

3. What attributes did Jesus possess that are also attributes of God?

4. Where is there a time prophecy pinpointing Messiah's arrival?

5. Where, in the Scriptures, does it speak of Jesus' dual natures?

Answering Jewish Objections to Jesus Volumes 1-4, by Michael L. Brown, Baker Books, 2000.

More Than a Carpenter by Josh McDowell, Tyndale House Publishers, Inc., 1977.

Why I Am a Christian: Leading Thinkers Explain Why They Believe, edited by Norman L, Geisler, and Paul K. Hoffman. Baker Books, 2001.

Baker Encyclopedia of Christian Apologetics by Norman L. Geisler, Baker Books, 1999.

CHAPTER 9 ~ *The Historical Resurrection*

Though this is probably more prevalent when viewing modern art, isn't it interesting how people can see or witness the same object or event yet express quite different interpretations? I guess there could be an array of explanations for this. One could be that the basis for their analysis just might be their level of understanding and knowledge regarding what took place. Such was the case one afternoon as Jeff and I ran errands with Nicole, who was five years old at the time.

Without acknowledging that we had noticed the same thing on the side of the freeway, Jeff and I glanced over at each other but refrained from any overt reaction. I guess our feelings were similar, in that we wanted to avoid explaining what we saw to our little girl, who was playing and singing so cheerily in the backseat of the car. Of course, nothing gets past the notice of a five-year-old.

"Mom," Nicole said excitedly, "I just saw three crosses on the side of the road over there." My husband and I, somewhat sorrowfully, once again looked toward each other, as if seeing who would explain to our little girl that it meant three individuals had somehow had lost their lives there. Seeing our saddened expressions, Nicole attempted to lighten the mood a bit and, therefore, immediately reassured, "Oh no, no, no—there was nobody on them!" At this, we were quite relieved.

From the variety of interpretations and perceptions of the event, I imagine the resurrection of Jesus comes with varying levels of understanding in much the same way. In my studies, I've read or heard everything from the idea that the resurrection is simply "a metaphor of our own sacrificial self-giving,"[142] to the theory that it was merely a fabrication by an unknown, switched-at-birth twin of

---

[142] Walter Martin and Dale Miller, *The Resurrection Debate*, available through the Walter Martin Religious InfoNet [www.waltermartin.com]; or write Box 25710, St. Paul, MN 55125).

Jesus, who had impersonated the risen Lord.[143] Everyone, no matter what their view—from metaphor to twin theory, to hallucination, to hysteria—can offer reasons why they believe what they believe about the historical resurrection of the Lord Jesus Christ.

However, what is important to remember, as a believer, is that you can offer evidence of the resurrection as well. The question to ask is, whose reasons are more reasonable to believe? That is the purpose of this chapter. Since the resurrection is the jewel in the crown of our faith, I want to be sure I present as many glorious facets of this jewel as is necessary. What I'd like to do is break things down a bit by using, as a foundation, just a few of the biblical prophecies that were fulfilled.

In all, there were twenty-seven Old Covenant prophecies fulfilled in one Man in one day. Simply amazing, isn't it? How comforting it is to know that the resurrection of our Lord is so much more than a metaphor. The reality of the resurrection of Jesus Christ is the redemption of our past, the reality of our today, and the hope for our tomorrow.

Now, let's go one step at a time through Jesus' betrayal, trial, and death—and the reason behind those dramatically changed lives that resulted.

The Pain of Betrayal

Even my close friend in whom I trusted, Who ate my bread, Has lifted up his heel against me (Psalm 41:9).

Judas Iscariot, who was one of the twelve, went off to the chief priests in order to betray Him to them (Mark 14:10).

I'm sure you would agree that it has to be one of the most emotionally painful experiences—not just the loss of friendship, but betrayal by a close friend. Has it ever happened to you? Have you ever felt the sting of a false friend? It is a heartbreaking wound that can go deep. If you have had such an experience, I hope your

---

[143] William Lane Craig and Robert Greg Cavin, *Dead or Alive? A Debate on the Resurrection of Jesus Christ,* available through New Life Resources, 1-800-827-2788.

attitude was one of restoration—that, though it was difficult, you at least attempted to reach out to that individual. Jesus, forever our example, showed us just how to respond to those who wound us, even in the midst of them drawing their sword.

Jesus did not hesitate to wash the feet of His betrayer. After the foot-washing, that beautiful picture of how we ought to serve one another, Jesus did not hide the fact that He was well aware of the evil plot against Him:

> "The Son of Man is to go, just as it is written of Him; but woe to that man by whom the Son of Man is betrayed! It would have been good for that man if he had not been born."[144]

Now, every time I read what happened next, what immediately comes to mind is the old lineup. I am sure if you have more than two little ones, you probably opted for this approach at your home as well. Just in case you are unfamiliar with it, it goes something like this: After gathering the children together, Mom and Dad will pose to them a scenario describing some unexplained shenanigans by a mystery offender. Mom and Dad then wait patiently for a reaction from the peanut gallery. Usually, the one who speaks most vigorously for his or her innocence is the guilty party. This principle seemed to apply at the last supper as well. After Jesus made His stunning disclosure regarding His betrayer, Judas immediately spoke up, saying, "Surely it is not I, Rabbi?"

Do you think Judas was just testing Jesus to see if He knew? Or was the searing of Judas' conscience not yet complete, and thus his guilt prompted his response? In any event, Jesus replied, "You have said it yourself."[145]

Jesus not only assured Judas that He was aware of the plot, but He sternly warned him of the horrible consequences of carrying out his dastardly deed. Jesus confronted him, yet for Judas, his path was set—he was determined. Jesus divulged to the Apostle John that the one to whom He offered the morsel of bread was

---

[144] Matthew 26:24
[145] Matthew 26:25

the one who would betray Him, and to Judas, it went. Once more, Jesus reached out to Judas: hand to hand and eye to eye.

Judas—whom Jesus had chosen to be among His closest companions, who had witnessed His miracles and acts of love and compassion, whom Jesus had trusted with the moneybag, though Judas helped himself to its contents,[146] was indeed the betrayer. Scriptures state that as soon as Judas ate the morsel, "Satan then entered into him."[147] How horrible that must have been. How incredibly awful it must be for those who dabble in the occult to be possessed by demonic spirits. Though demonic entities cannot possess a believer, how terrible it is to be oppressed by them. Satan himself entered into Judas and then led him to the chief priests and from there to Gethsemane.

"Do What You Have Come For"

When Judas was face-to-face with Jesus in the garden, *accompanied by a large crowd with swords and clubs*,[148] he said, "Hail, Rabbi," and then betrayed Jesus with a kiss.

In Matthew 26:50, Jesus then called Judas precisely what he was. Jesus said, "Friend, do what you have come for." Now, whenever I'd read that passage, I had always assumed Jesus might have been expressing some level of affection to Judas by calling him "friend." Once again, reaching out would seem consistent with Jesus' character. However, according to *The Complete Word Study Dictionary: New Testament*, the word "friend" in Greek, as used in this verse, can be rendered "selfish colleague, friendly opportunist, or an imposter."[149] Jesus again saw right through to the heart of the man and referred to Judas as an imposter there for the sole purpose of selfish gain.

I can only guess, because it seems so like Satan, that after accomplishing the devious deed of betrayal, he left Judas to himself

---

[146] John 12:4-6
[147] John 13:27
[148] Matthew 26:47
[149] Spiros Zodhiates, *The Complete Word Study Dictionary: New Testament* (Chattanooga, TN: AMG Publishers, 1992), p. 665

by withdrawing from him. He left Judas to suffer the weight of his guilt and the certainty of judgment. Jesus' words must have been ringing in his ears: "It would have been good for that man if he had not been born."[150]

Unlike Peter, whose denial times three brought him to godly sorrow, then to confession and repentance, Judas tried to cover his tracks by returning the money. Perhaps he thought, like so many who attempt to make things right apart from God, *If I try to fix it myself by returning the loot, surely this weight of guilt will be gone, and I will be absolved of any evil I've done.* He tried to do penance. It didn't work. (It never works, does it?) Judas knew that no act of his could clean the slate. Peter knew that no act of his could wipe his slate from having denied the Lord, so Peter took his guilt to God and was promptly forgiven and restored, then used mightily. Judas, however, instead of throwing himself on the mercy of a loving Heavenly Father, hanged himself.

> I said to them, "If it is good in your sight, give me my wages; but if not, never mind!" So they weighed out thirty shekels of silver as my wages. Then the LORD said to me, "Throw it to the potter, that magnificent price at which I was valued by them." So I took the thirty shekels of silver and threw them to the potter in the house of the LORD (Zechariah 11:12-13).

> When Judas, who had betrayed Him, saw that He had been condemned, he felt remorse and returned the thirty pieces of silver to the chief priests and elders, saying, "I have sinned by betraying innocent blood."
> But they said, "What is that to us? See to that yourself!" And he threw the pieces of silver into the temple sanctuary and departed; and he went away and hanged himself. The chief priests took the pieces of silver and said, "It is not lawful to put them into the temple treasury, since it is the price of blood." And they conferred together and with the money bought the

---

[150] Matthew 26:24

Potter's Field as a burial place for strangers (Matthew 27:3-7).

The Trial

He was oppressed and He was afflicted,
Yet He did not open His mouth;
Like a lamb that is led to slaughter,
And like a sheep that is silent before its shearers,
So He did not open His mouth (Isaiah 53:7).

While He was being accused by the chief priests and elders, He did not answer. Then Pilate said to Him, "Do You not hear how many things they testify against You?" And He did not answer him with regard to even a single charge, so the governor was quite amazed (Matthew 27:12-14).

Have you ever had the experience of being falsely accused? I think it can go hand-in-hand with a betrayal. Some time ago, an individual falsely accused me, telling others I had said something hurtful to another individual. I had no idea that for months this person was spreading this horrible lie. It deeply hurt me when I found out, and I was stunned at the people who believed it. After hours of long conversations and phone calls, someone finally decided to ask the individual whom I had supposedly hurt if this rumor was true. I was quickly exonerated. However, I will never forget how I felt about the possibility that people I love would think me capable of intentionally hurting someone else I also loved. This experience happened within a tiny circle of individuals close to me—knowing that pain, I cannot imagine how Jesus' heart must have hurt as He listened to those He came to die for, falsely accuse Him.

There stood Jesus before the chief priests and elders. His face lightly stained with streams of blood, which He sweated in the garden before His arrest. His extreme level of anxiety and anguish had prompted an unusual condition referred to as *hematidrosis*. This condition would also have left His skin fragile and very sensitive, only compounding the agony of the scourging yet to come. The same individuals who were so concerned with what was appropriate under the law regarding Judas' blood money in the temple treasury were perfectly fine with violating a myriad of other Jewish laws to rid themselves of the Man who threatened their position and authority.

Illegal Proceedings

In *The Trial of Christ: A Criminal Lawyer Defends Jesus*, Dee Wampler wrote:

> The condemnation of Christ was not based upon legal procedure and harmony with either the Mosaic Code or the Mishnah. He was never legally tried and convicted. The pages of human history present no stronger case of judicial murder than the trial and crucifixion of Jesus of Nazareth, for the simple reason that all forms of law were outraged and trampled underfoot in the proceedings instituted against Him.[151]

What were these illegal proceedings? The following are just a few:

• The arrest was illegal since it took place at night and through the agency of a traitor.

• The private examination before Caiaphas (or Annas) was illegal because it was also conducted at night, and no judge, sitting alone, could interrogate an accused person.

• The trial before the Sanhedrin was illegal on several counts. It took place at night. The location of the trial was illegal. Jesus had no defense representation. Caiaphas presented the charge instead of the leading witnesses. No two witnesses could agree. Jesus was told to confess. The Chief Priest voted first by rending his robe and then immediately declaring that Jesus deserved death, though Jesus was not guilty of the capital offense of blasphemy. First, He had never pronounced the name of God aloud (which could only be uttered once a

---

[151] Dee Wampler, *The Trial of Christ: A Criminal Lawyer Defends Jesus*, p. 3. For information on how to obtain this excellent booklet, write Dee Wampler, Attorney at Law, 1200-C East Woodhurst Drive, Springfield, MO 65804.

year in the sanctuary of the Temple by the high priest), and second, He was, and is, in fact, God incarnate!

Aside from the illegal points of Jesus' arrest and trial, Wampler also cited a variety of trial errors. Since Pontius Pilate found no fault in Him, and Herod sent Him back to Pilate, essentially acquitting Him as well, they should have freed Jesus. He definitely should not have been scourged, let alone delivered up to be crucified. Nevertheless, it all followed a divine plan.

The Unjust Verdict

Thus far as prophesied, Jesus was betrayed by a close friend and companion. He was then arrested by night by a detachment of Roman soldiers along with the chief priests, officers of the temple guard, and elders. The rest of His companions deserted Him; one even denied Him three times.

Jesus, this Man of love and truth, compassion, and mercy, Who brought hope and healing, then faced His false accusers. After this, the crowds who once adored Him, almost rioted until they persuaded Pilate by their pleas to crucify Jesus and free a notorious prisoner named Barabbas. Jesus then endured the horror of a Roman scourging, a sharp, thorny crown pressed down upon His brow, and the humiliation and pain of being beaten, mocked, spat upon, and then prepared for death on a Roman cross.

Oh, what our Lord endured for you and me! Is there anyone of us who would willingly, and with foreknowledge, suffer what He suffered? Is there any secret we would keep if we knew we would face such horror? Is there any cause according to our flesh for which we would suffer such torture? All this, even before Jesus went to the cross.

> I gave My back to those who strike Me, And My cheeks to those who pluck out the beard; I did not cover My face from humiliation and spitting (Isaiah 50:6).
> Just as many were astonished at you, My people, So His appearance was marred more than any man, And His form more than the sons of men (Isaiah 52:14).

Then [Pilate] released Barabbas for them; but after having Jesus scourged, he handed Him over to be crucified.

Then the soldiers of the governor took Jesus into the Praetorium and gathered the whole Roman cohort around Him. They stripped Him and put a scarlet robe on Him. And after twisting together a crown of thorns, they put it on His head, and a reed in His right hand; and they knelt down before Him and mocked Him, saying, "Hail, King of the Jews!" They spat on Him, and took the reed and began to beat Him on the head. After they had mocked Him, they took the scarlet robe off Him and put His own garments back on Him, and led Him away to crucify Him (Matthew 27:26-31).

His Death

He Himself bore the sin of many,
And interceded for the transgressors (Isaiah 53:12).

Jesus was saying, "Father, forgive them; for they do not know what they are doing" (Luke 23:34).

You might think me a bit odd, but every time I see someone wearing a cross I feel compelled to ask, and always in a very lighthearted tone, "Is that beautiful cross you're wearing a fashion statement, or are you totally on fire for the Lord Jesus Christ?" It is always fun to hear them respond with reverence for our Lord. There is instant fellowship, and I've met a sister or brother I will see again—if not in this life, in the next.

Unfortunately, more often than not, the individuals I ask, tell me they just like wearing the cross. They tell me they think the design is pretty. In other words, for them, it is reduced to a fashion statement. How heartbreaking and, when you think about it, how foolish this is. I often wonder if these same people would also wear a miniature noose, or the electric chair, or guillotine, or some other method of execution dangling about their neck, in 14-karat gold, spotted with diamonds. Or would they, not being Jewish, wear a

Star of David or, not being Buddhist, wear a Buddha around their neck or some other symbol of a religion they did not follow?

Perhaps you feel, as I do, that wearing the cross is a reminder of what our Lord suffered for us. It is a reminder that we are to pick up our cross daily and follow Him. Moreover, it is the symbol of our victory. The cross we wear is not for the sake of fashion. Like the tomb, it is empty; He is not there. Jesus proclaimed total victory when He declared from the cross, "It is finished."

According to Zodhiates, the Greek word for "finished" means "to make an end or to accomplish, to complete something, not merely to end it, but to bring it to perfection or its destined goal, to carry it through." Zodhiates goes on to say, "'It is finished,' meaning the whole work of salvation, the very purpose Jesus came into the world."[152]

Charles Spurgeon once said, "What meant the Savior, then, by this, 'It is finished'? He meant, first of all, that all the types, promises, and prophecies were now fully accomplished in Him."[153]

Years ago, while recording the compact disc series *Divine Appointments*, which is now the book *Engaging Encounters*, the companion resource to *Reasons for Faith*, a disciple of Sun Myung Moon, came into the studio to proselytize. It took a while for her to admit that she was promoting the Unification Church. We then began a dialogue on the subject of the crucifixion.

The cultist was convinced, because of her education through the Unification Church, that since Jesus was crucified and therefore died, God had to resort to Plan B. She expressed the notion that Jesus came to save the world, but they mistakenly crucified Him instead. As a result, we must now look to a new Messiah to finish the job correctly, and that would be the Reverend Sun Myung Moon. Her revelation of the Messiah took me quite by surprise. I would never have imagined the Jewish Messiah would be Korean. Apparently, neither would God!

---

[152] Zodhiates, p. 1375

[153] Charles H. Spurgeon, *Christ's Words from the Cross* (Grand Rapids, MI: Baker Books, 1981), p. 89

Plan A: Prophecy Fulfilled

Doesn't it comfort you to know that God never needs a Plan B? The crucifixion was nothing other than the fulfillment and culmination of every Old Covenant shadow or type concerning the event. The particulars of the crucifixion were prophesied from Genesis onward. The crucifixion itself was, in fact, God's plan for redemption long before humanity even existed to contemplate the forbidden fruit. I could go into much detail regarding the prophecies fulfilled, but for the sake of brevity, below are just a few prophecies concerning the events surrounding the crucifixion alone.

Dying Among Sinners

His grave was assigned with wicked men.
He poured out Himself to death,
And was numbered with the transgressors (Isaiah 53:9,12)

When they came to the place called The Skull, there they crucified Him and the criminals, one on the right and the other on the left (Luke 23:33).

Bruised Heel

In Genesis 3:15 God said to the serpent in judgment, "He shall bruise you on the head [crush your head], and you shall bruise him on the heel." Crucifixion is the only execution method that "bruises" the heel. And the crucifixion was part of the crushing victory over the power of Satan.

Pierced

They pierced my hands and my feet (Psalm 22:16).

The other disciples... were saying to [Thomas], "We have seen the Lord!"
But he said to them, "Unless I shall see in His hands the imprint of the nails, and put my finger into the place

of the nails, and put my hand into His side, I will not believe" (John 20:25).

Crucified

I am poured out like water, And all my bones are out of joint. (Psalm 22:14)

The above verse is a picture of what happens when the arms of a crucified person are stretched, and the full weight of the body drops down. The shoulders dislocate, or go "out of joint." Since crucifixion is death by asphyxiation, Jesus would have had to rise up on the spike in His feet, thus bruising the heel, to inhale, and then let Himself down again to exhale. Adding to His torture of having to move up and down on the cross to inhale and exhale was the fact that His back was flayed from the buttocks to the shoulders as a result of the Roman scourging—a horror truly unimaginable.

His Garments

They divide my garments among them,
And for my clothing, they cast lots (Psalm 22:18).

They cast lots, dividing up His garments among themselves (Luke 23:34).

Staring

They look, they stare at me (Psalm 22:17).

The people stood by, looking on (Luke 23:35).

Taunting

All who see me sneer at me;
They separate with the lip, they wag the head, saying,
"Commit yourself to the LORD; let Him deliver him;
Let Him rescue him, because He delights in him" (Psalm 22:7-8).

The chief priests also, along with the scribes and elders, were mocking Him and saying, "He saved others;

He cannot save Himself. He is the King of Israel; let Him now come down from the cross, and we will believe in Him. He trusts in God; let God rescue Him now, if He delights in Him; for He said, 'I am the Son of God'" (Matthew 27:41-43).

Thirst

I am weary with my crying; my throat is parched; My eyes fail as I wait for my God (Psalm 69:3).

My strength is dried up like a potsherd,
And my tongue cleaves to my jaws;
And You lay me in the dust of death (Psalm 22:15).

After this, Jesus, knowing that all things had already been accomplished, to fulfill the Scripture said, "I am thirsty" (John 19:28).

Offered Bitter Drink

They also gave me gall for my food
And for my thirst they gave me vinegar to drink (Psalm 69:21).

A jar full of sour wine [vinegar] was standing there; so they put a sponge full of the sour wine upon a branch of hyssop and brought it up to His mouth (John 19:29).

Words from the Cross

My God, my God, why have You forsaken Me? Far from my deliverance are the words of my groaning (Psalm 22:1).

About the ninth hour Jesus cried out with a loud voice, saying, "Eli, Eli, lama sabachthani?" that is, "My God, My God, why have You forsaken Me?" (Matthew 27:46).

No Broken Bones

I can count all my bones (Psalm 22:17).

Coming to Jesus, when they saw that He was already dead, they did not break His legs (John 19:33).

Jesus, as John the Baptist declared, was the Lamb of God who takes away the sin of the world. Jesus was the final Passover Lamb, and one of the requirements of such a lamb, according to Exodus 12:46, was that none of its bones were to be broken.

Brokenhearted

Reproach has broken my heart, and I am so sick. And I looked for sympathy, but there was none, And for comforters, but I found none (Psalm 69:20).

I am poured out like water, and all my bones are out of joint; My heart is like wax; it is melted within me (Psalm 22:14).

...and immediately blood and water came out (John 19:34).

A Wealthy Burial

His grave was assigned with wicked men,
Yet He was with a rich man in His death,
Because He had done no violence,
Nor was there any deceit in His mouth (Isaiah 53:9).

When it was evening, there came a rich man from Arimathea, named Joseph, who himself had also become a disciple of Jesus. This man went to Pilate and asked for the body of Jesus. Then Pilate ordered it to be given to him. And Joseph took the body and wrapped it in a clean linen cloth, and laid it in his own new tomb, which he had hewn out in the rock; and he rolled a large stone against the entrance of the tomb and went away (Matthew 27:57-60).

Plan B?

Because the crucifixion of Jesus Christ was the apex of God's divine wisdom and sovereign plan, there was never any need for a *Plan B*. Christ's suffering, and sacrifice on the cross was the ultimate expression of God's love for humankind. In John 15:13, Jesus said, "Greater love has no one than this, that one lay down his life for his friends."

When I think of the details of crucifixion—and I realize that Jesus knew every particular of what He would suffer, yet willingly faced it for me—how can I not fall on my face and call Him my Lord, and my God, and my King?

Jesus told us that dying for a friend was the supreme expression of love, yet while we were at enmity with Him, He died for us. No greater love or compassion is there than His precious love for us, which He expressed unreservedly at the cross.

> "Can a woman forget her nursing child
> And have no compassion on the son of her womb?
> Even these may forget, but I will not forget you.
> Behold, I have inscribed you on the *palms of My hands*."[154]

Ain't Nobody in Here but Us Linens!

They were on the road going up to Jerusalem, and Jesus was walking on ahead of them; and they were amazed, and those who followed were fearful.

And again He took the twelve aside and began to tell them what was going to happen to Him, saying, "Behold, we are going up to Jerusalem, and the Son of Man will be delivered to the chief priests and the scribes; and they will condemn Him to death and will hand Him over to the Gentiles. They will mock Him and spit on Him, and scourge Him and kill Him, and three days later He will rise again" (Mark 10:32-34).

Now after the Sabbath, as it began to dawn toward the first day of the week, Mary Magdalene and the other Mary came to look at the grave. And behold, a severe earthquake had occurred, for an angel of the Lord descended from heaven and came and rolled away the

---

154 Isaiah 49:15-16 emphasis added

stone and sat upon it. And his appearance was like lightning, and his clothing as white as snow. The guards shook for fear of him and became like dead men.

The angel said to the women, "Do not be afraid; for I know that you are looking for Jesus who has been crucified. He is not here, for He has risen, just as He said. Come, see the place where He was lying. Go quickly and tell His disciples that He has risen from the dead; and behold, He is going ahead of you into Galilee, there you will see Him; behold, I have told you" (Matthew 28:1-7).

Have you ever been so entrenched in your valley experience that you could feel the thistle touching your chin? Sometimes our response, as professing believers, can be puzzling. We retreat, we withdraw, and we imagine the worst scenarios, ones that never come to pass. Simply put, we break out the double-dip, chocolate-fudge-chip, almond rum ice cream and have ourselves a good old-fashioned pity party.

Then, to our surprise, the hand of God moves our mountain, and then sets us high atop His, so we can see from His perspective how the depth of our valley wasn't as deep as we thought. He lovingly sets us there until we can finally see that the mountain of our creation was simply a molehill after all. Our problem was twofold. One was our perspective from the valley, and the other was our lack of faith in God.

That's just where the disciples were after the crucifixion—minus the ice cream. Amid their despair and loss of Someone they dearly loved, Someone whom they believed to be the Messiah, with their pity-party in full swing, in came a stunning proclamation from unlikely sources. The women came to tell those in the upper room of the vision of angels and their order to inform the disciples of the reality of Jesus's resurrection. However, as often happens when it's hard to believe what the Lord already told us, the Scriptures state that the women's "words appeared to them as nonsense, and they would not believe them."[155]

---

[155] Luke 24:11

Peter, going into the tomb to see for himself, was not quite sure what had happened, but he "marveled." John's immediate reaction was unbelief, yet upon further examination of the grave and the position of the linen wrappings, and remembering that Jesus said He would rise from the dead, he then believed. However, both simply went home. The empty tomb was not enough to move them out, preaching with passion and power. (And we all know Thomas's famous, perhaps even sarcastic, declaration of unbelief.)

The tomb was empty—no doubt about it. Even the Jewish leaders believed the terrified guards—they knew His body was gone. The fact that they bribed the guards to report that the disciples had come and stolen the body proves this fact.

Where Did He Go?

Now, I must grant the fact that an empty tomb does not necessarily prove that Jesus rose from the dead. An empty tomb simply prompts the question, "Where did He go?" Also, if the Roman guards allowed themselves to be bribed by the Pharisees, perhaps they could have been bribed by the disciples as well. Maybe they were double-dipping. Perhaps they were paid to turn their backs for a few moments while the disciples sneaked Jesus' body out of the tomb.

However, would the disciples have attempted to steal Jesus' body to prove His resurrection? Is it possible that this would ever have entered their minds, especially since they were so skeptical regarding the testimony of the women? Would Jesus' followers, right after He had just been crucified for referring to Himself as God and King, then approach the Roman guards to ask for help in stealing the body so they could turn the world upside down with a phony resurrection story? Could they have said, "Excuse me, Mr. Roman Guard, who could be brutally killed if you left your post— would you just turn your head for a moment while we roll a two-thousand pound stone uphill so we can make it look as if our leader rose from the dead?"

Can anyone honestly imagine those fearful, grief-stricken men concocting a resurrection story? After all, the disciples did not fully grasp the things Jesus told them regarding His death and resurrection while He ministered among them. The concept of a crucified Messiah Who would return from the dead was foreign to them, especially since they understood that the Messiah would be King. Therefore, as Jesus hung on the cross, their thoughts were certainly not, *This is how the events are supposed to be—He is paying for our sin, and in three days we will see Him again!* No. They abandoned Him in the garden, fearing the same fate He met, and then despaired as He was laid in the tomb. Again, an empty tomb alone does not prove the resurrection. There has to be more.

He's Alive!

I think it is remarkable that, though Jesus was a man of sorrows and acquainted with grief, with the cross ever before Him, He still managed to maintain a sense of humor. To the Pharisees, He once said, "You strain out a gnat and swallow a camel."[156] Dry humor, but I think that illustration is rather funny when you picture it.

However, I especially wish I could have walked on the road to Emmaus to eavesdrop on the conversation heartbroken Cleopas, and the unnamed disciple had as they grappled over the events surrounding Jesus's death, burial, and empty tomb. Suddenly a Stranger walked along with them. The Stranger then expressed to those troubled disciples no knowledge of the subject concerning their impassioned conversation.

The stunned men concluded that the Stranger must have been a visitor, after all, everyone knew of the events surrounding the Nazarene. At that point, they were not aware they were speaking to Jesus, Himself. The Scriptures state, "their eyes were prevented from recognizing Him." The men, for that short trek, were divinely blinded.[157] They then began to tell the resurrected Jesus what

---

[156] Matthew 23:24

[157] For an article that might help to understand why our Lord temporarily blinded them please see: https://www.womeninapologetics.com/divinely-blinded/

happened to Him just days before. After they had updated their unexpected Traveling Companion on the events of that weekend, Jesus filled them in on the entire picture.

> He said to them, "O foolish men and slow of heart to believe in all that the prophets have spoken! Was it not necessary for the Christ to suffer these things and to enter into His glory?" Then beginning with Moses and with all the prophets, He explained to them the things concerning Himself in all the Scriptures.[158]

Isn't that always our way? We try to inform the Lord of what He already knows. Finally, when we take a moment to put our emotions aside and are willing to gain His perspective, we can receive the wisdom that's needed to help us through—wisdom, insight, and context directly from the heart of our Lord.

After arriving at Emmaus, the three men sat down for a meal, and as soon as He broke the bread, the two men recognized it was Jesus, and then He vanished. The two men then dashed back to the upper room to tell the other disciples. Jesus suddenly appeared there, where they, terrified, thought they saw a ghost. However:

> He said to them, "Why are you troubled, and why do doubts arise in your hearts? See My hands and My feet, that it is I Myself; touch Me and see, for a spirit does not have flesh and bones as you see that I have."[159]

I love what He said next. It's just such a guy thing—and again, I think it reveals something of His sense of humor. Jesus asked His terrified followers, "Have you anything here to eat?"[160] Now, imagine being in the middle of mourning the one person you love above all. Suddenly, you hear something; you then lift your gaze from your sorrow, only to see that he or she is standing right before you. Do you think it just might break the tension a bit if that person then asked, "Hey, ya got any food around here?" Somehow, I don't think Jesus was all that hungry. I think it was just His way of calming their fright, lightening up an intense situation,

---

[158] See Luke 24:13-35 for the entire account.
[159] Luke 24:38-39
[160] Luke 24:41

and resuming the intimacy He had with them the last time they broke bread.

In 1 Corinthians 15:5-8 the apostle Paul documented other appearances of the resurrected Lord:

> He appeared to Cephas [Peter], then to the twelve. After that He appeared to more than five hundred brethren at one time, most of whom remain until now, [are still alive to confirm this fact] but some have fallen asleep [have died]; then He appeared to James [Jesus' half-brother, who before the resurrection did not believe He was the Messiah, but who afterward became a leader in the church and wrote the epistle of James], then to all the apostles; and last of all, as to one untimely born, He appeared to me also.

On his way to murdering or imprisoning Christians, Paul (who wrote the words above) met the risen Lord and, as a result, turned from the church's heartiest persecutor into its heartiest proponent. How does one explain it apart from the resurrection?

Changed Lives

The apostles knew Jesus died. Nevertheless, there He stood, flesh, and bone. It was Jesus. They knew they did not see a ghost, nor a hallucination, or a fairy tale, but the resurrected Lord Jesus Christ. The apostle John later wrote:

> What was from the beginning, what we have heard, what we have seen with our eyes, what we have looked at and touched with our hands, concerning the Word of Life.[161]

The apostles knew what they had seen—they were eyewitnesses, and their lives dramatically reflected that fact. To me, this is the most substantial evidence for the resurrection; the changed lives of the apostles.

---

[161] 1 John 1:1

Because he saw the risen Lord, Peter changed from coward and fisherman to a man who, by the power of the Holy Spirit, led 3,000 people to faith in Jesus as the Messiah on the day of Pentecost. Later, in Acts 4:13, the Jewish leaders marveled at the confidence of Peter and John as they stood before them, and they could not help but note that the only conclusion could be that the two men had been with Jesus. Peter, according to church tradition, when in the hands of his executioners, requested to be crucified upside down—which he would never have done if he knew all along he bribed guards to steal Jesus' body.

Nearly all of the apostles—including Paul, who was beheaded—died a martyr's death. All except John, who penned the a gospel, three epistles, and the *Book of the Revelation of Jesus Christ* as an exile on the Island of Patmos. Now, if Jesus did not die, we have to wonder, even if the apostles did not die for what they proclaimed, what did they gain through spreading the gospel message? Certainly, by worldly standards, they lost it all, especially Saul, who became the Apostle Paul. Consider Paul's account of the sheer glamor of being a witness for Christ during the early days of the church:

> Five times I received from the Jews thirty-nine lashes. Three times I was beaten with rods, once I was stoned, three times I was shipwrecked, a night and a day I have spent in the deep. I have been on frequent journeys, in dangers from rivers, dangers from robbers, dangers from my countrymen, dangers from the Gentiles, dangers in the city, dangers in the wilderness, dangers on the sea, dangers among false brethren; I have been in labor and hardship, through many sleepless nights, in hunger and thirst, often without food, in cold and exposure. Apart from such external things, there is daily pressure on me of concern for all the churches. Who is weak without my being weak? Who is led into sin without my intense concern?[162]

---

[162] 2 Corinthians 11:24-29

I cannot fathom anyone deliberately going through that long list of hardships for a lie. There is no other explanation but that Paul—an intelligent, faithful Jewish man, a Pharisee among Pharisees—knew he met the risen Lord Jesus Christ on the road to Damascus.

There is no doubt that each of the apostles would have been able to share similar accounts as Paul. It took death to silence them. Each one boldly proclaimed the most incredible event surrounding any human being in history. There is, therefore, only one conclusion: It is a small thing for an infinite God with infinite power to have raised Jesus Christ from the dead.

FINAL THOUGHTS

When writing on the importance and meaning of the resurrection of Jesus Christ, the apostle Paul was rather no-nonsense. In 1 Corinthians 15:12-19, he wrote:

> Now if Christ is preached, that He has been raised from the dead, how do some among you say that there is no resurrection of the dead? But if there is no resurrection of the dead, not even Christ has been raised; and if Christ has not been raised, then our preaching is vain, your faith also is vain.
>
> Moreover, we are even found to be false witnesses of God, because we testified against God that He raised Christ, whom He did not raise if the dead are not raised. For if the dead are not raised, not even Christ has been raised, and if Christ has not been raised, your faith is worthless, you are still in your sins. Then those also who have fallen asleep in Christ have perished. If we have hoped in Christ in this life only, we are of all men most to be pitied.

Simply put, if Jesus Christ did not resurrect from the dead, we are without hope. We are self-deceived, and people should pity us since we base our faith upon fantasy.

However, Jesus Christ did rise from the dead. *He is risen!* And because He lives, I can do more than face tomorrow—I can face death itself because it has lost its sting. I will live eternally with Him in glory with a resurrected body just like His, and so will you.

We will eat, move from one dimension to another, all without the aches and pains of old age because our mortal body will have taken on immortality. As we saw in the previous chapter, Jesus was truthful in everything He said and did. He was indeed a good teacher—the best! Of the resurrection, He declared, "Destroy this temple [speaking of His body], and in three days I will raise it up."[163] Now, if He didn't raise His body as He said He would, that would make Him delusional or a deceiver, and once again, we are back to the conclusion of C.S. Lewis' poached egg comment of the previous chapter.

In one of the best Christian apologetics books I have ever read, *Scaling the Secular City*, Dr. J.P. Moreland wrote this regarding the resurrection:

> The resurrection of Jesus of Nazareth from the dead is the foundation upon which the Christian faith is built. Without the resurrection, there would have been no Christian faith, and the most dynamic movement in history would never have come to be.[164]

Jesus said, "I am the resurrection and the life; he who believes in Me will live even if he dies, and everyone who lives and believes in Me will never die."[165]

Jesus was not delusional, He was not a deceiver—we are not blind guides, and we need no pity—because Jesus Christ is alive with power, and this is the good news we have the pleasure and privilege to proclaim.

---

[163] John 2:19-21

[164] J.P. Moreland, *Scaling the Secular City: A Defense of Christianity* (Grand Rapids, MI: Baker Books, 1987), p. 160

[165] John 11:25-26

QUESTIONS & RESOURCES

1. What happened to Judas after he ate the morsel of bread given to him by Jesus?

2. What did Jesus mean when He said, "It is finished." What was finished?

3. Can you remember three specific Old Testament prophecies regarding the crucifixion?

4. Why do you think the disciples didn't believe the women's story?

5. Have you shared your resurrection account with anyone lately?

The Case for Christ by Lee Strobel, Zondervan Publishing House, 1998.

Christ's Words from the Cross by Charles H. Spurgeon, Baker Books, 1981.

Scaling the Secular City by J.P. Moreland, Baker Book House, 1987.

The Emmaus Conversation: An Eyewitness Account from the Unnamed Disciple, by Judy Salisbury, Logos Presentations 2020.

CHAPTER 10 ~ *The Gospel's Good News*

I will never forget the time I received a speeding ticket one lovely fall morning as I was on my way to Bible study. While the other women got a real chuckle out of it, I was still trying to settle down from the adrenaline rush I'd gotten when I'd first noticed the red-and-blue flashing lights illuminating my rearview mirror. I was mortified when the police officer cited me for speeding in a school zone. He asked me if I noticed the 20-mile-per-hour sign, but I had to admit I didn't. Later that day, I drove very slowly through the area once again and could not find the school-zone sign the officer mentioned.

When I received the formal ticket in the mail, I thought I would attempt to have the fine reduced to just plain old speeding. The fine for speeding in a school zone was hefty—and besides, I didn't like being accused of trying to turn small schoolchildren into speed bumps! Wouldn't you know it, about a week before I was to go to court, a brand-new sign on that road magically appeared? *Perfect!*

The day of my trial came, and I sat nervously in traffic court, feeling like an accused felon. Suddenly, the judge entered, and the words, "All rise," echoed throughout the courtroom. We stood and waited respectfully for the judge to take his seat. After the bailiff had called out each docket number, the accused stood before the judge to plead his or her case. I was so nervous my palms were sweating. A deep voice called my number, and I stood before the judge as I took my oath. With his glasses perched on the tip of his nose, he fumbled through my folder as I pleaded my case. "Your Honor," I humbly muttered, "there was no school-zone sign posted on the day I traveled down that road."

Nodding, he took off his glasses, closed the folder, looked straight into my eyes, and casually said, "Not guilty." *What! Did he say what I think he said? Maybe he thinks I'm someone else.* "You're dismissed," he said, then added with a grin on his face while gesturing gently with his hand, "and slow down next time."

Still stunned, I thanked him and got out of there as fast as I could. I kept looking back, waiting for someone to grab me by the collar, yelling, "Hey, you—Lead Foot—get back in here!"

The police officer cited me for speeding in a school zone, but because the sign wasn't posted at the time I drove through that unfamiliar area, the judge dismissed my case. In other words, what the judge communicated to me was, "You are free from the penalty of your sin—now go and sin no more." What a feeling it was to have my debt canceled. It felt great to have my penalty wiped out as if it never happened.

Have you ever had such an experience? As believers, we know the feeling of having the weight of our sin canceled by the Judge of the universe through Christ's work on the cross.

> When you were dead in your transgressions and the uncircumcision of your flesh, He made you alive together in Him, having forgiven us all our transgressions, having canceled out the certificate of debt consisting of decrees against us, which was hostile to us; and He has taken it out of the way, having nailed it to the cross.[166]

Jesus said, "Go into all the world and preach the gospel [good news] to all creation."[167] Indeed, the message of the gospel *is* good news. However, before we can share the good news, we must first address the bad news. It is the bad news that makes the good news not only necessary but also the greatest news humanity could ever have the opportunity to receive. The bad news is why Jesus had to die in the first place—and that will be our starting point for this chapter on why we believe the Gospel is good news.

First, we will look at humanity's fall from a state of innocence, then the consequences of that fall. Next, we'll look at a temporary solution to our fallen condition, and finally, the glorious permanent solution and restoration before our Heavenly Father.

---

[166] Colossians 2:13-14
[167] Mark 16:15

The Gift of Life

When I think of God's love in creating humankind in His image, according to His likeness, my heart is overwhelmed with love for Him. Whenever I read the account in Genesis 1:26-28, I just can't help the emotion.

God, like every parent, had high aspirations for His children. They were to have dominion over all creation. They were to rule over the birds of the air and over all sea creatures, and all land animals, and whatever happened to creep along our humble abode. They were to be faithful stewards of what God entrusted to them, and they were to multiply to the point of subduing the whole world.

Best of all, this husband and wife would have perfect unity with each other and pure intimate love and fellowship with God. Though His heart must have rejoiced over those He created in His image, it must have been bittersweet knowing that it would not be long before they'd rebel. In the chapter on evil and human suffering, I addressed the abuse of the gift of free choice. Therefore, I want to take a closer look at our first parents and what happened when they fell from grace.

Chatting with a Snake in the Grass

You just might want to take a moment to read Genesis, chapter 3, especially the part where the serpent charmed Eve. Eve knew that God's command was not to eat the fruit of *the tree of the knowledge of good and evil*. Nevertheless, you know how good we are, especially as women, at justifying just about anything. "It's a gorgeous dress, if I don't get it now I'll miss the sale. I know our budget is tight, and it's expensive, but when was the last time I bought a dress that really fit? Then I'll have something to wear for that dinner we have to go to six months from now." Or, "Oh, just one slice of that four-layer carrot cake won't hurt. My diet? Well, I've been really good today, and I even walked all the way to the mailbox this morning, I deserve a reward." I think we get it from our first mother.

After Eve's little exchange with the serpent, she did not seek counsel from God or her husband, who was with her at the time. Rather, the justification for sin was in full swing. Can you just hear her? "How simply wonderful this fruit looks. Surely, God wouldn't want to withhold anything good from us. My, I sure am hungry. Now, why walk three feet to that tree over there when, oh look, all I have to do is reach my hand out and—*oops*. Did you see that, Adam? It just slipped right off the branch. I hate to waste it by throwing it on the ground, especially when, according to that friendly serpent over there, it will make me wise. Now just think of how helpful that would be, particularly since I am supposed to be your helpmeet, Adam. Oh, I know what God said, but that helpful serpent seems to think God's just trying to keep us from being like Him!" Perhaps it wasn't quite like that—but Eve didn't waste much time between gazing, then grabbing, then gobbling.

Adam knew the command of God as well, and the Scriptures state that, again, he was with his wife when she ate the forbidden fruit. The serpent deceived Eve, and Adam did not intervene. Adam did not fulfill his role as leader and protector—instead, he listened to the voice of his wife and violated God's sole restriction.

And, surprise, surprise—the serpent lied. Adam and Eve remained unlike deity—at least in the way they desired—as the image of God within them became marred. After they ate the fruit, notice what followed:

- *They realized they were naked.* Suddenly, something foreign entered their consciousness: shame.

- *Religion entered the camp.* Adam and Eve attempted to save themselves from guilt and shame by sewing fig leaves together for clothes. This attempt is not unique to Adam and Eve. Many today believe they can cover their sin and shame through *good works* or *penance* as a means to *get right with God.* Adam and Eve tried to fix their sin problem apart from God's only method.

- *They suffered the loss of fellowship with God.* When Adam and Eve realized God was in the garden with them, instead of greeting Him and pursuing their heavenly Parent, they hid from His presence. God's question, "Where are you?" was not one of ignorance. God knew where Adam was—to a far greater extent than we know when our children are in some mischief. I believe the purpose of the question was to prompt Adam to reflect on the condition that he now found himself, which should have lead to confession and repentance.

• *They hid because of fear.* An emotion foreign to them, they suddenly feared God, and to be sure, they feared His impending judgment.

• *The blame game was in full swing.* Adam blamed his wife, and then he blamed God for creating her for him in the first place. Eve said, in essence, "The devil made me do it." Then there was the serpent—but we all know he never did have a leg to stand on.

Adam and Eve fell from their state of innocence, which resulted in spiritual death at once, then ultimately physical death. All of the creation suffered because of the free choice our first parents willingly made. They desired to be like God, *knowing* both good and evil, their supreme desire was to determine, in their hearts, right from wrong.

The Bad News

What a mess! Shame, religion (that is, doing their own thing apart from God), broken fellowship, fear, pride; I think our first parents got far more than they ever bargained. Did you notice that there was no confession, no accepting responsibility for their sin, no godly sorrow leading to repentance? They simply covered up, hid from God, and then when all else failed, they attributed their sin to anyone but themselves. Sound familiar? It is familiar because it is the human condition resulting from the fall. The prophet Isaiah described it perfectly:

> All of us have become like one who is unclean,
> And all our righteous deeds are like a filthy garment;
> And all of us wither like a leaf,
> And our iniquities, like the wind, take us away.
> There is no one who calls on Your name,

Who arouses himself to take hold of You;
For You have hidden Your face from us
And have delivered us into the power of our
iniquities.

Behold, the LORD's hand is not so short
That it cannot save;
Neither is His ear so dull
That it cannot hear.
But your iniquities have made a separation between
you and your God,
And your sins have hidden His face from you so that
He does not hear.[168]

It's a somber picture, isn't it? One that we all share, we are all guilty. Not one of us naturally seeks the presence of God. Instead, our iniquities move us farther and farther away from the intimacy of His presence.

Have you ever noticed that the last person you desire to talk to is the one you've offended? Do you realize that when you're out of God's will, the last thing you want to open is your Bible? Because inside it lies conviction, and who needs to read about self-control or taking every thought captive when we're indulging the flesh?

The above passage also speaks of God's *face* as *hidden* from a person caught up in the throes of their iniquity. The face is the source of blessing—and when we sin, He figuratively hides His face from us. Remember, it is not that God *cannot* hear when we call out to Him, but that He *will not* or will refuse to hear until we repent.

I remember praying about and for things when I lived apart from God—and the non-answers I received, I mistook as meaning that the phone was off the hook in heaven. I thought the reason why was that perhaps God didn't exist, or that He was merely aloof.

---

[168] Isaiah 64:6-7; 59:1-2

However, what I ought to have done was shift the focus from my wants list to addressing what I needed to address: the fact that I was a sinner, lost and without hope. My sinful condition and the realization of it was terrible news for me. How easy it would have been to keep denying these fundamental truths or keep trying to measure my righteousness or sinfulness according to humanity's standards. My denial of my sin condition reminds me of the following words of that great seventeenth-century preacher, Stephen Charnock: "Those that never had a sense of their own vileness, were always destitute of a sense of God's holiness."[169] Ouch!

God's holiness—the one element we most forget. God is holy and just, and as such, He cannot let sin go unpunished. The choice God could make is to wipe all humankind off the face of the earth or make provision for them. How thankful I am that He chose the latter.

A Temporary Solution

Now for the good news: God did not leave Adam and Eve in the fig leaves. (Not because they looked ridiculous, and leaves would never suffice for those upcoming cold winter nights.) Through the substitutionary death of an animal, God set a requirement to deal with their sin and shame. God's provision for atonement has always been through blood sacrifice. "The LORD God made garments of skin for Adam and his wife and clothed them."[170]

Exodus 12 outlined the first Passover. The children of Israel were to sacrifice an unblemished lamb, which they would eat, and its blood they would smear upon the two doorposts and the lintel of their homes. When the Lord saw the applied blood, death passed over their house. The blood of the Passover lamb would save Israel's firstborn during that final plague in Egypt.

---

[169] Stephen Charnock (1628–1680), *The Existence and Attributes of God*, vol. 2, reprint ed. (Grand Rapids, MI: Baker Books, 1996), p. 192

[170] Genesis 3:21

The necessity of a blood sacrifice to satisfy the righteous wrath of God is throughout Scripture. Leviticus 17:11 gives us the reason why:

"The life of the flesh is in the blood, and I have given it to you on the altar to make atonement for your souls; for it is the blood by reason of the life that makes atonement."

Leviticus 17:11 is an amazingly accurate statement from a biological perspective. Since blood oxygenates the cells, brings nourishment throughout the body, and carries away its waste, the flesh cannot live without blood flow. Blood truly is what sustains biological life; in other words, *the life of the flesh is* literally *in the blood.*

On a spiritual level, Hebrews 9:22 states, "according to the Law, one may almost say, all things are cleansed with blood, and without shedding of blood there is no forgiveness."

Thus, God instituted the tabernacle and temple sacrifices to atone for the sin of the individual, Passover was for the sin of the family, the Day of Atonement covered the sin of the nation, and the Final Sacrifice was the satisfactory requirement to atone for the sin of the world. The purpose of the Messiah was to be that Final Sacrifice for final atonement.

The Picture of a Final Sacrifice

Nowhere in the Scriptures is there a more vivid picture of the purpose of the Messiah than Isaiah 53. Dr. Barry Leventhal, the academic dean, and professor at Southern Evangelical Seminary, wrote the following regarding his encounter with this passage as a young Jewish man seeking answers:

I vividly remember the first time I seriously confronted Isaiah 53, or better still, the first time it seriously confronted me. Being rather confused over the identity of the Servant in Isaiah 53, I went to my local rabbi and said to him, "Rabbi, I have met some people at school who claim that the so-called Servant in Isaiah

53 is none other than Jesus of Nazareth. But I would like to know from you, who is this Servant in Isaiah 53?"

I was astonished at his response. "Barry, I must admit that as I read Isaiah 53 it does seem to be talking about Jesus, but since we Jews do not believe in Jesus, it can't be speaking about Jesus." Not only did his so-called reasoning sound circular, it also sounded evasive and even fearful. There are none who are as deaf as those who do not want to hear.[171]

Take a moment, if you will, to read Isaiah 53. Included in that chapter is a perfect definition of sin. The first half of verse 6 reads:

> All of us like sheep have gone astray,
> Each of us has turned to his own way.

The passage above outlines our problem. Sin is the result of turning to our own way instead of God's way. For example, if you decide you want to go out on a foreign mission field, but the Lord's will is that you serve faithfully in your fellowship, though your intentions are noble, you are choosing to turn to your own way. You are outside God's will and are thus walking in sin. Does this surprise you? If it does, I'm pretty sure you're not alone. Thankfully, we find the solution in the second half of that verse.

> But the LORD has caused the iniquity of us all
> To fall on Him.

There it is in one verse: the problem and the solution. As we read this entire passage of Scripture, we cannot help but recognize the prophecies as fulfilled in Jesus. According to verse ten, the Servant would "render Himself as a guilt offering." Not only that, but this Servant would also render Himself up willingly.

We find the final perfect picture of the atonement in verse eleven:

> As a result of the anguish of His soul,
> He will see it and be satisfied;
> By His knowledge the Righteous One,

[171] Norman L. Geisler and Paul K. Hoffman, eds., *Why I Am a Christian: Leading Thinkers Explain Why They Believe* (Grand Rapids, MI: Baker Books, 2001), p. 213

My Servant, will justify the many,
As He will bear their iniquities.

In other words, God would see this guilt offering as a satisfactory, substitutionary, atoning sacrifice. The Servant of Isaiah 53 would bear the sin of others upon Himself, thus obtaining their justification before God. However, the good news keeps getting better:

> Therefore, I will allot Him a portion with the great,
> And He will divide the booty with the strong;
> Because He poured out Himself to death,
> And was numbered with the transgressors;
> Yet He Himself bore the sin of many
> And interceded for the transgressors.[172]

He will intercede on our behalf. He will mediate our case before the Father as an attorney on the part of fallen, broken humanity. Is it any wonder why the Old Covenant saints longed for the Messiah? All the sacrifices of the Old Covenant were but a shadow for the fulfillment of that Final Sacrifice yet to come.

The Glorious Fulfillment

Jesus said, "Do not think that I came to abolish the Law or the Prophets; I did not come to abolish but to fulfill."[173] It saddens me to think of just how many professing Christians there are who are unfamiliar with the Old Testament. I'm sure you can see how vitally important knowledge of the Old Testament is for understanding the gospel message and why Jesus had to die; why He had to shed His blood. All the Old Testament passages we've read thus far help us to understand New Testament passages like the following:

> We have been sanctified [set apart] through the offering of the body of Jesus Christ once for all.
> Every priest stands daily ministering and offering time after time the same sacrifices, which can never take away

---

[172] Isaiah 53:12
[173] Matthew 5:17

sins; but He, having offered one sacrifice for sins for all time, sat down at the right hand of God.[174]

The Holy Spirit testifies to us; for after saying,

"THIS IS THE COVENANT THAT I WILL MAKE WITH THEM

AFTER THOSE DAYS, SAYS THE LORD:

'I WILL PUT MY LAWS UPON THEIR HEART,

AND ON THEIR MIND I WILL WRITE THEM,'"

He then says, "AND THEIR SINS AND THEIR LAWLESS DEEDS I WILL REMEMBER NO MORE."

Now where there is forgiveness of these things, there is no longer any offering for sin.[175]

Thus, with the atoning sacrifice of Jesus Christ—the final Passover Lamb, the Lamb of God who takes away the sin of the world—the sacrificial system for sin came to a halt. To use the words of our Lord from the cross, "It is finished." Death, the penalty for sin, was conquered through Christ's resurrection. The resurrection of Jesus Christ broke Satan's power over death, and this is why Jesus had first to die—so that in rising from the dead, He would overcome the final penalty for sin. Arthur W. Pink, an itinerant Bible teacher of the early 1900s, wrote:

God's holiness is manifested at the Cross. Wondrously and yet most solemnly does the Atonement display God's infinite holiness and abhorrence of sin. How hateful must sin be to God for Him to punish it to its utmost deserts when it was imputed to His Son![176]

No More Separation

The moment Jesus Christ died on the cross, the veil in the temple (as thick as a man's hand is long) tore from top to bottom, as we read in Matthew 27:51. No longer is the congregation separated from the Holy of Holies and the presence of God. Jesus Christ took the penalty of our sins upon Himself and restored our

---

[174] Hebrews 10:10-12

[175] Hebrews 10:15-18

[176] Arthur W. Pink, *The Attributes of God* (Grand Rapids, MI: Baker Books, 1975), p. 43

intimate communion with the Father that was broken in the garden. So great was that final sacrifice on the cross that those who figuratively apply the blood of the Lamb of God to the doorposts of their heart are cleansed from their sin, saved from sin's penalty, and given access to the presence of the Holy Father.

At the Cross, the ultimate in divine justice was satisfied, and the ultimate in divine love was expressed as the ultimate penalty was paid for the sin of the world. As Savior, Jesus is the Lamb of God, who willingly offered His body to pay a debt the world could never pay. While we were still sinners, while we were still enemies of God, Jesus Christ died for us:

> By this the love of God was manifested in us, that God has sent His only begotten Son into the world so that we might live through Him. In this is love, not that we loved God, but that He loved us and sent His Son to be the propitiation [the required satisfaction] for our sins.[177]

We can only find restoration of fellowship, image, and right standing in the sacrificial death of Christ upon the cross. Nothing and no one else will do. Made in His image spiritually, though sin marred that spiritual image, we now have an opportunity to be conformed to the image of His Son and our Savior, Jesus Christ.

Believe and Receive

Romans 6:23 is a powerful summation of the gospel message: "The wages of sin is death, but the free gift of God is eternal life in Christ Jesus our Lord." You might think it strange for the apostle to modify the word *gift* with the word *free*. After all, aren't all gifts *free*? A gift that is not free isn't a gift, is it? I think the Apostle Paul was making an important point by stating it just that way. His words are powerful and straightforward. You don't deserve it, and you didn't earn it.

Nevertheless, this leads us to our next question. How do we receive this *free gift*? We find the explanation in Romans 10:8-10:

---

[177] 1 John 4:9-10

"THE WORD IS NEAR YOU, IN YOUR MOUTH AND IN YOUR HEART"—that is, the word of faith which we are preaching, that if you confess with your mouth Jesus as Lord, and believe in your heart that God raised Him from the dead, you will be saved; for with the heart a person believes, resulting in righteousness, and with the mouth he confesses, resulting in salvation.

By faith, we verbally confessed Jesus Christ as our Lord—and the result of believing that God raised Him from the dead is a life change and exchange from our will to His. God's grace saves us through faith in the resurrection of Jesus Christ, and we acknowledge Him as Lord and Savior of our lives.

Now, what kind of belief or faith is this that we possess? It is a faith built upon the bedrock of fact. It is a faith built upon what you've read throughout this book. How unfortunate it is that many people quote Hebrews 11:1—"Now faith is the assurance of things hoped for, the conviction of things not seen"—almost as if this verse indicates that the faith a believer proclaims is simply blind faith. Thankfully, our faith in the Lord Jesus Christ, His atonement, and resurrection, does not flow from fumbling around blindly. God does not want us to believe in ignorance since His Word commands us to "examine everything carefully; hold fast to that which is good."[178]

Spiros Zodhiates defines the Greek word for "faith" used in Hebrews 11:1 and Romans 10:8 as follows:

"That persuasion is not the outcome of imagination but is based on fact, such as the reality of the resurrection of Christ (1 Cor. 15), and as such it becomes the basis of realistic hope."[179]

Unlike other world religions, ours is "based on fact" and "the reality of the resurrection of Christ." We have faith in God not based on sentiment or emotion but upon the verifiable fact that God raised Jesus Christ from the dead.

---

[178] 1 Thessalonians 5:21

[179] Spiros Zodhiates, *The Complete Word Study Dictionary: New Testament* (Chattanooga, TN: AMG Publishers, 1992), p. 1162

I think that if I had to base my faith upon my emotions, I would constantly doubt my salvation. Some moments I feel particularly saved—like when I am sharing Christ with a seeker. However, at other times a hurried, or sour mood might prompt not only me but others to doubt my salvation as well. How many times have we heard unbelievers, after expressing their particular spiritual idea, defend it by saying, "I feel it's true" or, "It just feels right."

No doubt, we can all raise our hand when asked if our emotions or *feelings* have ever deceived us. Fear, pride, anger, lust, depression, and the list can go on; as members of the human race, we have all *been there*. Rather than be led by what deceives us, we can stand firm in that no matter how we *feel*, God did indeed raise His Son from the grave, and salvation for us all is possible through Him.

An Opportunity for Everyone

Jesus is the Jewish Messiah, but not for our Jewish friends and family only; He is the Messiah to the Gentile as well. Matthew, applying Isaiah 42 to Jesus, wrote:

> BEHOLD, MY SERVANT WHOM I HAVE CHOSEN;
> MY BELOVED IN WHOM MY SOUL IS WELL-PLEASED;
> I WILL PUT MY SPIRIT UPON HIM,
> AND HE SHALL PROCLAIM JUSTICE TO THE GENTILES...
> AND IN HIS NAME THE GENTILES WILL HOPE.[180]

There is hope for Jew and Gentile alike:

> For there is no distinction between Jew and Greek [Gentile]; for the same Lord is Lord of all, abounding in riches for all who call upon Him; for "WHOEVER WILL CALL UPON THE NAME OF THE LORD WILL BE SAVED."[181]

---

[180] Matthew 12:18,21
[181] Romans 10:12-13

Every human being on this planet has an opportunity to respond to God. God's Word implores us that when we feel His tug in our conscience when we know He is beckoning us to come to Himself, we are not to harden our heart, we are to respond. He is compassionate and longsuffering. He is a God who said, as quoted by the apostle Paul, "ALL THE DAY LONG I HAVE STRETCHED OUT MY HANDS TO A DISOBEDIENT AND OBSTINATE PEOPLE."[182]

When I think of my years apart from Him, I realize how often He stretched out His loving hand to me. Regretfully, all I did was slap it back. Perhaps you have a similar testimony. All of us—including me—like sheep, have gone astray. Through it all, thankfully, He never gave up. He simply kept reaching out until we responded to His love.

Children of God

Along with the gift of eternal life through our Lord and Savior, Jesus Christ comes a magnificent change in position—a change in our eternal standing before the Father:

> As many as received Him, to them He gave the right to become children of God, even to those who believe in His name, who were born, not of blood nor of the will of the flesh nor of the will of man, but of God.[183]

Now, some might argue that all humans are God's children. However, I think we must consider this concept in light of what the Scriptures state and not what tickles our ears. I am sure you have, just as much as I received e-mail or messages from believers and unbelievers alike with what on the surface might sound good, but is quite heretical in its concept of who is a child of God. Consider the following message I once received:

> Make a wish before you read this poem. Did you make a wish? If you don't make a wish, it won't come true—last chance to make a wish.

---

[182] Romans 10:21
[183] John 1:12-13

FOR TODAY AND EVERYDAY. May today there be peace within YOU. May you trust your highest power that you are exactly where you are meant to be. May you not forget the infinite possibilities that are born of faith. May you use those gifts that you have received, and pass on the love that has been given to you. May you be content knowing you are a child of God.

Let this presence settle into your bones and allow your soul the freedom to sing, dance, and to bask in the sun, it is there for each and every one of you. Send this to seven people within the next five minutes and your wish will come true. Hope you're having a great day!!!

Though I was one of the seven who received this message, I never did find out if the sender's wish came true. We should be quite thankful that our faith and relationship with God and the blessings He bestows are not the results of making a wish or sending an e-mail or instant message. Though this message has a quip about God, its essence spotlights the *self*. These types of sentiments and thinking break my heart, and unfortunately, they are prevalent. All too often, people think that simply because something has the word *God* in it, it must be true—it must portray God and how we can approach Him accurately. I think it is tragically heretical and sad for the author of the above message to have reduced God to a lucky charm.

Now, did you notice that the one mention of God was not really about God, but about the recipient? "Be content knowing that you are a child of God." How unfortunate that a beautiful gift from God, the gift of spiritual adoption that we received as believers, is so often perverted to reinforce humanity's desire to do his or her *own thing*.

The Need for Rebirth

The Bible speaks plainly regarding the identity of God's children. Paul wrote in Ephesians 2 that when we were apart from God, we were, by nature, children of wrath who walked according to the lusts of our flesh and our mind. In the parable of the seeds and the weeds, Jesus referred to the good seeds as the sons of the kingdom, and the weeds as the sons of the evil one.[184] The apostle John wrote in 1 John 3:10:

> By this the children of God and the children of the devil are obvious: anyone who does not practice righteousness is not of God, nor the one who does not love his brother.

We were once born of flesh by earthly parents, but we were born again in Christ, at which time we became children of God.

In His conversation with Nicodemus, a ruler of the Jewish people, Jesus said, "Truly, truly, I say to you, unless one is born again he cannot see the kingdom of God."[185] Like many, Nicodemus had a difficult time receiving this spiritual truth—the truth of spiritual rebirth. Jesus explained:

> "That which is born of the flesh is flesh, and that which is born of the Spirit is spirit. Do not be amazed that I said to you, 'You must be born again.'"[186]

Unlike Nicodemus, the apostle Peter grasped this truth as is evident by his explanation in 1 Peter 1:22-23:

> Since you have in obedience to the truth purified your souls for a sincere love of the brethren, fervently love one another from the heart, for you have been born again not of seed which is perishable but imperishable, that is, through the living and abiding word of God.

When you became a genuine child of the living God, it meant, "you have not received a spirit of slavery leading to fear again, but you have received a spirit of adoption as sons by which we cry out, 'Abba! Father!'"[187] The word *Abba* means that you can cry out to God as "Father, my Father!"

Perhaps you're talking with a friend whose concept of God is distorted by an alcoholic or otherwise abusive earthly father. The

---

[184] Matthew 13:38
[185] John 3:3
[186] John 3:6-7
[187] Romans 8:15

alarming number of deadbeat dads and absentee fathers leave fatherless children with one place to turn to for their example—and that's television. Sadly, we've gone from *Father Knows Best* to *Father Knows Nothing.* If the media does portray him, they usually make his character the bumbling fool.

Therefore, the idea of God as a male figure is tough enough, but as *Father*—well, that can be a significant obstacle for people with a fractured view. If this is the case, explain to your hurting friend that, unlike an earthly father who can fail or disappoint her, our blessed Heavenly Father, Who never changes, is always there to listen compassionately and lovingly to her heart's cry.

In his book, *Knowing God,* J.I. Packer superbly explained our adopted relationship with our perfect Father:

> There are no distinctions of affection in the divine family. We are all loved just as fully as Jesus is loved. It is like a fairy story—the reigning monarch adopts waifs and strays to make princes of them. But, praise God, it is not a fairy story: it is a hard and solid fact, founded on the bedrock of free and sovereign grace. This, and nothing less than this, is what adoption means. No wonder John cries, *"Behold, what manner of love!"* When once you understand adoption, your heart will cry the same.
>
> If God in love has made Christians His children, and if He is perfect as a Father, two things would seem to follow, in the nature of the case.
>
> First, the family relationship must be an abiding one, lasting forever. Perfect parents do not cast off their children. Christians may act the prodigal, but God will not cease to act the prodigal's father.
>
> Second, God will go out of His way to make His children feel His love for them and know their privilege and security as members of His family. Adopted children need assurance that they belong, and a perfect parent will not withhold it.[188]

---

[188] J.I. Packer, *Knowing God* (Downers Grove, IL: InterVarsity Press, 1973), pp. 216, 225

I think the concept of spiritual adoption is almost too astonishing to grasp. God draws us to Himself by His loving-kindness, and then we have an opportunity to choose either to remain, children of wrath, at enmity with Him—or to cry "Abba, Father" and receive the Spirit of adoption as His child. God loves us with an everlasting love and grants us perfect assurance. He turns us, poor waifs, into wealthy heirs in His kingdom.

FINAL THOUGHTS

It is a trustworthy statement, deserving full acceptance, that Christ Jesus came into the world to save sinners, among whom I am foremost of all. Yet for this reason, I found mercy, so that in me as the foremost Jesus Christ might demonstrate His perfect patience as an example for those who would believe in Him for eternal life.[189]

Have you ever felt like the foremost sinner of all? Oh, how the enemy of your soul would like to convince you that you are without hope! "Blew it again, didn't you?" he whispers in your ear. Nevertheless, you have an advocate with the Father, Jesus Christ, your Lord.

It gives us confidence and strength of faith to know that Jesus now speaks on our behalf because, by God's enormous grace, we have forgiveness. Perhaps Stephen Charnock summed up this sentiment best when he wrote the following:

Without sin the creature [would] not [have] been miserable: had man remained innocent, [he would] not [have] been the subject of punishment; and without the creature's misery, God's mercy in sending His Son to save His enemies could not have appeared. *The abundance of sin is a passive occasion for God to manifest the abundance of His grace.*[190]

Now, while we don't go right ahead and willingly give God an opportunity to manifest the abundance of His grace, isn't it

---

[189] 1 Timothy 1:15-16

[190] Charnock, *The Existence and Attributes of God,* vol. 1, p. 533, emphasis added.

grand knowing our sins are forgiven and forgotten at the moment of our repentance?

God's abundant grace. Ephesians 2:8 reminds us that it is by God's grace we are saved from our sins and the wrath of God's judgment. Salvation came to us through faith, as a free gift of God—not according to our works, which would prompt our boasting, "Isn't God lucky to have me?" However, in humility, recognizing our need, we bow before the throne of grace and accept it. Oh, how hard it is for sinful humanity to do just that! We fell in pride, and we continue in our lost state in pride, for salvation comes by a willful act of humility before God.

I am continually amazed at how many people I speak with, whose questions are answered to their satisfaction, refuse to believe. As I mentioned in a previous chapter, the answers we offer simply remove obstacles to the conversion of the soul. Some will never believe, even if One rises from the dead.[191] Nonetheless, never stop sharing the good news, and certainly never stop praying for them.

Gamaliel had it right in Acts 5:34-39. If the message preached is of men, it will eventually come to nothing—however, if it is of God, nothing can stop it, and those who fight against it will find themselves fighting God.

As we know, many people would rather fight against God and all He stands for rather than kneeling before Him, offering Him the adoration He deserves. However, at some point, they most certainly will bend the knee.

We find in Philippians 2:6-11 an amazing summation of Jesus, the God-man:

> Although He existed in the form of God, did not regard equality with God a thing to be grasped, but emptied Himself, taking the form of a bond-servant, and being made in the likeness of men. Being found in appearance as a man, He humbled Himself by becoming obedient to the point of death, even death on a cross.

---

[191] Luke 16:31

> For this reason also, God highly exalted Him, and bestowed on Him the name which is above every name, so that at the name of Jesus every knee will bow, of those who are in heaven and on earth and under the earth, and that every tongue will confess that Jesus Christ is Lord, to the glory of God the Father.

Are you sharing the Lord with someone you love who refuses to believe? Never stop praying on their behalf that the Lord would soften his or her heart to receive Him before it's too late.

To sum it all up, lest we ever forget or become confused, what our Lord and Savior Jesus Christ saved us from, consider something called the "sin tax." In case you are unfamiliar, a sin tax is a sales tax tacked onto vices such as alcohol and cigarettes. Now, can you imagine if there were a tax for every one of our sins, sins we've committed in thought and deed? Our national debt would be paid in full in no time. However, we would all find ourselves in debtor's prison, which I suppose would be more commonly known as Hell, because we could never afford to pay all the tax we'd owe.

The good news is that Jesus left the glories of heaven to become a man. He suffered at the hands of sinful humanity and died to pay our *sin tax* upon the cross—a price impossible for us to pay. He then rose from the dead, conquering the ultimate penalty for sin and thus freeing us from bondage to the enemy of our soul. Moreover, when we are finally called to our eternal home in glory, we will praise Him throughout all eternity as brothers and sisters, joint-heirs with Christ in God's adopted family. Now, I don't think good news can get any better than that!

QUESTIONS & RESOURCES

1. Of whom does Isaiah 53 speak? What one verse shows both our problem and the solution?

2. Why is blood sacrifice necessary? What passage explains this? What does it mean?

3. What's so good about the Good News?

4. Can you explain what it means to be *adopted* into God's family? What does it mean to be a *child of God*?

5. Define our relationship with God before and after coming to Christ.

I Talk Back to the Devil by A. W. Tozer, Wingspread Publishers, 2008.

Knowing God by J.I. Packer, InterVarsity Press, 1993.

Through the Windows of Heaven by Walter Martin and Jill Martin Rische. Broadman & Holman Publishers, 1999.

CHAPTER 11 ~ *My Life is My Witness*

My nose hurt. No kidding, my nose hurt from smelling all those candles. I simply could not make up my mind—the selection was plentiful. Perhaps you can identify if you've ever been to one of those candle parties and sniffed your way to a sore nose. Even coffee grounds didn't clear away the *sassy-but-nice pumpkin-spice* scent from my nasal passages.

The following week I received an invitation to a home-and-garden party—two weeks later, a cookware party. A week after I spent twenty-five bucks for a spatula, I was invited to a cosmetics party. I never imagined the women in this little community could be such party animals, but there I was, invited to one in-home shopping party after another, after another.

It was remarkable how each hostess was as excited as the next regarding her offering of wares. That excitement was contagious and made an impact on my wallet. At the candle party, after the speaker revealed the plan for how we could become sales representatives as well, a few women took advantage of the offer. Several other women signed up to host a party in their homes, and out went the circle of invitations all over again. Thus, if my nose wasn't sore enough the first time around, surely I'd have two or three more opportunities.

I must say I did have a lot of fun. However, the majority of women at those parties were believers—and I couldn't help but think, *Wouldn't it be great to offer the best plan of all right here and now?* What amazed me was how each hostess couldn't wait to tell us gals about her party and the different items we might have the opportunity to purchase. Suddenly these women, and many others just like them, became bold spokeswomen—apologists if you will—for their in-home shopping parties.

Oddly enough, the vast majority of women I talk with about sharing the Lord comment, "Oh, I'm not comfortable talking to people about the Lord. I'm just not gifted in that area." Then they quickly end our conversation with, "My life is my witness," or, "I'm a silent witness."

How unfortunate it is that many women who can speak enthusiastically regarding their in-home shopping party feel they cannot adequately communicate their testimony for Christ. I understand their unease, but I also know the Holy Spirit will give them the tools they need—and surely, there is nothing more exciting to share than the hope of redemption. However, it seems to me that occasionally the comment, "My life is my witness," or, "I'm a silent witness," is offered more as an excuse to remain silent than as a tactic for winning souls for eternity.

What's a Witness?

By definition, a witness, however, cannot be silent. A witness is someone who attests to a fact or event. A witness is one who gives public testimony, one who furnishes evidence. That is the definition of the word *witness*. Yes, our life is *a* witness—it's the loudest witness we have. If Christianity is true, it should, therefore, permeate every area of our lives. Nevertheless, as witnesses, we must also give public testimony—we must furnish evidence for what we witnessed.

Being a witness is not as hard as you might think. The purpose of this chapter is to encourage you to let your life, which includes your verbal proclamation, be a powerful witness in three distinct areas: the home, the church, and the world.

How My Life Is My Witness in the Home

My husband and I have a little arrangement. He takes care of the outside of the home while I take care of the inside. He mows I vacuum. He deals with the overgrown ferns and thistle—I take care of the overgrown stack of dishes in the sink and laundry in the hamper. He plants and waters, I decorate. Now, I happen to think I got the better end of the deal because I love decorating. Since I am a bargain-hunter through and through, I feel I've achieved quite a victory whenever I find a special little something that enhances a spot in my home—for at least half of what it's worth. For me, this is a conquest. Usually, when I make a significant find, I am immediately on the telephone to my mother-in-law, scoring points for being a wise wife with the finances.

Now, as the decorator of the home, I understand how important it is to attend those candle parties. We love the fragrance of spice during the holidays—and in the spring, a lovely floral scent. The fragrance in the home is essential. However, what is more important to the house, I desire to make into a home, is the aroma of my life. Second Corinthians 2:14 reads:

> Thanks be to God, who always leads us in His triumph in Christ, and manifests through us the sweet aroma of the knowledge of Him in every place.

"The knowledge of Him in every place." I think one of the best ways to manifest His knowledge in our favorite place is to fulfill the call of Deuteronomy 6:4-7:

> Hear, O Israel! The LORD is our God, the LORD is one! You shall love the LORD your God with all your heart and with all your soul and with all your might. These words, which I am commanding you today, shall be on your heart. You shall teach them diligently to your sons and shall talk of them when you sit in your house and when you walk by the way and when you lie down and when you rise up.

Passing our faith on to our children is the highest calling. It is vitally important to be a living witness in the home to those hearts tender toward God and whose spirits are sensitive to Him. The truth is, though God gave us such a sober charge in Deuteronomy 6, He has readied the soil for the seed of our witness.

I am always astonished at how spiritual small children can be. When Nicole was quite tiny, I used to quote to her—and very dramatically—John 1:1-5,14. Remembering that I had done this with Nicole, one day, I decided to recite it in the same manner to our then three-year-old son, Mikael.

> In the beginning was the Word, and the Word was with God, and the Word was God. He was in the beginning with God. All things came into being through

Him, and apart from Him nothing came into being that has come into being. In Him was life, and the life was the Light of men. The Light shines in the darkness, and the darkness did not comprehend it.

And the Word became flesh, and dwelt among us, and we saw His glory, glory as of the only begotten from the Father, full of grace and truth.

He was mesmerized. When I finished, solely for curiosity's sake—because I had never explained it to him—I asked, "Mikael, who is the Word?"

He said, without a moment's hesitation and with as much passion as he could muster, "Jesus! And He is alive, and He *wose fron da* dead, and He is alive!" I was stunned. Now that he's an adult, and a United States Marine, his abiding love for Christ has not wavered.

We are to teach our children diligently the things of the Lord. It is impossible to do that silently, especially since God commanded us to "talk of them when you sit in your house and when you walk by the way and when you lie down and when you rise up." We are to seize every moment we can as an opportunity to plant the Word of God and to cultivate a genuine love for Him in their hearts.

You might be thinking, *But Judy, aren't most things caught, not taught to our children?* Quite true. That is why we must not forget the first part of Deuteronomy 6: "You shall love the LORD your God with all your heart and with all your soul and with all your might."

The children are indeed watching. If perhaps you don't have small children, maybe you have grandchildren—or an aged parent or an unbelieving husband in the home. Whichever the case might be, someone is watching you, even your neighbor across the fence.

Indeed, our love for and devotion to God are more contagious than the excitement of a candle party. Moreover, enthusiasm for God prompts our verbal witness. We cannot help it. Oh, how important it is for that sincere love devotion to be in our hearts so we can be the witness in our home, day to day, that the Lord calls us to be.

For Jeff and me, knowing we were faithful to the call of planting our children's feet on a firm foundation in Christ, once they became adults, we had peace knowing they alone are accountable before the Lord for their adult choices—good or bad.

When Your Reasons are Rejected

Perhaps you are one of the many mothers out there who will read this and feel a burning desire to scold, "That's easy for you to write, Judy, but you don't know what it's like to have a child turn their back on all you've taught them." Oh, yes, I do!

I have a tremendous heart for those parents of wayward children and want to encourage you to refuse to give up on your child, prayer, or your firm stand and testimony before the Lord.

It was 2010 when a young man from our community in his early twenties beguiled our then seventeen-year-old daughter. I will tell you, and so will Nicole (to whom this book is dedicated), without a moment's hesitation that he was the only one who could have enticed her. She had had affection for him since she was only eight-years-old. There were folks in our community who, with only a surface knowledge of him, immediately praised the relationship. He knew *Christianeeze*, which allowed him to say all the *right things*. He attended church and church gatherings with us and was even baptized.

When it was plain that Nicole was firmly under his influence, and after he showed his true colors, only then did others in our community come out of the woodwork to warn us of what kind of person he really was. Unfortunately and obviously to all, by then it was simply too late.

By eighteen, Nicole chose to learn life and spiritual lessons the hard way, as she cast off all we warned her about him and all we taught her about the Lord. On the night after we celebrated her graduation from high school with honors in June 2011, she allowed this person (with the help of his parents), to lead our only daughter out of our home, into theirs, and eventually to join him in his evil excesses.

As she later told us, this abusive man was a pro at luring young teen, virgin girls away from their family and into his arms as he boasted about this behavior to another young man whom he encouraged to do the same while in Nicole's presence. At the time, it was apparent to him that his plans to isolate her were in place, and her ego was not yet bruised enough to admit to her parents, or anyone else, that she had made a horrible mistake. Her heels drove in further.

It was a time of tough love. We took heat from believers and even some family members who called us unloving for not coddling or enabling our daughter during that time. Many of those folks had wayward adult children of their own and felt we should reach out and help her as her life became more difficult, as they had done with their rebellious children. I am so thankful to our dear friend and pastor, Denny Martinez and his wife, Lynette, for standing firmly by us, which gave us the strength to survive what was the most painful journey of our lives as parents.

In a phone conversation with rebellious Nicole, Pastor Denny could not have been clearer to describe to her his thoughts on her behavior in light of God's Word. At the time, Nicole hated him for confronting her and telling her the truth. As parents, no matter how difficult, we knew we had to stand firm against what she yoked herself to because we knew, and she knew deep in her soul, that what we taught her was the truth.

Through that horrible time, Nicole knew her parents stood on solid ground. We knew that after the horror of whatever she would experience, she would need to come home to our strong foundation in Christ, and she could not find us wavering. The other important facet of all this was that our son, eleven-year-old Mikael, examined our reactions as well. He witnessed us, though in tremendous pain, not waiver or enable our daughter, who we loved deeply, but would not coddle as she shook her fist at God.

Oh, how we praise our Lord that that time, though a horror for us, was a brief one, and yet those were the longest two and a half years of our lives. God is so good, gracious, and faithful because it was at a women's conference I was leading where Nicole re-committed her life to the Lordship of Jesus Christ and prayed for Him to use that experience to help her warn others.

At this writing, Nicole is in her late-twenties, a godly wife to our wonderful son-in-law, (Pastor Denny, performed their wedding ceremony), and is a loving mommy to our adorable little grandson.

Nicole's love and heart for teen girls and young women who find themselves with beguilers allow her to speak to them with authority. Her experience apart from the Lord cemented her faith *in* Him, and she continues to pray for Him to use her.

The Prodigal Example

Some children need to shake their fist or turn their backs to test the authenticity of God and the faith of those around them. Just ask Franklin Graham, and many other preachers' kids, who learned the lesson in like manner.

To this day, Nicole comments that Pastor Denny, with his harsh phone conversation, was the only person aside from her parents, who were willing to tell her the truth. She strongly rebukes those parents who taught their rebellious children to love the Lord but who then coddles or enables them in an attempt to gain them back.

The Prodigal Father did not enable his sinning son. He did not hand his son steak because he couldn't bear the thought of his boy eating corncobs with the hogs. He did not *slip him a few bucks* after he blew his inheritance on shameful living to stay in his son's good graces. That father allowed the son to feel the full weight of his decision while that faithful father stood firm in the Lord. Upon the son's return, dad rejoiced and forgave him, and then reminded others to do the same. (Oh, how important that extension of total forgiveness is.) Dad kept his eyes on the horizon for the son's return. On more than one occasion, Nicole has commented,

"Mom, who knows how long I would have been spinning if you and dad made life easier for me during that time."[192]

It all comes down to this. Yes, I do love Jesus Christ more than I love my children—or anything else for that matter. Some children need to test that by seeing it lived out in shoe-leather. Was it brutal, painful, and horrible? Yes. Did Jesus carry us through? There is no doubt about it. In fact, it was at that time, though excruciatingly painful to bring myself to the point of actually sitting at my desk, that I wrote the book, *More Than Devotion*. I do not believe that book would have had nearly the depth it does, had I not walked that valley as I pressed hard into the Everlasting Arms.

The Woman in the Mirror

One of the things I love about living a life in Christ is that it is not a shallow existence. Scriptures like 2 Corinthians 13:5 and Romans 12:2 encourage us toward a more in-depth view of ourselves and our relationship with the Lord:

> Test yourselves to see if you are in the faith; examine yourselves! Or do you not recognize this about yourselves, that Jesus Christ is in you unless indeed you fail the test?

> Do not be conformed to this world, but be transformed by the renewing of your mind, so that you may prove what the will of God is, that which is good and acceptable and perfect.

A. W. Tozer posed a compelling question: "What comes into your mind when you think about God?" He then noted that "Worship is pure or base as the worshiper entertains high or low thoughts of God."[193] Before we can hope to be a witness for Christ

---

[192] It is important to note that I do not mention my children without their permission. Just so ya know, Nicole gave a hearty thumbs up after reading this section before we went to print. Her hope and mine is that this account will help others who painfully find themselves in a similar circumstance.

[193] 137-1. A.W. Tozer, *The Knowledge of the Holy* (New York: Harper & Collins, 1961), p. 1

at all, we must first test our hearts and be willing to ask ourselves that tough Tozer question.

The Christian life is one of self-examination and reflection. It is a faith that penetrates deep into the inner man or woman, where the Lord can do His healing and cleansing work. While this can be a painful process, we must allow the Lord to bring the less than godly attitudes, habits, and behaviors before our eyes that we have either justified or denied, so He can help us deal with them promptly. When we are willing, He moves us toward wholeness and holiness. Suddenly family and friends around us witness the radical transformation of our lives, and it is the testimony we can't help but verbally proclaim—the glory of God cleansing us from the inside out.

Are You Ready to Be Transformed?

Jesus Christ transforms us when we submit to His Lordship—when we see sin as He sees it, and we desire to do something about it. As I mentioned in an earlier chapter, how can you know if you're in the Lord's will? Simply lift it up and ask the Lord, "Does this please You?' and wait for His reply in your conscience. When we wait for the answer and obey His voice regarding what concerns us, our lives will never be the same. Ezekiel 11:19-20 is a passage that means a great deal to me:

> "I will give them one heart, and put a new spirit within them. And I will take the heart of stone out of their flesh and give them a heart of flesh, that they may walk in My statutes and keep My ordinances and do them. Then they will be My people, and I shall be their God."

Though the above passage in Ezekiel concerns first the nation of Israel, I am also a living example of God taking a heart of stone and replacing it with a heart of flesh. Before giving my life to Christ, I was quite emotionally detached. I could turn my feelings off like a light switch and feel nothing toward another human being outside of myself, what a horrible, sick existence. I imagine that I must have been at the height of my emotional dysfunction by the time He saved me.

Though it wasn't an easy process and at times was downright painful, God so transformed my heart that I now find it hard to worship without tears streaming down my face. She who hadn't cried for years now finds it hard to get through a 20-minute song service. Somehow, when I feel those tears upon my cheeks, I am reminded of the miracle God performed in my life. How can I remain silent?

So how are you doing in the self-examination department? Do you profess Jesus Christ as Lord, yet your life seems to go on like business as usual? While I was on the road as a sales representative, in a small hotel room in Morgan Hill, California, all by my lonesome, I was driven to pick up a Gideon Bible left in the nightstand drawer. That night I read 1 John 2:4, and I was immediately convicted. When I wrestled with the truth of that passage, it drove me to solemn self-examination, and then to my knees.

> The one who says, "I have come to know Him," and does not keep His commandments, is a liar, and the truth is not in him.

No Lordship, no life change, and ultimately the unholy trinity I worshiped was *me, myself, and I*. However, once the Lord indeed took residence in my heart, the results were a radical transformation and a passionate love for God.

When we allow the Lord to cleanse and heal us, day by day, we can pursue His presence like never before. "If anyone is in Christ, he is a new creature; the old things passed away; behold, new things have come."[194] As new creatures in Christ, we find that He suddenly becomes the delight of our everyday conversation. We cannot help but speak of Him to others.

How many brides have you known who did not regularly speak of their betrothed? Have you ever met a bride who was not longing for her wedding day? Since, as believers, we are referred to

---

[194] 2 Corinthians 5:17

in the Scriptures as *the bride of Christ*, how about you? Are you a bride who loves to talk about your Groom, one who longs for her wedding day? I pray this is the case.

How My Life Is My Witness in the Church

I love my sisters in the Lord. We are a family, indeed. That I love them is evidence of the radical transformation that God performed in my life. God has given me such a heart and love, not only for my sisters in Christ, but for my sisters in Adam as well: one group to encourage in the Lord, the other to lead to His love, forgiveness, freedom, and gift of eternal life.

My sisters in Christ have taught me so much—I am indebted to them. What would I have done had they not shared their gift of hospitality so an old corporate woman could learn how to be a loving hostess? I am so thankful for those sisters who, when my children were small, willingly babysat when my husband and I needed a night out together, or when the Lord called me to minister in another city or country.

The love we share is genuine, unwavering, and supernatural. When I speak to a group, I am almost heartbroken to leave; I love my sisters so. It does not matter that I have just met them that weekend—I love them all. I love listening to them share their hearts, and I am humbled when God grants me an opportunity to offer a word of encouragement or pray for them about a particular need—from weight loss to a wayward child. It is always a blessing to receive cards or messages from women I prayed with, who are excited to share what God accomplished in some particular matter. This is our living witness in the church, and it is the fulfillment of 1 John 4:7:

> Beloved, let us love one another, for love is from God; and everyone who loves is born of God and knows God. The one who does not love does not know God, for God is love. By this the love of God was manifested in us, that God has sent His only begotten Son into the world so that we might live through Him. In this is love, not that we loved God, but that He loved us and sent

His Son to be the propitiation for our sins. Beloved, if God so loved us, we also ought to love one another.

Indeed, we ought to love one another. Unfortunately, like any family, we sure can have our little scraps and disagreements. Nevertheless, the Holy Spirit is the tie that binds our hearts in one accord, and our response to one another is unique to the church of Jesus Christ. I will never forget, on my 1994 trip to Russia, holding the face of a young Russian woman as tears streamed down our faces for the joy of the love of God we shared. Even though we could not communicate with words since we had a language barrier, our hearts and spirits spoke volumes. The love she and I expressed without words is a love I wish the whole world knew, love many would never think possible—and it isn't, apart from an abiding relationship with the living God through Christ.

The Witness of Unity

Colossians 3:12-17 encourages us to remember who we are in the family of God and how we ought to respond to one another:

> As those who have been chosen of God, holy and beloved, put on a heart of compassion, kindness, humility, gentleness and patience; bearing with one another, and forgiving each other, whoever has a complaint against anyone; just as the Lord forgave you, so also should you. Beyond all these things put on love, which is the perfect bond of unity. Let the peace of Christ rule in your hearts, to which indeed you were called in one body; and be thankful. Let the word of Christ richly dwell within you, with all wisdom teaching and admonishing one another with psalms and hymns and spiritual songs, singing with thankfulness in your hearts to God. Whatever you do in word or deed, do all in the name of the Lord Jesus, giving thanks through Him to God the Father.

If I had the opportunity to select any passage that would encourage women to let their lives be a powerful witness in the church, I think I would simply quote Philippians 2:1-2 since the Scriptures always state it best:

> If there is any encouragement in Christ, if there is any consolation of love, if there is any fellowship of the Spirit, if any affection and compassion, make my joy complete by being of the same mind, maintaining the same love, united in spirit, intent on one purpose.

And may that purpose be to glorify God in all we say and do before everyone, whether they are in Christ or Adam. This desire and movement toward unity is our life witness in the church—and it is evident to all that our love is genuine, tangible, unwavering, and without hypocrisy—a love that is indeed a supernatural gift of God.

How My Life Is My Witness in the World

One of the advantages of having left my job in the corporate world was that I had an opportunity to Christmas shop during the week when everyone else was at the office. Unfortunately, as you know, the closer it gets to midnight on Christmas Eve, the busier the shopping malls become. On one such holiday season, I decided to venture out with my then, five-year-old daughter, Nicole, as we found ourselves in a large shopping mall for a few last-minute gifts just two days before Christmas. It seemed to me that no matter what store we entered, crowds were thick, and the lines were long. After a while, my stomach told me it was time for lunch, and we decided to grab a bite to eat.

The timing was perfect. As one couple left a sandwich-shop counter, we managed to settle into their empty seats. A cheery young woman waited on us, and it struck me how graciously she handled the crowds while maintaining a bright smile. My daughter noticed it as well. Nicole leaned into me and whispered, "She's really nice, isn't she?"

"Yes, Honey, she sure is," I agreed as I sank my teeth into my sandwich.

After a few minutes, I noticed my daughter trying to get her attention. As the young woman raced back and forth, happily filling her customer's orders, Nicole kept patiently saying, "E'scuse me... e'scuse me."

Finally, the lady heard my five-year-old's soft voice and asked, "Oh, I'm sorry—did you need something?"

"Can I ask you a question?" Nicole asked eagerly.

"Sure," came her expectant reply.

"Do... do you know Jesus?"

Somewhat startled, then looking at me, she said, "Well, yeah... I guess so... I mean... I've been to catechism and all." Then leaning close to Nicole's face, she said, "Yeah, I guess I do."

Nicole's countenance radiated with joy, and looking as if she were about to burst, she energetically stated, "I *love* Him!" The young lady's face turned beet-red. She could plainly see that this little girl loved God, and not only that, but also that she couldn't wait to tell others. Suddenly it became challenging for me to swallow my turkey-and-cheese on wheat with that large lump in the middle of my throat.

When our life is our witness in the home, it positively influences the world around us—just as much as if we were out there ourselves. Seeing my little girl's beaming love for Jesus and her desire to be His witness to others in the world around her made me so want to follow the charge that Jesus gave to all believers in Matthew 28:18-20:

> All authority has been given to Me in heaven and on earth. Go therefore and make disciples of all the nations, baptizing them in the name of the Father and the Son and the Holy Spirit, teaching them to observe all that I commanded you; and lo, I am with you always, even to the end of the age.

Jesus called us to bear fruit for the kingdom. He called us to the formidable task of making disciples, or students, of the Lord and His Word—not merely moving folks to an intellectual assent but to a vibrant relationship with Himself. We are to help those we lead to Christ to grow in their faith and knowledge of Him so they can then make disciples of others whom they point to Christ as well.

Perhaps you are married but don't have children, or maybe you have grown children and are an empty-nester. Maybe you are a single woman—a corporate woman as I once was. Oh, how mightily God can use you at your place of business. I can't help but think of one friend of mine who, after realizing other believers surrounded her at her workplace, decided to start a once-a-week prayer meeting before the day began.

The impact of her decision was significant, primarily since she works at a county prison. Knowing that she and other believers meet for prayer, other co-workers—whom she never anticipated would talk with her about her faith—have unexpectedly approached her. My friend is more than happy to meet with them after work and is available to do so now that her children are off to college. Though she's a bit intimidated at times, she is thrilled with the opportunities; never imagining the Lord would use her this way.

We're Equipped for an Exciting Assignment

Answering the call of the Great Commission can seem overwhelming, but our Lord and Savior never calls us to a task without adequately equipping us to accomplish it. How blessed we are to live in a nation where we have access to a wealth of resources to help us become equipped or more confident in fulfilling Jesus' command. I cannot help but feel that we will be held a bit more accountable because of the overwhelming amount of access we have to Christian radio, Christian bookstores, Christian websites, and faithful fellowships.

The apostle Peter wrote:

> Sanctify Christ as Lord in your hearts, always being ready to make a defense to everyone who asks you to give an account for the hope that is in you, yet with gentleness and reverence.[195]

---

[195] 1 Peter 3:15

The Apostle Paul complements that charge in Colossians 4:5-6:

> Conduct yourselves with wisdom toward outsiders, making the most of the opportunity. Let your speech always be with grace, as though seasoned with salt, so that you will know how you should respond to each person.

When I think of what those two passages must look like as part of our life witness, I am reminded of *The Pilgrim's Progress* by John Bunyan. Bunyan's book is a thoughtful and creative example of the believer's walk in this world. It is filled with challenges to the faith and sound answers to those challenges. The life of Christian (the pilgrim) is one of testifying for the Lord, a life of defending his faith uncompromisingly yet graciously.

Being a life witness in this world is not always a comfortable or easy thing to do. Fortunately, Jesus knew that going into all the world would be a challenging prospect—one that would require nothing less than being filled with the Holy Spirit and His power. Where is this more needed than when we testify of the Lord to our closest family and friends—those who remember us before we became new in Christ? Jesus said, "A prophet is not without honor except in his own hometown, and in his own household."[196]

Yes, it isn't always comfortable sharing the Lord, but it sure is exciting. Some missionaries we support in Sudan, whose lives are always in danger, tell us with high confidence that they are "living the book of Acts." They are people who can identify with Philippians 3:14: "I press on toward the goal for the prize of the upward call of God in Christ Jesus."

Indeed, we press on. Does the Lord call all of us to travel to distant lands? No. Does He call each one of us to write a book or speak before thousands of people? No. Would He like us to seize the divine appointments He places before us in our home or neighborhood, our workplace or grocery store, on the job, or perhaps right at our front door? You bet!

---

[196] Matthew 13:57

God is on the move, and He wants us to join Him in reaching the lost for eternity. Now is certainly an appropriate time to join the fray! True faith in God is not passive, it's active, as Stephen Charnock notes: "God is active, because He is spirit; and if we be like to God, the more spiritual we are, the more active we shall be."[197]

The Great Commission is just that. It is *great*. Though it can seem overwhelming, nonetheless, by God's grace, our hearts should burn for those who don't know Him. Each of us has a job to do as siblings in the family of God, because:

> How will they call on Him in whom they have not believed? How will they believe in Him whom they have not heard? And how will they hear without a preacher? How will they preach unless they are sent? Just as it is written, "HOW BEAUTIFUL ARE THE FEET OF THOSE WHO BRING GOOD NEWS OF GOOD THINGS!"[198]

May the Lord give you grace as you bring your beautiful feet to those who need Him—those who are right under your nose.

FINAL THOUGHTS

Philosophy professor and Christian Apologist J.P. Moreland wrote the following concerning what his relationship with Jesus Christ meant to him:

> I repeatedly return to the conviction that Jesus of Nazareth is simply peerless. He is the wisest, most virtuous, most influential person in history. I can't even imagine what the last two thousand years would have been like without His influence.
>
> There is no one remotely like Him. The power of His ideas, the quality of His character, the beauty of His personality, the uniqueness of His life, miracles, crucifixion, and resurrection are so far removed from any other person or ideology that, in my view, it is the

---

[197] Stephen Charnock (1628–1680), *The Existence and Attributes of God*, vol. 1, reprint ed. (Grand Rapids, MI: Baker Books, 1996), p. 202

[198] Romans 10:14-15

greatest honor ever bestowed on me to be counted among His followers.

Not only is it an unspeakable honor to be one of His followers, it is also by far the greatest opportunity to gain a life of meaning and to become what we all know we ought to be.[199]

I cannot say it better than Dr. Moreland. Jesus Christ brought us to a place of reconciliation with God. In Him, we are free from the bondage of a life of sin, the bondage of the terror of death, and the bondage of intuitive knowledge of God's wrath through judgment all because:

God, being rich in mercy, because of His great love with which He loved us, even when we were dead in our transgressions, made us alive together with Christ (by grace you have been saved), and raised us up with Him, and seated us with Him in the heavenly places in Christ Jesus, so that in the ages to come He might show the surpassing riches of His grace in kindness toward us in Christ Jesus.[200]

How can we remain silent in the face of that? When you share the blessed truth of the gospel of Jesus Christ, questions usually arise. I pray that this guide will help you to answer them. I also pray that you will take the time to read the resources I've suggested. Nothing can compare to being used by God to impact the lives of others—and He desires to use *you*.

I find that reasons for my faith and the opportunity to share them produce confidence in God, which displaces fear that leads to bondage. I sincerely think that if more believing women would grasp the importance of knowing what they believe and why many self-help books would be rendered unnecessary.

Perhaps you have friends or family members who believe, yet continue to struggle in their lives and faith. It's true—life sure can seem to toss us to and fro. I find that when circumstances of my life

---

[199] Norman Geisler and Paul K. Hoffman, eds., *Why I Am a Christian: Leading Christian Thinkers Explain Why They Believe* (Grand Rapids, MI: Baker Books, 2001), p. 264

[200] Ephesians 2:4-7

become more complicated and the thistle does hit my chin, having sound reasons for my faith is something tangible amid uncertainty. Sound reasons for belief are reminders that the God I serve and the hope I hold are as rock-solid as the Chief Cornerstone in whom I have never been disappointed. Nor will I ever be.

> For I am convinced that neither death, nor life, nor angels, nor principalities, nor things present, nor things to come, nor powers, nor height, nor depth, nor any other created thing, will be able to separate us from the love of God, which is in Christ Jesus our Lord.[201]

---

[201] Romans 8:38-39

QUESTIONS & RESOURCES

1. What is the command of Deuteronomy 6:4-9?

2. What does a life in Christ mean to you concerning the inner woman?

3. What is the Great Commission?

4. How can your life be a witness in your home, church, and the world?

5. How do we respond to wayward adult children? Who is our example?

Love Your God with All Your Mind: The Role of Reason in the Life of the Soul by J.P. Moreland. NavPress Publishing Group, 1997.

Pictorial Pilgrim's Progress by John Bunyan, Illustrated by Joanne Brubaker. Moody Press, 1960. (This was the version my children enjoyed.)

More Than Devotion: Fifty Days of Remembrance and Resolve by Judy Salisbury, Logos Presentations, 2020 (this is the most revised version).

ABOUT THE AUTHOR

Judy Salisbury, President, and Founder of Logos Presentations has been equipping Christians to share the gospel more effectively while helping believers to live a vibrant life in the faith since the start of her multifaceted organization in 1994. This former radio talk show host has served on her local fire department since 2005 and volunteers as a firefighter, an EMT-I.V., EMS Evaluator, and as the Crisis Care Counselor.

Judy speaks nationally on a wide variety of topics such as Christian living, apologetics, and emotional trauma for secular and faith-based audiences. She is the author of several works, including *Engaging Encounters (the companion resource for Reasons for Faith)*, *More Than Devotion*, *Calamity Care*, and *The Emmaus Conversation*.

Judy and Jeff are proud parents and grandparents. The family enjoys an occasional marshmallow roast at their home on the outskirts of Mount St. Helens volcanic National Park in Washington State. For more information on Judy Salisbury or the work of Logos Presentations, or to schedule Judy to speak at your next event, please visit www.JudySalisbury.com.

MORE RESOURCES BY JUDY SALISBURY

Engaging Encounters

Your Guide to Apply Reasons for Faith

Judy Salisbury

FOREWORD BY DR. DAVID GEISLER

THE EMMAUS CONVERSATION

AN EYEWITNESS ACCOUNT

FROM THE UNNAMED DISCIPLE

JUDY SALISBURY

JUDY SALISBURY

MORE THAN DEVOTION

FIFTY-DAYS OF REMEMBRANCE AND RESOLVE

The Relevance Of Revelation

Thirty-One Days to Radical Revival

JUDY SALISBURY

Calamity Care

My 31-Day Spiritual Guide to Thrive

JUDY SALISBURY

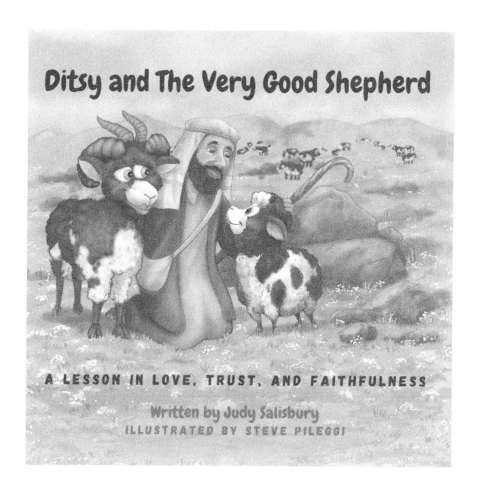

Ditsy and The Very Good Shepherd

A LESSON IN LOVE, TRUST, AND FAITHFULNESS

Written by Judy Salisbury

ILLUSTRATED BY STEVE PILEGGI

Made in the USA
Monee, IL
18 March 2024

54692504R00152